Representing Modernist Texts

I0895447

Representing Modernist Texts
Editing as Interpretation

Edited by George Bornstein

Ann Arbor
The University of Michigan Press

Copyright © by the University of Michigan 1991
All rights reserved
Published in the United States of America by
The University of Michigan Press
Manufactured in the United States of America

1994 1993 1992 1991 4 3 2 1

Library of Congress Cataloging-in-Publication Data

Representing modernist texts : editing as interpretation / edited by
George Bornstein.
p. cm.
Includes bibliographical references and index.
ISBN 0-472-09439-4 (alk. paper). — ISBN 0-472-06439-8 (pbk.
alk. paper)
1. English literature—20th century—Criticism, Textual.
2. American literature—20th Century—Criticism, Textual.
3. Modernism (Literature)—Great Britain. 4. Modernism
(Literature)—United States. 5. Transmission of texts. 6. Editing.
I. Bornstein, George.
PR478.M6R4 1991
820.9′0091—dc20 91-25452
CIP

British Library Cataloguing in Publication Data

Representing modernist texts : editing
as interpretation.
I. Bornstein, George
808.02

ISBN 0-472-09439-4
ISBN 0-472-06439-8 pbk

For Joshua

Acknowledgments

The preparation of this book has reminded me once again of the extent to which texts are socially constituted and of the limits of original intention. I should like to thank, first, the contributors to this volume and, second, the staff of the University of Michigan Press, particularly Joyce Harrison and Colin Day. The College of Literature, Science, and Arts of the University of Michigan provided welcome financial support, particularly through the efforts of Deans Peter Steiner and Edie Goldenberg, along with my chairman Bob Weisbuch. David Holdeman was a splendid research assistant. Finally, I should like to thank my family, and especially the one-year-old dedicatee of this volume, for putting up with both me and the project with such support and joy.

Grateful acknowledgment is made to the following publishers, organizations, and individuals for permission to reprint copyrighted materials:

New Directions Publishing Corporation for material from *Trilogy* by H.D., copyright 1944 by Oxford University Press, copyright renewed 1973 by Norman Holmes Pearson.

New Directions Publishing Corporation for material from *Paterson* by William Carlos Williams, copyright 1963 by Florence Williams.

New Directions Publishing Corporation, agent, for previously unpublished material by William Carlos Williams, Copyright © 1991 by William Eric Williams and Paul H. Williams.

New Directions Publishing Corporation, agent, for previously unpublished material by Ezra Pound, Copyright © 1991 by the trustees of the Ezra Pound Literary Property Trust.

Marianne Craig Moore, Literary Executor for the Estate of Marianne Moore, for unpublished letters and other unpublished material by Marianne Moore. All rights reserved.

Harcourt Brace Jovanovich, Inc. and Faber and Faber Ltd. for material from a letter from T. S. Eliot to Richard Aldington, 17 November 1921, from *The Letters of T. S. Eliot, Volume I: 1889–1922,* edited by Valerie Eliot, copyright © 1988 by SET Copyrights Limited.

Eudora Welty for permission to reproduce a letter to Noel Polk, 26 November 1984.

Contents

Introduction: Why Editing Matters
George Bornstein 1

Text and Interpretation in the Poems of W. B. Yeats
Richard J. Finneran 17

Editing William Carlos Williams
A. Walton Litz and Christopher MacGowan 49

Excavating the Ideological Faultlines of Modernism: Editing Ezra Pound's *Cantos*
Ronald Bush 67

Canon, Gender, and Text: The Case of H.D.
Lawrence S. Rainey 99

Complete with Omissions: The Text of Marianne Moore's *Complete Poems*
Andrew J. Kappel 125

The Two Audens and the Claims of History
Edward Mendelson 157

Intentional Error: The Paradox of Editing Joyce's *Ulysses*
Vicki Mahaffey 171

Textual Criticism as Feminist Practice: Or, Who's Afraid of Virginia Woolf Part II
Brenda R. Silver 193

Censorship and Self-Censorship in the Fiction of D. H. Lawrence
Eugene Goodheart 223

Where the Comma Goes: Editing William Faulkner
Noel Polk 241

Contemporary Textual and Literary Theory
Michael Groden 259

Notes on Contributors 287

Introduction: Why Editing Matters

George Bornstein

The modernist writers' editorial sophistication often outstripped that of their critics. "With plenty of printers, plenty of paper, plenty of ink, it is manifestly idiotic that we couldn't have the editions we want," exploded Ezra Pound with typical exasperation about the effort to produce his own edition of Guido Cavalcanti.[1] Sixty years later, the situation has changed little, except that we may be more uncertain about the kinds of editions we want. Of course, many of the major modernists themselves functioned as editors, of both their own work and that of others. Pound, for example, famously performed one type of editorial labor in bringing Eliot's *Waste Land* to a publishable state, a second type in his role as editor-impressario for various small magazines, and still a third in his extensive editing of finished volumes, whether of Cavalcanti, Confucius, or the Imagist poets. With his usual exuberance, he even hoped that his elaborate Genova edition of Cavalcanti would "serve as a model for edition [*sic*] of such texts as are worth the trouble."[2] Yeats produced editions all his life, from the early recuperations of neglected Irish writers through the monumental three-volume edition of Blake (1893) and more modest one-volume Spenser (1906), and on to the Indian writers of his later years, after the turn of the century helping to direct the Cuala Press as well. Most importantly, from 1895 onwards Yeats periodically reordered his own work to date, setting both canon and text with elaborate revision and rearrangement. And Virginia Woolf described her ownership of Hogarth Press as making her the freest woman in England to express her opinions, while Eliot, as a last instance, worked for nearly his entire career as an editor for Faber in London.

Both their astute sense of literary politics and their respect for documentary transmission led the major modernists to enmesh themselves in a wide range of editorial activities. They saw clearly that editors set the field of literary study, both by deciding what works came to the public and by determining the form in which those works appeared. Part of the extraordinary success of the modernists in canon formation came from their attention to editorial presentation of new or neglected writers, whether in little magazines (such as *Poetry, Little Review,* or the larger *Dial*) or in books from both small presses (Shakespeare and Company, Cuala, or Hogarth) and major publishers (Faber, Oxford, or Macmillan). Chief among those new writers were the modernists themselves, of course, whose works reached influential though—especially for the poets—usually not large audiences through such outlets. The main target of the modernists' editorial labor was often their own art. Their effort to control the process of textual production involved not only authority over the text itself but also determination of the form in which it appeared to the public and influence over institutions of transmission, whether magazines, anthologies, or entire publishing houses.

Critics of modernist literature have been slow to see the importance of editing both to the literature they study and to its transmission and reception. Perhaps fewer students of modernism than of any other period (except, of course, the postmodern) have even been aware of such questions. Thus, one can have a distinguished book on Yeats impervious to the careful sequencing by which his poems speak to and undercut each other within individual volumes, or an article about gaps in Stevens's "An Ordinary Evening in New Haven" based solely on the truncated eleven-section version in *Selected Poems* with no awareness of the fuller thirty-one-section version in *The Auroras of Autumn* and *Collected Poems*. More important, critics have proceeded as though the modernist texts somehow come to them transparently innocent of textual and theoretical choices rather than being the product of such choices. In that sense, the editor has come to occupy the position often assigned to hegemonic ideology by literary theory—invisible because the choices generated seem natural and inevitable rather than constructed and contingent.

The situation has begun to change partly because of the scale and impact of modernist editing projects, perhaps most prominent among them the publication of Valerie Eliot's edition of *The Waste Land: A Facsimile and Transcript of the Original Drafts* in 1971 and of Hans Gabler's synoptic edition of *Ulysses* in 1984. Publication of the *Waste Land* drafts led immediately to realization of the personal dimension of that poem and of the extraordinary editorial contribution of Ezra Pound toward its final shaping. Only recently have scholars begun to ponder the deeper implications of that edition: the arbitrariness of excluding all but the final published form of a work, the dissolution of the notion of a single author, and the role of social forces in the literal constitution of a text. Similar points have emerged forcefully from publication of the new version of Joyce's *Ulysses,* less from the reading text on the rectos than from the synoptic text on the versos of the three-volume edition. Perhaps most importantly, the books, articles, and conferences generated by that controversial enterprise have sensitized modernist critics at large to the highly problematic physical status of the texts on which they lavish such attention. Those questions, too, are implicit in the wide range of modernist editing projects at the present time, whether aiming to present manuscript materials as in the James Joyce Archive or the Cornell Yeats, or new reading texts of major authors or works, as with the Macmillan Yeats, the Princeton Auden, the Cambridge Lawrence, the Hogarth Woolf, or the Library of America Faulkner. The essays in the present volume all foreground textual and editorial problems and theories; before introducing them I should like to comment briefly on some of the chief practical and theoretical issues.

Perhaps of greatest concern to practical criticism of modernist literature is the unstable nature of the physical texts. As Fredson Bowers observed in his classic 1958 lecture on "Textual Criticism and the Literary Critic":

> We should be seriously disturbed by the lack of contact between literary critics and textual critics. Every practising critic, for the humility of his soul, ought to study the transmission of some appropriate text. If he did, he would raise such an outcry that we should no longer be reading most of the great English and American classics in texts that are inexcusably corrupt. We should no longer complacently accept the sleazy editing that even today too often marks the presentation of works of literature to the student and to the general public.[3]

Bowers peppered his essay with spectacular critical misfires derived from reliance on faulty texts from *Hamlet* to the modernist writers, in the process demolishing the idea that such questions pertain only to literature from earlier periods. His memorable examples included F. O. Matthiessen's famous gloss on the phrase "soiled fish of the sea" in Melville's *White-Jacket:* "hardly anyone but Melville could have created the shudder that results from calling this frightening vagueness some 'soiled fish of the sea' . . . the unexpected linking of the medium of cleanliness with filth, could only have sprung from an imagination that had apprehended the terrors of the deep, of the immaterial deep as well as the physical." Unfortunately, "soiled" was a typesetting error for "coiled" in the edition that Matthiessen used rather than what Melville actually wrote. Bowers discovered an example from modernist literature in dismissing William Empson's claim in *Seven Types of Ambiguity* that the ambiguous syntax in lines 10–12 of T. S. Eliot's "Whispers of Immortality" was "the point of the poem"; Bowers showed instead that Empson's quotation derived from a printing that reversed the punctuation at the end of lines ten and eleven to create a confusion that Empson had compounded by himself inadvertently mispunctuating line twelve in quotation. Such instances may be multiplied with ease from the canon of modernist literature. No American edition of Henry James's novel *The Ambassadors* published before 1957 had chapters 28 and 29 in the correct order, while the confusion over the proper text of Joyce's *Ulysses* began with the first edition in 1922, in which Shakespeare and Company inserted a notice apologizing "for typographical errors unavoidable in the exceptional circumstances."[4] Clearly, critics need to know at least enough about editing to choose appropriate editions rather than ones flawed in ways that undermine the critic's own point.

The same principle applies to larger units of an author's work. For example, Yeats's devotion to arranging his volumes into coherent sequences has long been well known, but no collected edition until Richard Finneran's *Poems* in 1983 printed the final poems in the order specified by Yeats himself.[5] Before that, the widely used *Collected Poems* had run together under the heading "Last Poems" two separate collections—the original *New Poems* (1938) and the poems from posthumously published *Last Poems and Two Plays* (1939), the latter in an order contradictory to Yeats's own instructions for that volume. Finneran's edition restored both the separation between *New Poems* and *Last Poems* and Yeats's own manuscript ordering of *Last Poems*. The results are startling. In the botched *Collected Poems* amalgamation, the expanded "Last Poems" begins with "The Gyres" and ends with "Under Ben Bulben," reflecting a static and impersonal point of view with little sympathy for human suffering. In contrast, Yeats's own orderings as restored by Finneran make "New Poems" begin with the stony "The Gyres" ("What matter though numb nightmare ride on top / And blood and mire the sensitive body stain?") but end with the more compassionate "The Municipal Gallery Revisited" ("And I am in despair that time may bring / Approved patterns of women or of men / But not that selfsame excellence again") and "Are You Content."[6] Correspondingly, "Last Poems" does not end with the superhuman "Under Ben Bulben" but rather begins with it, and ends instead in the "foul rag and bone shop of the heart" of "The Circus Animals' Desertion" and the avowal of human love in the envoi "Politics." The Yeats ordering restored by Finneran had been available to scholars since Curtis Bradford's work twenty years before,[7] but few had consulted it for their own analytic or theoretic arguments about Yeats's later poetry.

The examples so far derive from a traditional theory of editing, one that would postulate the notion of an ideal "correct" text, measured against which extant texts show various degrees of "corruption" that the editor seeks to remove. That theory finds its theoretical underpinning in the line of thought articulated in W. W. Greg's classic essay "The Rationale of Copy-Text" and elaborated by Fredson Bowers and, more recently and perhaps more flexibly, by G. Thomas Tanselle.[8] Such a position usually comes to rest on the principle of "author's final intention," whereby the editor (or critic) seeks first to understand and then to implement the final intention of the author regarding the reading of his or her text. Seemingly diametrically opposed to the New Criticism with its "intentional fallacy" ruling out the author's intentions from criticism altogether, traditional textual theory in some ways conspires with the New Criticism in that both posit a unique status for the art work as well wrought urn, at once unitary, authoritative, and superior to historical contingency, the product instead of an autonomous creative artist. With the virtual extinction of textual scholarship as a field of graduate training today in major universities, such a limited notion of editorial theory and practical application is as far as most literary critics and theorists get.

The essays in this volume seek less to update Bowers's examples for the present-day study of modernist texts than to explore the implications for literary critics and theorists of the recent revolution in editorial theory itself. Such editorial theory often begins from the position succinctly put by Jerome McGann in his influential *A Critique of Modern Textual Criticism:* "editors cannot follow the guidance of a rule of final authorial intentions in determining the texts they will print because final authorial intention is a deeply problematic concept."[9] The problems pertain to all three terms—final, author, and intention—often in ways that parallel their problematizing in contemporary theory as well. Together, they challenge traditional views of the "authority" of a text, as well as the notion that there can be such things as definitive, authoritative texts, or even definitive and authoritative apparatuses. Difficulties in applying a Greg-Bowers model of editing to modern texts derive not only from differences between premodern and modernist texts, or from the fact that we know so much more about the composition and publication of modernist works, but also from fundamental assumptions in the theory itself.

It is perhaps easiest to see the problems with the term *final,* which seems to privilege the latest version of an author's text over all others. But why should that be so? For example, if W. B. Yeats published "The Wanderings of Oisin" first in 1889, revised it heavily for *Poems* (1895), and continued to tinker with it for nearly forty more years of publication up through *Selected Poems* (1929) and *Collected Poems* (1933), why should the last published version (or a later manuscript if that could be established as showing "final intentions") have exclusive claim to authority? And what would the twenty-three-year-old Yeats have thought of a series of successively older men revising his youthful work? Which of Marianne Moore's versions of her famous poem "Poetry" should have authority—the original forty-line version of 1919, the intervening ones of thirteen or thirty lines, or the final 1967 one of three lines? Faced with such questions, editorial theorists have tended recently to favor concepts of versions or stages over single authoritative texts. Writing from the cusp between structuralism and poststructuralism, the German theorist Hans Zeller argued in 1975 that "a version is a specific system of linguistic signs, functioning within and without, and authorial revisions transform it into another system. . . . in principle a new version comes into existence through a single variant" and that "A new version implies a new intention" before going on to critique received notions of authorial intention and textual error as well.[10] More traditional Anglo-American scholars like Donald Reiman and Stephen Parrish mount similar critiques against final intention as leading to final or authoritative single-state texts. In an article entitled "'Versioning': The Presentation of Multiple Texts," Reiman supports "'versioning,' as distinguished from 'editing'" because

> it is both more useful and more efficient to provide critics and students with complete texts of two or more different stages of a literary work,

> each of which can be read as an integral whole, than to chop all but one version into small pieces and then mix and sprinkle these dismembered fragments at the bottoms of pages, or shuffle them at the back of the book as tables of 'variants' or 'collations.'[11]

Similarly, the general editor of the Cornell Wordsworth, Stephen Parrish, resists the notion that "rejected drafts, discarded variants, abandoned versions" should be "looked upon as false starts, misjudgments, or lapses of taste on the part of the poet, all happily rectified as the work, by obedience to some inner logic, reaches final form. That form, after all, represents the poet's 'final intention.'" Instead, Parrish "would plead the autonomy and the validity of each steady state of the text as it changes in confused, unpredictable ways, through patterns which the author may never have foreseen, let alone 'intended.'"[12]

Zeller, Reiman, and Parrish thus all posit replacing the single text with a series of texts. In that view, the "text" of, say, Marianne Moore's "Poetry" would be all published versions of that much-revised poem, perhaps together with chief manuscript versions. Such conceptions have already become established in the Romantic literature on which Parrish and Reiman (like McGann) principally work. Contemporary readers know both the 1805 and the 1850 versions of Wordsworth's *Prelude,* along with the two-book version of 1799, disseminated in texts like the widely used Norton Critical Edition of *The Prelude 1799, 1805, 1850.*[13] The procedure has been applied to literature still more canonical. Some of the most exciting controversies in Shakespearean studies derive from Michael Warren's 1976 suggestion that the differences between the quarto and folio versions of *King Lear* are best explained not by a quest for an idealized lost text of which we have two corrupt copies but rather by the hypothesis that the quarto and folio should be treated as two distinct versions reflecting Shakespeare's deliberate revision of the play. Variously elaborated in the essays of *The Division of the Kingdoms,* that hypothesis has recently come to fruition in Warren's four-part *Complete King Lear, 1608–1623.*[14] Such speculations offer an interesting middle ground between stable, unitary notions of the text on the one hand and poststructuralist freeplay of endless deferral on the other. They clearly dislodge the notion of one privileged form for a text exercising authority over all other forms and, indeed, constituting their teleological ground. Yet they provide a limit to *différance* by limiting the deferral to a finite sequence of versions constituting the bound of that particular text (though not, of course, of intertextuality). Most conspicuously, they establish a physical, literal, and empirical level of meaning to such terms as revision, erasure, instability, and writing itself.

The same logic that leads to destabilizing the "final" form of a work also opens terms like *author* and *intentions* to interrogation. Most obviously, the "author" changes over time, so that Yeats at sixty is a different author from Yeats at thirty, or the aged American Auden from his younger English self. But even a given author at a given moment often displays not a monolithic singularity of purpose or desire, but rather a multiplicity of them embodied in a multiplicity of intentions. Indeed, the notion of "intention" itself tends to dissolve under examination into a bundle of different intentions that may be in harmony but also may be at cross-purposes and contradiction with each other. And some theories would argue for assigning the "author" function not to an isolated originator of a text but rather to the more extended social network that produces a text and of which he or she is but a part. Rather than pursue those distinctions formally, I should like instead to emphasize that examination of the three terms *final, authorial,* and *intention* will frequently lead us away from an ahistorical conception of the art work toward one of its historical situation and contingency.

Such historical grounding has always been a part of textual scholarship. Things could hardly be otherwise, given the preoccupation of descriptive and analytical bibliography with books as physical objects, and of the elaboration of such insights by textual criticism itself. Fredson Bowers himself sounds remarkably *au courant* with theoretical developments of the 1990s when he calls in the 1950s for considering works like Whitman's "Passage to India" "just as a material object."[15] Indeed, a problem with contemporary "materialist" studies is that they are often not materialist enough, but instead innocent or primitive in their treatment of a book as a literal material object. Textual scholarship must necessarily always remind us that any embodied form of a text is a contingent product of concrete historical and economic institutions rather than a transparent conduit of an author's unmediated words. For example, the famous two "lost" Cantos (LXXII and LXXIII) of Pound's epic have one set of meanings if we detect their presence solely as a gap in the old New Directions text, a second set in their original publication in the Italian fascist journal *Marina Repubblicana* (1945), a third set in Mary de Rachewiltz's Italian edition (1985), and still another set when placed not in their numerical sequence but rather at the end of the New Directions printing of 1986. *Any* text is an edited text, and critics and theorists neglect the principles of its editing and construction at their peril. A full textual inquiry will necessarily remind us of the many social and historical forces besides the author that contribute to the constitution of a text. Hence, an important work like McGann's *Critique of Modern Textual Criticism* takes as a chief object the argument "for a socialized concept of authorship and textual authority."[16] And Peter Shillingsburg's influential recent overview in *Scholarly Editing in the Computer Age* identifies four different orientations—the historical and the sociological along with the aesthetic and the authorial.[17]

As a group, the essays in the present volume touch on all four of the orientations identified by Shillingsburg. While they all posit the importance of editorial and textual matters, they do not subscribe to a single school. Rather, the authors come from different generations and approaches, and represent the variegated range of contemporary textual theory rather than any particular school of it. Some subscribe to author-based theories of editing, others to socially constituted views of the text; or again some may view texts as historically discrete entities to be reproduced in facsimile while others see no way of avoiding individual aesthetic choices by editors. Like editors in general, few contributors exclusively favor any one approach, and the same individual usually draws on two or more in the course of an essay as of an edition. What does unite the contributors is a firm belief in the potential of contemporary literary criticism and theory and of contemporary textual scholarship and theory to enrich each other. Some of the essays highlight editorial theory or the actual construction of editions, and others highlight textual scholarship or the archaeological recuperation of various states of a text. They all emphasize the implications of new developments in editorial and textual theory for the study of literature at the present time.

The first two essays, on W. B. Yeats and on William Carlos Williams, grow out of the experience of distinguished editors constructing editions of two major modernist poets. Richard Finneran records his initial surprise that the two-volume 1949 edition of Yeats's *Poems* was too flawed to serve as basis for his *Poems: A New Edition* of 1983, revised as *Poems* in 1989. Instead, problems with punctuation, title, order, and even composition of the canon necessitated a much-altered volume. Even such small matters as the exclusion of an initial definite article could change the protagonist of "The Man and the Echo" from a specific to a generic figure, while the exclusion of a mere comma alters the line "What matter, we are but women" from voicing limitation (or worse) to instead avowing heroic aspiration. In tracking those and much larger issues like the order of the poetry through both his own edition and some of those that appeared upon expiration of copyright outside the United States last year, Finneran reminds us that such editions are necessarily constructed through the contingent decisions of their editors. Unusually for the exponent of an author-based theory like his own, Finneran thoughtfully concludes that a "definitive editon" is a mythical chimera and that an editor will always have to employ his or her own judgment. Correspondingly, A. Walton Litz and Christopher MacGowan begin from an author-based theory that would restore the chronology of Williams's work but find that theory leading to complex choices about whether to print poetry and prose in Williams's mixed-genre volumes, about which text of revised poems to reproduce, and even about which poems to include. Acute enough with the *Collected Poems,* textual problems become even more so with *Paterson* because the social and economic factors behind many textual changes are themselves part of the poem's themes and are incorporated into the poem as embodied process rather than as finished statement. As Williams himself wrote to Louis Zukofsky, "most modern work is written to be printed and cannot be considered to exist until it is so."[18] A particular problem with Williams's texts is the changing visual layout of the poems on the page, and Litz and MacGowan contribute to a neglected aspect of editorial theory in highlighting the semantic aspect of spatial design in modernist poetry.

The next two essays, on Pound and on H.D., feature textual scholarship more than editorial theory. Ronald Bush begins with the problems created by the *lack* of a scholarly text of Pound's *Cantos,* particularly a variorum or genetic one that would enable reconstitution of lost earlier states of the poem. Instead, the current reading text (loyally kept in print by New Directions over the years) necessarily erases earlier stages of the poem as they first appeared. As a result, Pound's opus has been open to revisionary poststructuralist attacks upon it as a closed, totalized, ultimately fascistic or sexist system. Using both manuscript materials and earlier printings of the *Cantos,* Bush instead argues for the poem as more open, contingent, and tentative than many of its critics allow. He shows, for example, that objectionable sections of Canto VI were late additions interpolated into the poem after the original 1919 version had been published three times (in *Dial* of 1921, in *Poems 1918–1921,* and in *A Draft of XVI. Cantos* of 1925), just as the current invocation of Mussolini at the beginning of *The Pisan Cantos* belongs to a very late stage of the compositional process and obscures the original and more humane beginning of that section. Bush's examination of the problem of the ending of the poem in the *Drafts and Fragments* section argues that our inability to determine how Pound wanted the physical text to conclude, and the shifting conclusions created by his publishers and others, suit the open nature of the poem better than the more totalizing endings desired by both admirers and detractors. Similarly, Lawrence Rainey argues for distinguishing between an H.D. constructed by the spate of posthumous editions and supporting criticism in the 1980s and the original H.D. constructed by the works that she allowed to appear during her own lifetime. In contrast to the current notion of a great original and democratic artist suppressed by a patriarchal order, Rainey uses bibliographical evidence to suggest instead a picture of H.D. metamorphosing under the patronage of her lover Winifred Ellerman (Bryher) into a coterie author content to have her work appear in tiny, expensive editions from Ellerman's press with colophon notices such as "This edition, of 100 copies, has been printed by friends of the author for private circulation." Rainey finds, too, that in contrast to more financially hard-pressed modernist authors like Pound, Moore, or Yeats, H.D. published very little critical prose, less than an article a year, and that her later verse appeared most often in periodicals controlled by Bryher. Some readers will find Rainey's reassessment of H.D.'s achievement controversial, but all will have to take account of the publication history that he here recuperates.

While the canons of H.D. and Pound have swelled considerably since their deaths, those of Marianne Moore and W. H. Auden shrank surprisingly during their authors' own lifetimes. In both cases, current "collected" or "complete" editions in fact omit numerous passages and poems, and they often contain heavily revised texts as well, so that "selected and revised" would be a better sobriquet for them. Moore's most characteristic technique of revision was deletion and pruning, as her *Complete Poems* prominently informed readers by announcing that "omissions are not accidents." Andrew Kappel's essay charts the several forms of omission in Moore's revisions, including dropping entire poems, dropping passages from poems in increasingly obvious fashion, and removing a work like her famous "The Steeple-Jack" from its original sequence to let it stand alone. Kappel relates the resistance toward totality and finality in the original title of that sequence, "Part of a Novel, Part of a Poem,

Part of a Play," to the pervasive modernist suspicion of authority also at work in titles like "Notes toward a Supreme Fiction" and even *The Cantos*. He concludes with examination of the celebrated deletions in Moore's "Poetry," where the resultant gaps insert a characteristic modernist gesture into the poem. In "The Claims of History and the Claims of the Two Audens" Edward Mendelson explores the problems for editor and critic alike created by a poet who radically revises and excises his own work, a particularly acute problem with Auden after his move to America in 1939 but one already present in the earlier gatherings. Mendelson identifies two poles of editorial choice—a "fading-coal" model in which the earliest text of a poem deserves priority as closest to the author's original imaginative vision, and a "gothic-tower" model favoring the author's final version as the product of a mature craftsmanship. The new Princeton *Complete Works* will adopt a policy of printing the contents and version of each of Auden's books as they first appeared between hard covers, in contrast to the policy of the *Collected Poems* of 1976, which offers Auden's final reshaping of his canon. The new edition will thus restore famous deleted poems like "September 1, 1939," whose political nature reminds us of the political dimension of all editorial choices. The treatment of the musical revue *The Dance of Death* accentuates that dimension by raising the question of what to do about changes made in the interests of stage presentation (including censorship) or of following the meter of the musical settings. Such stage changes recapitulate a central question in contemporary editorial theory, namely whether the work is constituted by its author as sole creator or by a more collective process of composition and dissemination.

Questions of constitution and dissemination permeate the essays on James Joyce and on Virginia Woolf. In her essay on Joyce, Vicki Mahaffey calls attention to the growing prominence of the computer in preparing editions like Hans Gabler's of *Ulysses*. The versos of Gabler's three-volume edition offer a "synopsis" of different stages of the text's autograph composition from final draft through the last set of proofs. That procedure highlights the conception of writing as process rather than product; the corresponding definition of copy-text becomes the most important as well as the most controversial aspect of the edition, and in some ways aligns Gabler's procedure with theoretical views of multiple versions. Mahaffey concludes that Gabler is conservative in his valuing of authorial intention but radical in his decision to define that intention as multiple and changing. Indeed, the edition implies that an editor's authority may be as provisional and contingent as an author's, as examination of the problems created by Joyce's "deliberate errors" shows. The concept of multiple versions of a work also underlies "Textual Criticism as Feminist Practice." There Brenda Silver explores the mutual tendencies of both feminist criticism and textual scholarship to break through surfaces of established texts in order to bring to light submerged ones. The recent history of Woolf scholarship illustrates her point, as early versions of Woolf's work have become available in original editions—for example, *The Pargiters,* part of which became *The Years* and part *Three Guineas; Melymbrosia,* which became *The Voyage Out;* and *Pointz Hall,* which became *Between the Acts.* The existence of multiple versions has led to debate about whether the later ones "improve" the earlier texts aesthetically or whether instead they "parget" (whitewash) the original anger of the earlier drafts. One view sees Woolf's revisions as "self-editing," the other as "self-censorship." Silver proposes a model of reading "both ways" that would not privilege either version but rather take the composite one as a whole. That procedure would view the text neither in the common New Critical way as a given object of interpretation nor in the common poststructural one as an invention of interpretation, but rather as a palimpsest composed of its chief constituent stages.

Censorship also plays a leading role in the essay on D. H. Lawrence, particularly the social censorship that caused him to suppress his erotic frankness. For example, under pressure from the English publisher of *The White Peacock* Lawrence reluctantly emended the passage "God—we were a passionate couple and she would have me in her bedroom while she drew Greek statues of me" to "Lord—we were an infatuate couple—and she would choose to view me in an aesthetic light." Such extreme cases form an interesting crux for theories of editing that view the text as socially constituted rather than authorially devised. Eugene Goodheart uses several volumes of the Cambridge edition of Lawrence to argue surprisingly that following a historically oriented view may in many cases reinforce social censorship or repression, and that following authorial "intention" (however complicated that term) may ultimately support the potentially subversive role of art. Like other contributors to the volume, Goodheart does find that social contexts, authorial intention, and the editor's aesthetic judgment all contribute to editorial decisions. Noel Polk takes a somewhat similar position in his essay on editing

William Faulkner. Beginning with the collapse at least for modernist literature of Greg's distinction between substantives and accidentals, Polk concludes that a "definitive" edition of Faulkner may be impossible. He views his own series of Faulkner editions for Random House and Library of America as attempts to "de-edit" Faulkner and instead to get into print editions as close to Faulkner's typescripts as possible. Like other contributors, Polk finds the concept of "intention" continuously problematic in a way that facilitates thinking of *Sanctuary* as a composite rather than unitary text composed of two equally valid versions, and of writing as a process rather than a product.

The concluding essay on "Contemporary Textual and Literary Theory" foregrounds many of the issues explored through particular cases earlier in the volume. Michael Groden investigates relations among text, author, and social context by interrogating the linked pairs first of author and authorial intention and then of work and text. Like other contributors, Groden finds problems in the traditional editorial concepts of final authorial intentions and of the art work itself, both of which covertly accord with the seemingly anti-intentionalist views of the New Criticism. His historical overview of the development of contemporary editing culminates in an exploration of alternatives to mainstream, author-centered theories like G. Thomas Tanselle's recent adaptations of Greg-Bowers principles. Those alternatives include the broader but still author-centered theories of Peter Shillingsburg (which distinguish an "intention to mean" from an "intention to do" and argue that an editor can recover only the latter), the sociological orientation of Jerome McGann, and more recent work with various poststructural roots. An important benefit for textual scholarship appears to lie in literary theory's recent reconceptions of the term *author,* just as a benefit for literary theory lies in textual scholarship's careful distinctions between a work of art and its embodiment in any given physical text. Groden's essay, like all those in this volume, is meant not to limit the range of inquiry but rather to explore its potential scope. Students of modernism may come belatedly to the relation between editorial and literary theory, but for that reason they may be able to stimulate substantial reconceptualizations. Contemporary technology may sometime satisfy Ezra Pound's wish and make it possible for us to have the editions we want; the union of contemporary textual and literary theory would go a long distance toward helping us understand what and how those editions would mean.

NOTES

1. *Rime* Mss., Ezra Pound Center, Beinecke Library, Yale University, as quoted in David Anderson, *Pound's Cavalcanti: An Edition of the Translations, Notes, and Essays* (Princeton: Princeton University Press, 1983), xxvii.

2. Ibid.

3. Fredson Bowers, *Essays in Bibliography, Text, and Editing* (Charlottesville: Published for the Bibliographical Society of the University of Virginia by the University Press of Virginia, 1975), 300–301. The following examples from Melville and from Eliot may be found on 320–21 and 322, respectively.

4. For discussion see William Proctor Williams and Craig S. Abbott, *An Introduction to Bibliographical and Textual Studies* (New York: Modern Language Association, 1985), 4; and Charles Rossmann, "Introduction," *Studies in the Novel* 22 (Special Issue on Editing *Ulysses,* Summer 1990): 113.

5. Discussions of Yeats's arrangement of his poems in significant orderings include, among others, Hugh Kenner's well-known essay "The Sacred Book of the Arts," in his *Gnomon* (New York: McDowell, Obolensky, 1958), 9–29, reprinted most recently in *Critical Essays on W. B. Yeats,* ed. Richard Finneran (Boston: G. K. Hall, 1986); Hazard Adams, *The Book of Yeats's Poems* (Tallahassee: Florida State University Press, 1990); and my own "Remaking Himself: Yeats's Revisions of his Early Canon," *Text* 5 (1991): 339–58.

6. W. B. Yeats, *The Poems,* ed. Richard J. Finneran (New York: Macmillan, 1983, rev. 1989), 293, 320, and 348. For more on the ordering of *Last Poems* see Finneran's monograph *Editing Yeats's Poems: A Reconsideration* (London: Macmillan, 1990).

7. See Curtis Bradford, "The Order of *Last Poems," Modern Language Notes* 76 (June 1961): 515–16, and *Yeats's 'Last Poems' Again,* Yeats Centenary Papers 8 (Dublin: Dolmen Press, 1966).

8. W. W. Greg, "The Rationale of Copy-Text," *Studies in Bibliography* 3 (1950–51): 19–36.

9. Jerome J. McGann, *A Critique of Modern Textual Criticism* (Chicago: University of Chicago Press, 1983), 68.

10. Hans Zeller, "A New Approach to the Critical Constitution of Literary Texts," *Studies in Bibliography* 28 (1975): 240–41.

11. Donald H. Reiman, *Romantic Texts and Contexts* (Columbia: University of Missouri Press, 1987), 169, 170.

12. S. M. Parrish, "The Whig Interpretation of Literature," *Text* 4 (1988): 344–45 and 349.

13. William Wordsworth, *The Prelude 1799, 1805, 1850,* ed. Jonathan Wordsworth, M. H. Abrams, and Stephen Gill (New York: Norton, 1979).

14. Gary Taylor and Michael Warren, eds., *The Division of the Kingdoms*

(Oxford: Clarendon, 1983); and Michael Warren, ed., *The Complete King Lear, 1608–1623* (Berkeley: University of California Press, 1990), four parts.

15. Bowers, *Essays*, 309.

16. McGann, *Critique*, 8.

17. Peter L. Shillingsburg, *Scholarly Editing in the Computer Age* (Athens, Ga.: University of Georgia Press, 1986).

18. See below, Litz and MacGowan, "Editing William Carlos Williams," n. 2. Further quotations not documented in my introduction itself are drawn from subsequent essays in the volume and are fully documented in those essays.

Text and Interpretation in the Poems of W. B. Yeats

Richard J. Finneran

Shall we not find in our new texts
Things to be cherished like the thought
Of the Definitive Edition?

—With apologies to Wallace Stevens

In the beginning was the Word, and the Word was *Poems* (1949). Heralded by a Prospectus that claimed "for some time before his death, W. B. Yeats was engaged in revising the text of this edition of his poems, of which he had corrected the proofs"; described by Allan Wade in *A Bibliography of the Writings of W. B. Yeats* (1951) as "The Definitive Edition"; certified by Mrs. Yeats to Russell K. Alspach as a volume that "fully warranted the word 'definitive,'" for which "WBY had corrected the proof and arranged the poems in the order he wanted" and had made "the final corrections"; adopted by Alspach and Peter Allt as the copy-text for the magisterial *Variorum Edition of the Poems of W. B. Yeats* (1957): seldom has textual apotheosis been so swift or so certain.[1]

Four years after the publication of *Variorum Poems,* a lone voice of dissent emerged. Curtis Bradford, having discovered a manuscript table of contents that precisely matched the contents and arrangement of the Cuala Press *Last Poems and Two Plays* (1939), ventured the heretical suggestion that the differences in the Macmillan *Last Poems & Plays* (1940) and all later editions might not be authorized (*EYP:AR,* 4). A few years later, after an extensive study of the manuscripts which resulted in *Yeats at Work* (1965), Bradford compounded his heresy by suggesting that perhaps Yeats's punctuation was superior to that of his "editors and copy editors" (*EYP:AR,* 35n.16).

Bradford was a major Yeatsian, rather more than merely a voice crying in the wilderness. His arguments, especially about *Last Poems,* received significant acceptance among other Yeats scholars. But no changes were made to the *Variorum Poems* or to the *Collected Poems* (1950, 1951), which continued to be reprinted with texts based on the 1949 "Definitive Edition." The critical enterprise of explication and interpretation likewise continued on its way, virtually unaffected. Readers read, students studied, and professors professed the Word as inscribed in *Poems* (1949) and its derivatives.

In 1976, I was commissioned by Macmillan, London, and the Yeats Estate to undertake a new edition of Yeats's poetry. I began with the assumption that although *Poems* (1949) might require some small emendation, it would surely provide the basic text.[2] However, it quickly became clear that the volume could not bear such a burden: that it was defective in contents, in order, and in text. In fact, *Poems* (1949) was both less and more than advertised: it was *not* a "Definitive Edition," a final, pure emanation from the master's hand; it *was* the product of the silent but active intervention of both the poet's widow, Mrs. W. B. Yeats, and Yeats's principal editor at Macmillan, London, Thomas Mark. In the end, the collection was to serve as the copy-text for only one lyric (the first of "Two Songs Rewritten for the Tune's Sake"), and then only because of the (probable) loss of a manuscript or typescript (*EYP:AR,* 55–57).

My work resulted in *The Poems: A New Edition* and *Editing Yeats's Poems,* both published in 1983. These have now been superseded by *The Poems,* revised edition (1989), which includes four additional lyrics as well as the inevitable minor corrections in both text and notes; and by *Editing Yeats's Poems: A Reconsideration* (1990), revised and expanded to draw on new archival materials and to address some matters raised by reviewers of the 1983 volumes. My edition of Yeats's poetry was not offered—and could not have been offered—as a new "Definitive Edition." Indeed, by 1983 the very concept of such an artifact had been largely discredited by textual scholars. With Yeats's poetry the notion is especially problematic for several reasons, ranging from his notorious handwriting to his lifelong habit of revising and rearranging his verse. Rather, I tried to present Yeats's poems as they stood at the time of his death, in terms of both text and arrangement. This meant rejecting the great bulk of the posthumous emendations introduced by Mrs. Yeats and Thomas Mark as early as the Cuala Press *Last Poems and Two Plays* and trying to reproduce what Yeats in fact did or clearly intended to do, rather than what others assumed he would have done—or should have done.

With the expiration of all Yeats copyrights outside of the United States on 1 January 1990, other editions of the poetry are rapidly becoming available. Three are presently in print. From a textual standpoint, those by Augustine Martin and Daniel Albright are, as Jerome McGann has noted, "either naive or appalling."[3]

In his edition of the *Collected Poems* (1990), Augustine Martin simply rearranges the canon to his liking.[4] "Upon a Dying Lady," for instance, is moved from *The Wild Swans at Coole* to *Responsibilities;* "Reprisals" is inserted into *Michael Robartes and the Dancer;* "The Gift of Harun Al-Rashid" is placed before *The Tower;* and so forth. The result is a text never seen before, never conceived of by Yeats, and, some might hope, "a thing never known again" (*P,* 303).

In his edition of *The Poems* (1990), Daniel Albright at least uses an order more or less derived from the unpublished Edition de Luxe of the 1930s.[5] But Albright proceeds to rewrite and especially to repunctuate the poems according to his own preferences. As he explains, only his inability to "contrive" something better forced him to print the opening lines of "Sailing to Byzantium" as Yeats left them (Albright, xlix). But in many other places, unfortunately, his ingenuity did not fail him.

The dangers of editing by intuition and its effects on interpretation are well illustrated by Albright's commentary on a passage from "The Gift of Harun Al-Rashid." As this episode is typical of the problems that confront all editors of Yeats, and as it also illustrates the timeless axiom that a little (and a secondhand) acquaintance with manuscript evidence is a dangerous thing, it is worth examining in detail. The passage reads:

> . . . I cannot hide the truth
> That wandering in a desert, featureless
> As air under a wing, can give birds' wit.
>
> (*P,* 445)

Albright explains:

> Sometimes every modern text is mistaken. "The Gift of Harun Al-Rashid", 1. 28, reads, according to Mark and Finneran alike: "As air under a wing, can give birds' wit." However, in an early magazine printing, the apostrophe is absent. The apostrophe ought to be absent;

> *birds* must be dative, not genitive; in fact in an early draft this line read, "Even as the air has given a bird wits" (Stallworthy, *BL*, p. 68), where the genitive construction is impossible. (Albright, 1)

The invocation of Mark, rather than of Yeats, will doubtless hoodwink most readers into thinking that "birds' wit" first appeared posthumously. In fact, it is found in *The Cat and the Moon and Certain Poems* (1924); *The Tower,* including the revised edition (1928, 1929); and both the English and American printings of the *Collected Poems* (1933). Moreover, the close variant "bird's wit" is found in both *The Dial* (June 1924) and *A Vision* (1925). Albright's preferred dative form occurs only in *English Life and The Illustrated Review* (January 1924), a text that was significantly revised for *The Dial.*

Albright's citation of the manuscript materials is likewise incomplete and inaccurate. First, he relies on another scholar's transcription rather than the actual manuscript. Unfortunately, in an atypical error Stallworthy mistranscribes "a birds wits" as "a bird wits"; moreover, he neglects to indicate that the entire passage up to "a birds wits" is canceled by a vertical stroke.[6] Second, Albright conflates two lines: the phrase occurs not at the end of "Even as the air has given" but at the end of the following line, most of which is canceled by an additional horizontal stroke: "~~Even as the air gives this~~ a birds wits."[7] Since the apparent antecedent for "this" is "the truth," the genitive construction is not "impossible" but almost inescapable: i.e., "the air has given this truth the wits of a bird."

That "birds' wit" is correct is confirmed by other manuscripts of "The Gift of Harun Al-Rashid" only briefly mentioned by Stallworthy. There are two states of a complete typescript. The first state exists in duplicate and was doubtless the source for the January 1924 printing. The line was typed "As air under a wing can give birds wit." On both, Yeats added a comma after "wing" and a period after "wit". On one he also revised to the possessive, "bird's" (SB, 24.1.021, 030). A second state of typescript shows many of the revisions for *The Dial.* Here the line was typed "As air under a wing, can give birds wit." Yeats again revised to the possessive, "bird's" (SB, 24.1.041). Finally, based on this revised typescript, Yeats prepared a holograph of the first 118 lines of "The Gift of Harun Al-Rashid." This may have been used as partial copy for either *The Cat and the Moon* or *The Tower.*[8] In any case, Yeats has clearly written "As air under a wing, can give birds' wit" (SB, 24.1.050).

The proper reading is sufficiently unusual that it might well have been queried either by Yeats's sisters when producing *The Cat and the Moon and Certain Poems* for the Cuala Press and/or by Thomas Mark when producing *The Tower* for Macmillan, but proofs for those volumes do not survive. We do have, however, the 3 August 1932 revised page proofs of the Edition de Luxe *Poems*. Mark introduced revisions in lines 26 and 30 that Yeats silently accepted, but line 28 is passed over. Either Mark had already queried "birds' wit" and been informed that it was correct, or he saw nothing to question.

In sum, the bulk of the evidence strongly supports the possessive, "birds' wit." Proper interpretation might do the same. In Albright's text, Kusta Ben Luka is stating that he cannot hide forever his knowledge about the wit of birds. Leaving aside the fact that the verb should thus be "gives," not "can give," why would the speaker apologize for his disclosure? Such avian information need scarcely be sequestered until "fitting time has passed"; nor would one be likely to describe it as "A mystery that else had found no chronicler / But the wild Bedouin" (*P,* 445), a people not generally known as ornithologists. In Yeats's text, the truth is so esoteric that it can give *man* wit like that of birds, birds being used as an emblem of the supernatural (note the speaker's later reference to "All my fine feathers" [*P,* 450]). It is precisely because of the "mystery" of such truth that "In after time they will speak much of me / And speak but fantasy" (*P,* 445). One can hope that if Albright's edition is reprinted, Yeats will be allowed to speak for himself.

The third recent edition (more are to follow) is *Yeats's Poems,* edited by A. Norman Jeffares.[9] This repeats the fundamental mistake of Allt and Alspach in using *Poems* (1949) as copy-text. In fact, though, Jeffares has produced the first Construct-a-Text Edition of Yeats's poetry, as the textual apparatus provides "Corrections of Misprints or Other Alterations Made to the Copy Text" (3 pp.), "Possible Emendations of the Copy Text" (16 pp.), and "Possible Emendations from Copy Submitted for the Proposed Dublin Edition" (1 p.)[10] Astonishingly, "printed sources only are cited as authority for corrections or alterations in the copy text, or for suggested possible emendations of it" (Jeffares, 644). Hazarding to edit Yeats's poems, particularly the last works, without recourse to manuscript evidence is extraordinary. As matters stand, any readers who venture into the sixteen-page list are left to their own devices to choose between, for instance, the *American Mercury* versus the *London Mercury* or *Last Poems and Two Plays* versus *Last Poems & Plays.*

As a short but very interesting example, consider the key variant in a lyric from *New Poems* (1938):

The Spur

You think it horrible that lust and rage
Should dance attendance upon my old age;
They were not such a plague when I was young;
What else have I to spur me into song?

(*P,* 312)

Jeffares offers not "attendance" but "attention," the reading of the *London Mercury* (March 1938), *Last Poems & Plays* (1940), and the posthumous printings before 1983. Although a diligent reader can discover "attendance" as a "possible alternative," with *New Poems* as the source (Jeffares, 656), one cannot learn from Jeffares that "attendance" is supported by a vast array of primarily contemporary documents—letters to Ethel Mannin and Dorothy Wellesley, all the working manuscripts as well as the final corrected typescript in the National Library of Ireland, a corrected copy of *New Poems,* and the typescripts sent to Scribner's for the Dublin Edition in June 1937 and again in the spring of 1939. On the other hand, after the *London Mercury* "attention" resurfaces only on the Macmillan Coole Edition proofs version of *Last Poems* (28 June 1939), which became the source for the posthumous printings.[11]

It is of course possible to believe that Yeats revised "attendance" to "attention" on the lost proofs for the *London Mercury* but proceeded to forget the revision while working on *New Poems* as well as when dictating corrections to that volume; and to further suppose that Mrs. Yeats forgot it when submitting copy to Scribner's in 1939. But how likely is such a sequence? One inevitably turns in such instances to evaluation, to interpretation. Would Yeats have sacrificed the vivid image of lust and rage as courtiers to the aging poet, particularly when the Renaissance context is reinforced by the reference to "plague"? Indeed, the *OED* definition of "to dance attendance" as "'to attend,' . . . usually with some shade of sarcasm or contempt," not only fits the poem perfectly but is supported by quotations from Heywood (1562) and Burton (1621).[12]

In brief, it seems clear that from both an editorial and an interpretive perspective, "attendance" is the preferable reading, "attention" at best a "possible alternative." But as Jeffares's editorial procedure discounts the archival materials, few readers of *Yeats's Poems* will stumble upon "attendance" and even fewer be inspired to adopt it.[13]

As another example, consider the conclusion of "Cuchulain Comforted" (ll. 19–25):

'Now we shall sing and sing the best we can
But first you must be told our character:
Convicted cowards all by kindred slain

'Or driven from home and left to die in fear.'
They sang, but had nor human notes nor words,
Though all was done in common as before,

They had changed their throats and had the throats of birds.

January 13, 1939

(*P*, 332)

Except for the addition of a missing quotation mark (l. 22) and of a comma in the date, this text follows the final corrected typescript in the National Library of Ireland (*EYP:AR*, 98–99). Ignoring that typescript, Jeffares adopts the wording in the first printed text, *Last Poems and Two Plays;* adds the posthumous changes in punctuation first found on the Coole Edition proofs of *Last Poems;* and deletes the date found on those proofs as well as in all printed editions, including *Poems* (1949):

'Now must we sing and sing the best we can,
But first you must be told our character:
Convicted cowards all, by kindred slain

'Or driven from home and left to die in fear.'
They sang, but had nor human tunes nor words,
Though all was done in common as before;

They had changed their throats and had the throats of birds.

(Jeffares, 456)

As the question of Yeats's punctuation remains to be discussed, I shall not pause over those differences (ll. 19, 21, 24), except to note that although Jeffares lists the typescript readings as a "possible alternative" (Jeffares, 660), citing *Last Poems and Two Plays* as the "source," he relies on that same printing to suggest that the deletion of a quotation mark (l. 22) is an equally "possible alternative," when virtually no reader would wish to make such an emendation. And only in the explanatory notes can a reader discover "13 Jan. [sic] 1939 (appended to text *P* (1949))" (Jeffares, 635).[14]

More interesting, of course, are the substantive differences: "we shall sing" / "human notes" versus "must we sing" / "human tunes" (ll. 19, 23). An argument can be made for either. The readings in *The Poems* (1989) are derived from a typescript that was used as the setting copy for the Cuala Press edition and of which a retyped version was submitted to Scribner's. In the process of correcting the Cuala proofs, Mrs. Yeats (presumably) decided to adopt the revisions Yeats had made on the original of an earlier typescript but not on its surviving carbon. Complicating the issue is the fact that only on the carbon of this earlier typescript do we find the correction of an obvious typing error, "the man / The man" (ll. 17–18). If we could determine whether the typescript followed in *The Poems* (1989) was contemporary or posthumous, the debate might be nearer to resolution, but such a determination seems unlikely.[15]

Our uncertainty mirrors that of Yeats, who in the holograph manuscript wrote "notes", then revised it to "tunes", but must have again changed his mind when dictating the first typescript. Inevitably, then, we fall back on interpretation. For example, I have argued for "notes" partly because the spectral nature of the Shrouds seems to me enhanced if they lack not merely human melodies but indeed human sounds (would one indeed expect a Shroud / bird to be singing, say, "The West's Awake"?); and partly because it creates a double rhyme ("notes nor words" / "throats of birds") at the end of this, Yeats's only *terza rima* lyric. But the problem with Jeffares's edition is that neither "we shall sing" nor "human notes" are contained therein, since they did not appear in print until 1983. Thus to him they are not—as they certainly were to Yeats—"possible alternatives."[16] In sum, Hugh Kenner's description of Jeffares and *Yeats's Poems* is persuasive: "Mr. Jeffares's eclecticism follows nothing coherent. An old-fashioned editor who prints what he happens to like, he has fussed into printed status what we surely don't need . . . ."[17]

Although we shall refer again to the work of Albright, Jeffares, and Martin, we now proceed to further examples of how the revised texts in *The Poems* (1989) affect interpretation. We might consider this under several headings, beginning where most readers begin.

Titles

There are only a few changes in title in the revised edition of *The Poems* (1989), but they are not without interest. For example, the initial article in "The Man and the Echo" is first found on the Cuala proofs of *Last*

Poems and Two Plays. There is no contemporary support for that addition, as all four typescripts and both January 1939 printings offer "Man and the Echo," which was therefore adopted in the new text.[18] It seems clearly superior for a poem that is less about W. B. Yeats—despite the biographical allusions in the opening stanza—than about generic Man, facing the moment of death. One might note the shift from "I" to "we" near the end of the lyric:

> O rocky voice
> Shall we in that great night rejoice?
> What do we know but that we face
> One another in this place?
>
> (*P*, 346)

A more complex editorial problem concerns the section title for the poems that fall between *The Winding Stair and Other Poems* (1933) and *New Poems* (1938). Yeats's last known title was "Poems 1933–1937," which he lit upon in late January 1937 and reaffirmed that June. However, most of the lyrics in question were published in *New Poems* in 1938, and thus it is now impossible to retain Yeats's working title. For *Poems* (1949) Mark and/or Mrs. Yeats employed the awkward "From 'A Full Moon in March,'" even though for the *Collected Poems* (1933) the parallel "From 'The Green Helmet and Other Poems'" had been replaced by simply "The Green Helmet and Other Poems." Warwick Gould's statement that a June 1937 list of contents for the Scribner Edition "included Yeats's own annotation that 'from "A Full Moon in March"' should be used as a subsection title" (Jeffares, 728) is, like much else in his Appendix 6 of *Yeats's Poems*, simply erroneous.[19]

In my edition I offered "Parnell's Funeral and Other Poems," a heading that occupies a full page in *A Full Moon in March*.[20] Although it is no more authorized or "definitive" than other options, it has the virtue of highlighting the opening poem of the section, surely one of Yeats's most impressive responses to Irish politics, a lifelong preoccupation.

Punctuation

Much has been made of Yeats's disdain for punctuation and his inability to punctuate—rather too much, I think. As with most matters involved in editing Yeats, the documentary evidence is fundamentally inconclusive. Against such well-known statements as the remark to Robert Bridges that "I do not understand stops. I write my work so completely for the ear that I feel helpless when I have to measure pauses by stops & commas"—usually quoted without reference to the context, Yeats being deferential to the Poet Laureate about an anthology reprint—should be balanced by his less familiar statement upon returning a proof of "Sailing to Byzantium" to his publishers: "Through vacillation over the punctuation of the first stanza I have made a blotted proof but I think it is clear" (*EYP:AR*, 35, 35nn. 15–16). Moreover, many of Yeats's manuscripts show him carefully adding punctuation, usually at a late stage of composition.

Essentially, those who object to Yeats's punctuation believe in the theory of delegation—that he required others to punctuate for him. Albright, for instance, claims that "an inattentive, half-blind, possibly dyslexic poet must rely on his editors. . . ." Yeats "wanted his poems to look finished . . . but he could not fulfil this wish without aid" (Albright, xlviii). Likewise, Gould quotes a letter from Mrs. Yeats to Thomas Mark on 17 April 1939 (as usual, the italics are Gould's): "WBY wrote to you in September (or October) 1932 about punctuation and generally asking your help, *without which he knew he could never get his work into the final form he wished*" (Jeffares, 739n.5). Ignoring the inherent flattery of the occasion, Gould takes this at face value.[21] One is left to wonder how the maladroit poet ever managed to publish anything during the thirty years or so before he came into contact with Mark, or even thereafter in various periodicals or with several other publishers.

Since I do not accept this vision of a Yeats prostrate at the threshold of the demiurge Semicolon, in my text I attempted to present his own punctuation. This policy resulted in numerous differences from all previous editions. Not all these revisions are improvements; not all (despite Poe on Hawthorne) are significant to interpretation; not all are indisputably correct. But as one example consider the opening of "The Lady's Second Song":

> What sort of man is coming
> To lie between your feet?
> What matter we are but women.
> Wash; make your body sweet;
> I have cupboards of dried fragrance
> I can strew the sheet.
> *The Lord have mercy upon us.*
>
> (*P,* 299)

This is the text as found in *New Poems* (1938), including the copy in which Mrs. Yeats apparently recorded Yeats's later corrections (*EYP:AR*, 66, 62–63). The repunctuation of the stanza began when Mrs. Yeats added a comma after "fragrance" on the typescript sent to Scribner's in the spring of 1939. On the Coole Edition proofs of *Last Poems*, Thomas Mark not only accepted that change, but he also added a comma after "what matter" (as well as another in l. 19). The additional punctuation was first published in *Last Poems & Plays*. Martin (314) and Jeffares (417) follow this posthumous text, though the latter allows for the deletion of the commas in his list of "Possible Emendations." Albright offers a comma after "fragrance" but not after "matter."

Which of these versions is a reader to read and interpret? Although the additional punctuation is not supported by the extant typescripts, one can sympathize with those who want something at the end of line five. But what? Surely a semicolon is at least as good as Mrs. Yeats's comma? If in 1939 Mark had opted for a colon or a dash or even a period, would anyone now be moved to question his choice? If there is no punctuation authorized by Yeats, if there is no inevitable solution, and if the passage makes perfect sense as written, is emendation necessary? In this instance, I think, whatever choice one makes will have little effect on interpretation.

However, "What matter, we are but women" presents rather another situation. Mark's comma presents a speaker who accepts her subservient position, making the lyric fit ammunition for feminist attacks on Yeats. Yeats's text opens up the possibility of rather the opposite image, a speaker who sees herself as certainly the equal of man, if not indeed someone dominant in sexual matters. In other words, a single unauthorized comma can radically alter our understanding of an entire poem, indeed in this instance of an entire sequence. This is arguably the most spectacular example of the case that can be made for Yeats's punctuation instead of his editors', but there are many others—and not only in the late poems.

The Order of the Poems

Certainly the most controversial difference between *The Poems* (1989) and *Poems* (1949) is the overall arrangement of the poetry. As there is a chapter in *Editing Yeats's Poems: A Reconsideration* and a lengthy Appendix in *Yeats's Poems* on the topic, I offer here the shortest possible summary.[22]

On the page proofs for the unpublished Macmillan Edition de Luxe, prepared in 1931 and checked by Yeats in 1932, the poems are in a quasi-chronological arrangement, with "The Wanderings of Oisin" at the head of the volume and the other narrative poems interspersed among the lyrics. When the *Collected Poems* was in preparation in 1933, Macmillan suggested a two-part division: their motivation was primarily commercial. In what remains his only documented comment on the matter, Yeats agreed, expressing his "delight" at the suggestion (*EYP:AR*, 154).[23] *His* motivation is unknown. Yeats planned to use the two-part format for the unpublished Scribner Edition as early as 1935, and he followed through with that plan when submitting copy in June 1937. Shortly thereafter, he arranged with Macmillan for an expanded edition of the *Collected Poems* in 1939 (*EYP:AR*, 156). The 1949 *Poems* uses the order of the Edition de Luxe proofs, whereas the two-part arrangement is retained in the posthumous and expanded editions of the *Collected Poems,* including the 1956 American volume, which is described—almost surely with Mrs. Yeats's blessing—as the "Definitive Edition, With the Author's Final Revisions" (*EYP:AR*, 166).[24]

I have omitted some details, but those are the basic facts. Essentially, the Edition de Luxeites argue that Yeats's poetic heart and soul were always with the quasi-chronological scheme, and that he accepted the arrangement of the *Collected Poems*—described by the most vociferous de Luxeite as a "pot-boiler" or a "money-spinner"—only for financial gain.[25]

Again, there has yet to materialize a "smoking gun" that would resolve the issue on purely editorial grounds.[26] In a future electronic edition of Yeats's poetry, such as Jerome McGann has called for, no doubt either the F1 key or Alt + 0 will enable the reader to toggle between the competing formats. But even then, one version will presumably have to be the default arrangement; or, if one opts for windows, that on the top or on the right. Thus in answer to the complaint that I presume "that one must choose *either* the *Edition de Luxe or* the *CP* order" (Jeffares, 745), yes, Virginia, short of the discovery of a lost codicil to Yeats's will or the reappearance of his supernatural Instructors, readers—and editors—must make such a choice.[27]

Having examined the evidence on both sides, McGann concludes that the question is "moot"; Kenner finds it not something to "get agitated about."[28] To the extent that Yeats sanctioned both arrangements at different times and that the surviving archive does not *absolutely* validate one scheme over the other, McGann is certainly accurate (cf. *EYP:AR*, 170). In that few if any of us begin reading Yeats's poetry at page one and persevere until the end, Kenner is also quite correct. Yet I still believe our choice of formats has significant consequences for interpretation.

Indeed, the choice speaks to our understanding both of the poetry and of the poet. The Edition de Luxeites offer us a poet who for his publisher and agent is "an easy tool / Deferential, glad to be of use," someone who, as Gould writes, was "happy to accept 'some rearrangement' if it were judged on his behalf that to do so would be in his interests" (Jeffares, 722).[29] The alternate view presents a poet who was always open to the advice of others but who reached his own decisions.[30]

The Edition de Luxeites offer us a poet who is content to reserve the superior arrangement of his work for a strictly limited audience and who is moreover prepared to let this arrangement remain a trade secret while he is alive, in the interim allowing an inferior format to be published, reprinted, and read throughout the world. The alternate view presents a poet who is concerned that his work be available in its best form to any interested reader and who prefers to live to witness the event.

The Edition de Luxeites offer a canon that begins by stressing its Irish and its epic dimensions, and that continues to aspire to the conventional long poem as late as "The Gift of Harun Al-Rashid" in 1928. The alternate view presents a canon that begins by stressing its English origins and its lyric form, and one in which the long poems are understood as a kind of adjunct to the fundamentally lyric achievement.

What we face, then, are questions of audience, of subject matter, of genre. These questions concern not only us, editors and readers attempting to choose between competing formats; they also concerned Yeats himself. On the question of subject matter, for instance, I recently discovered that as early as 1891 he went through *The Wanderings of Oisin and Other Poems* (1889) and made up a list of "Irish Poems" versus "Arcadian" poems, noting (with pride or with anguish?) that the volume contained "46 pages of poems on non-Irish subjects."[31] Nearly a half-century later we find him, in what was intended as the preface to *Poems* in the Scribner Edition, explaining that "I owe my soul to Shakespeare, to Spenser and to Blake, perhaps to William Morris, and to the English language in which I think, speak, and write; . . . everything I love has come to me through English; my hatred tortures me with love, my love with hate."[32]

We might conclude this section by reconstructing Yeats in London on Tuesday, 22 June 1937. Two weeks earlier he had reaffirmed (as he had in January 1937) his choice of the two-part arrangement of his poetry for the Scribner Edition; on 11 June Mrs. Years had forwarded to New York (via his agent) a corrected copy of the *Collected Poems.* Now, on 22 June, he had met with Macmillan and planned an expanded edition of the *Collected Poems* in 1939. Returning to the Athenaeum, he found in his mail a check for some £600 (a rather considerable sum), the first installment from a fund established by an American Testimonial Committee to guarantee financial security for the remainder of his life. He wrote some letters, to Oliver St. John Gogarty and Dorothy Wellesley. He then set to work on the prefaces for the Scribner Edition.[33]

As he sat in the drawing room of the Athenaeum, its two-story windows open to the light of a late English afternoon, and began to compose—"A poet writes always out of his personal life, in his finest work out of its tragedy . . ." (*E&I,* 508)—did he recall some lines from "The Grey Rock" (*P,* 104) and say to himself

> I regret that this important essay will be attached to an inferior arrangement of my poems; I regret that the Edition itself will be bought by virtually all of my American benefactors, many of them virtual strangers. But what could I do? My publisher and my agent wanted "divergence," to ensure the financial success of the Edition de Luxe. Have the words I wrote so many years ago—Lady Gregory's favorite passage in all my poems—returned to vex me?
>
> You had to face your ends when young—
> 'Twas wine or women, or some curse—
> But never made a poorer song
> That you might have a heavier purse. . . .
>
> Have I broken "the Muses' sterner laws" and renounced the right "To troop with those the world's forgot / And copy their proud steady gaze"?

Perhaps. Or did he look forward to attaching his essay to nothing less than what he then considered the best possible embodiment of his life's work, an expanded version of the arrangement he had given to his reading public four years earlier?

There is of course no record of Yeats's thoughts on that summer afternoon; readers—and editors—must think for themselves.

The Order of [*Last Poems*]

We now come to the most visible difference between the revised edition of *Poems* and the previous texts, the order and contents of *Last Poems*. Again, the facts can be quickly summarized. A manuscript table of contents demonstrates that the 1939 Cuala Press *Last Poems and Two Plays* was arranged by Yeats. The typescripts submitted to Scribner's in the spring of 1939 suggest that it was Mrs. Yeats's idea to add to the volume the three poems from *On the Boiler.* A letter from Mrs. Yeats to Thomas Mark on 14 June 1939 demonstrates that it was his suggestion to move "Under Ben Bulben" from the front to the rear of the volume, and that Mrs. Yeats readily agreed, despite knowing that she was violating her husband's design. The fact that the further rearrangement of the volume is found on the Coole Edition proofs of *Last Poems,* and was thus accomplished within less than two weeks after the receipt of her letter, suggests that Mark was responsible for the other extensive changes.[34]

In *The Poems* (1989) I thus restored the division of *New Poems* (1938); and, with Yeats's contents and order, [*Last Poems,* 1938–1939]. (It remains unknown whether "Last Poems" was Yeats's title or his wife's.) One might think that those decisions are about as certain as anything can be in editorial matters. However, Phillip L. Marcus has reminded us that we do not know what Yeats might have done with *Last Poems* once he came to include them, without the two plays, in a collected edition of his verse. That is indisputable. But Marcus then proceeds to offer what I have described as the rather silly notion (*EYP:AR,* 80n.5) that, given our ignorance of what Yeats might have done, we would do as well as to reject the only arrangement he is known to have approved and replace it with that constructed by Mrs. Yeats and Thomas Mark: an order "not authorially sanctioned but prepared by individuals whose judgment Yeats usually trusted and arguably reflecting what he would have done or would have wanted to have done better than does the Cuala volume."[35] As Eliot might have said, after such logic, what forgiveness? Indeed, Marcus's essay is a classic document of the *What If?* school of editing, above whose entrance portal is carved the motto not

"Know thy document" but "Every man/woman his/her own editor." Fortunately, the editors of the other recent editions have not seen fit to matriculate.[36]

The significance of the proper order and contents of *Last Poems* has been discussed by Curtis Bradford, Stanley Sultan, M. L. Rosenthal, and, most recently, Hazard Adams, and there is no need to rehearse their arguments. I would add only two comments. First, I don't think even Yeats was *always* able to find an appropriate spot for every poem in the canon; thus even the best of commentaries based on such a premise are at times guilty of a certain degree of over-ingenuity—e.g., if a particular poem doesn't extend or refine the ideas of its predecessor, then surely it provides a crucial contrast, and so on.

More important, perhaps, we might consider the closure of the collection in light of the debate over the proper arrangement of the poems. If, as I think, Yeats in the last few years of his life conceived of his poetry in the two categories of "Lyrical" and "Narrative and Dramatic," perhaps we can understand his choice of closing poems in a new light. In the penultimate poem, "The Circus Animals' Desertion," he reviews his efforts in narrative poetry ("The Wanderings of Oisin") and drama itself (*The Countess Cathleen* and *On Baile's Strand*), finding them less than satisfactory. "Old themes," "old songs or courtly shows," they are now firmly a part of his past. Though "but a broken man," at the end of the poem he returns defiantly to his origins, to "the foul rag and bone shop of the heart" (*P*, 347–48). What issues forth as his final poetic statement is what we would expect, a lyric, "Politics": a lyric about love, a lyric about the impossibility of love, a lyric about love and politics, a lyric about youth and age. Those were Yeats's themes; that was Yeats's form.[37]

Textual Revisions

It is doubtless the dream of every editor to be able to publish previously unknown materials. Truth be told, there is relatively little of that in my edition. *The Poems* (1989) does include three early works discovered by John S. Kelly as well as, after a change of heart, the posthumously published "Reprisals";[38] but there are only a few places within the canonical poems where entirely new readings are offered: "Brown Penny," "Ribh denounces Patrick," and part two of "Three Marching Songs" are perhaps the major instances.

The last involves the correction of a misreading of Yeats's holograph correction on the final typescript (*EYP:AR*, 102–3). Yeats clearly intended

> We were not born in the peasant's cot
> Where man forgives if the belly gain.
>
> (*P*, 334)

In *Last Poems and Two Plays,* the first line was read correctly, but an unauthorized change was introduced into the second:

> We were not born in the peasant's cot
> Where men forgive if the belly gain.

In *Last Poems & Plays,* the sense of the passage was inverted:

> Were we not born in the peasant's cot
> Where men forgive if the belly gain?

Clearly, that version, also used in *Poems* (1949), creates a meaning quite the opposite of what Yeats intended.[39]

The changes to "Brown Penny" and "Ribh denounces Patrick" are found on the copy of the *Collected Poems* submitted to Scribner's in June 1937. The revision to the later lyric is perhaps the more interesting (*EYP:AR*, 57). Yeats revised

> An abstract Greek absurdity has crazed the man—
> Recall that masculine Trinity. Man, woman, child (a daughter or a son)
> That's how all supernatural stories run.

to

> An abstract Greek absurdity has crazed the man,
> A Trinity that is wholly masculine. Man, woman, child (daughter or son)
> That's how all supernatural stories run.
>
> (*P*, 284)

Yeats's revision places the emphasis where it belongs—not on the doctrine of the Trinity ("Recall that masculine Trinity," followed by a pause) but on its sexuality, or better, its asexuality: "A Trinity that is wholly masculine." In the process Yeats is able to introduce a wonderful homophonic pun on "wholly"/"holy" while at the same time retaining the original (if for him unusual) nineteen-syllable line.[40]

We need to admit that it doesn't take a vast amount of critical ingenuity to put forth an argument favoring reading X over reading Y, as even I have just done. We also need to remind ourselves that as the examples of, say, Wordsworth and Whitman demonstrate, the poet doesn't always know best—or at least we don't think that he does.[41] Thus a skeptic could argue that Yeats made the revision only so that the Scribner Edition would contain some unique readings. It could further be suggested that there is a loss involved in deleting the direct address to the listener/reader, "Recall that masculine Trinity," a device also used in the opening lyric of *Supernatural Songs*—"Because you have found me in the pitch-dark night"/"With open book you ask me what I do" (*P,* 283).

Thus one cannot say that the revision is inherently "correct" or "definitive," or even that it represents Yeats's "final intentions," a term once widely venerated but now at meetings of the Society for Textual Scholarship barely whispered in dark corners. A new variorum or an electronic edition of Yeats's poetry will doubtless offer both readings; bereft of that luxury, why did I adopt the revised text? Primarily for the simple reason that it represents Yeats's last known version. Yet had a sudden attack of senility overcome the master and caused him to write something like "An abstract Greek absurdity has crazed the man— / Let's chat about that macho Trio," I think (or at least I hope) that I would have retained the earlier text, relegating the revision to the virtually eternal darkness of an appendix.

A Final Example

We might end by returning to "Politics," not only the final poem in the lyric canon but also a small masterpiece.

Politics

'In our time the destiny of man presents its meanings in political terms.'
—Thomas Mann

How can I, that girl standing there,
My attention fix
On Roman or on Russian
Or on Spanish politics,
Yet here's a travelled man that knows
What he talks about,

And there's a politician
That has both read and thought,
And maybe what they say is true
Of war and war's alarms,
But O that I were young again
And held her in my arms.

(*P*, 348)

Comparing this text, taken from the *London Mercury* of January 1939 without emendation, with those of the posthumous printings, we find only four differences, but they are significant (*EYP:AR*, 123). First, the epigraph. Perhaps more accurately, the anti-epigraph, as the poem itself disproves its thesis. By attaching it to "Politics" Yeats deliberately gives the misleading impression that he is *au courant* with the latest developments in European literature, and in particular with the most recent thoughts of Thomas Mann. Thus one might suppose that "meaning" rather than "meanings," first found on the Coole Edition proofs, was simply the correction of a quotation. In fact, though, Yeats appropriated the epigraph from an essay by Archibald MacLeish in the March 1938 *Yale Review.* Yeats's "meanings" is precisely Mann as quoted by MacLeish. A printed source in Mann has not to my knowledge been traced; indeed, it is likely that MacLeish quoted from a speech he had heard during Mann's recent American lecture tour. That Mrs. Yeats or Thomas Mark was able to locate a printed source during a few weeks in the spring of 1939 is, to say the least, extremely improbable. Rather, "meaning" is either an unnoticed misprint or, more likely, a "correction" based on the view that the singular "destiny" requires a singular "meaning," a conundrum I will leave to better students of grammar than me—I mean I.[42]

The virtue of preserving Yeats's "meanings" is not only that it suggests the complexities involved in man's "destiny" but also that it verifies MacLeish's essay as the originating occasion of the poem. When Yeats cited the article in a letter to Dorothy Wellesley on 24 May 1938, he could be confident that his epistle would be preserved and eventually published (remember, we're dealing with someone who in 1913 offered to "improve" his earlier letters for the benefit of Katharine Tynan's autobiography!). Indeed, "Politics" is on one level a direct refutation of MacLeish's article. After some admiring remarks, remarks Yeats was happy to quote to Wellesley, MacLeish went on to offer what had become the standard criticism of Yeats by the poets of the 1930s:

> The later poetry of Yeats, because of Yeats's somewhat isolated situation in Ireland and because of Yeats's age, has not been called upon to employ the results of the poetic revolution at the point where those results may prove to be most useful. Yeats has moved only briefly and unwillingly at the point where the poetic revolution crosses the revolution in the social and political and economic structure of the post-war world, which so deeply concerns our generation in this country. But it is precisely at that point that the greatest victories of modern poetry may be won.[43]

One can imagine Yeats's reaction: "somewhat isolated situation in Ireland" . . . "age" . . . "briefly and unwillingly" involved in the realities of the twentieth century. "Politics" is his response, intertextuality with a refined vengeance. Presented with a choice between current affairs or romantic love, Yeats—having had more than enough experience of both—will always choose the latter. What's more, he'll go down with his colors flying and his guns blazing, Thomas Mann, Archibald MacLeish, and all the rest be damned.

One last contribution of MacLeish's essay to the poem: it doubtless provided a source for the closing image. Early in his article MacLeish quotes what he calls "the anonymous poet of the Western Wind":

> O western wind when wilt thou blow
> That the small rain down can rain:—
> Christ, that my love were in my arms
> And I in my bed again.[44]

As Mary FitzGerald has suggested to me, by concluding his lyric canon with an allusion to this, one of the earliest lyrics in the language, Yeats is not only suggesting the timeless nature of the theme of love, but also perhaps presenting himself as the current if not the final inheritor of the English lyric tradition, the "last romantic," taking for his theme "traditional sanctity and loveliness" (*P,* 245). This would be altogether in accord with his decision to open his canon not with "The Wanderings of Oisin" but with "The Song of the Happy Shepherd."

The second variant concerns the punctuation at the end of line four. In correcting the proofs for the Cuala volume, Mrs. Yeats changed Yeats's comma to a question mark, and this is found in all posthumous printings before 1983. This revision suggests that the first four lines are asking a question, which of course they are not. The speaker knows before he begins that it is impossible to be interested in politics in the presence of youthful beauty. Yeats's punctuation (the "run-on sentence," if you must) also nicely matches the conversational tone of the poem. Finally, Yeats had always been fond of the single-sentence poem, and to have his final lyric employ that form is altogether fitting.[45]

The third revision occurs in line eight. The final typescript of "Politics" as well as the version in the *American Mercury* reads "has read and thought." However, the *London Mercury,* the Cuala proofs, the Cuala volume, and the corrected Cuala proofs sent to Scribner's all offer "has both read and thought," with a comma rather than a period. The Coole Edition proofs revert to "has read and thought." *Last Poems & Plays* and *Poems* (1949) retain that reading but give a comma at the end of the line instead of a period.

It would be impossible, of course, to refute a suggestion by, say, a *What If?*er that "both" was an error by the *London Mercury* not detected until after the Cuala volume had been published. But although one could easily enough ascribe the change in punctuation to a typesetter, the addition of "both" would be an unusual typesetting error indeed. Moreover, it is virtually certain that Yeats read proofs for the *London Mercury* (*EYP:AR,* 86; cf. 121n.50).

The evidence, then, strongly supports "both" and the comma as authorial, and it seems clear that the *London Mercury* text is indeed superior. Not only is it improved metrically—"that has both read and thought" instead of "that has read and thought"—but also it offers a more biting commentary on politicians. By implication, most politicians at best read or think (probably most do neither); here's an atypical one who has somehow managed both, and yet even his conversation still pales in comparison with the attraction of "that girl standing there."[46]

Finally, the closing punctuation mark. In the Macmillan *Last Poems & Plays,* the period was replaced by an exclamation mark, almost surely a revision by Thomas Mark. As argued above, I simply do not believe that Yeats failed to understand the difference between those two closures. Mark's version of "Politics" ends with a sense of triumph, some might say masculine bravado (or worse). Yeats's "Politics" ends with a note of wistful regret and perhaps with the great hunger and longing of the

Western Wind closing. In Mark's poem the speaker almost seems to project a tryst with the "girl." In Yeats's poem the speaker is aware of the impossibility of any union, aware, as Yeats wrote elsewhere, that "Bodily decrepitude is wisdom" (*P,* 265).[47]

Albright and *The Poems* (1989) give what is almost certainly the last version seen by Yeats, that in the *London Mercury.* Martin offers a posthumous, emended text, first published in 1940 and thereafter accepted as standard until at least 1983. Rejecting two of the posthumous changes but accepting the others, Jeffares presents a new, hybrid "Politics." It is impossible to say with certainty that any one of these is "correct" or "definitive." Indeed, one's preference for a particular text is as much a matter of "literary criticism" as of "textual scholarship," even though the relationship between those endeavors has only recently come to be appreciated. To that juncture we now turn.

Conclusion

In an important recent essay, D. C. Greetham has persuasively demonstrated the virtues of seeing the relationship between literary theory and textual theory, arguing that "different theoretical perceptions . . . result in differing texts."[48] In Greetham's terms, Jeffares's *Yeats's Poems* seems most closely related to reader-response theory, perhaps especially to the version most cogently developed by Jerome McGann, "the so-called 'social' school of textual criticism" (Greetham, 11). That is, Jeffares's edition is based on the premise that the intervention of Yeats's "delegates, his wife . . . and his trusted editor," is an essential part of the text of the poetry; thus he generally declines to "overturn the *textual* decisions inevitably left by the dead poet to be settled by his widow and editor" (Jeffares, 707). To argue that a surviving text is an unfinished document awaiting the refining fires of the writer's heirs and/or "trusted editors" has, of course, a long (if usually less than honorable) history in textual scholarship.

McGann correctly describes Albright and Martin as other than "highly trained textual scholars and theorists" (494), and it is more difficult to characterize their work. They both seem less concerned with the *source* of their texts—Martin simply adopts the 1950 English *Collected Poems,* Albright never clearly indicates his copy-text[49]—than with what can be done to improve Yeats's poems. For Martin, this mainly applies to arrangement; for Albright, mainly to punctuation. For an editor to take on authorial or quasi-authorial status might now be thought to derive from deconstruction; but from the perspective of editorial theory it is little more than an extension of the method employed by Jeffares. Instead of "Yeats would have expected these emendations" we have "Yeats should have wanted these emendations."

My edition of *The Poems* (1989) is based primarily on "writer-based theories" (Greetham, 6), in that I have attempted to present Yeats's last known versions of his poems with as little emendation as possible. I differ from some other editors using this approach, however, in arguing the fundamental impossibility of arriving at a "Definitive Edition," suggesting instead that "individual readers will always be required to evaluate the texts offered them in a particular edition against their own sense of Yeats as a poet" (*EYP:AR*, 175). Indeed, much of this essay has been an example of that process, whether the debate was about something as (relatively) small as a question mark in "Politics" or as large as the overall arrangement of the poetic canon.

Of course I do not anticipate full agreement with my conclusions; but I hope that my work has provided readers and critics with the complete record—including the relevant manuscript materials, materials ignored by Albright, Jeffares, and Martin—so that their own judgments can be fully informed. Indeed, one could adapt Henry James's biblical phrasing and say that "in the House of Yeats's Poems are many texts": most of them placed there by Yeats himself, in the process of composition and revision that ended only with his death; some of them placed there by error, whether by printers and proofreaders or by editors mistranscribing a manuscript or lacking access to a particular document; some of them placed there by editors believing that their intervention is required so that the contemporary documents can be "to perfection brought" (*P*, 302).

Greetham has quite accurately commented that "literary critics have all too often assumed that . . . 'any text will do'" (4). If nothing else, perhaps this essay has shown that for all aspects of Yeats's poetry, the Age of Textual Innocence is lost, and we must now learn to live and to interpret in a wilderness of multiple texts, of multiple arrangements. But if we are forever exiled from an earlier era of "manifold illusion," it is as well to remember that "man's life is thought" (*P*, 289).

NOTES

1. See my *Editing Yeats's Poems: A Reconsideration* (London: Macmillan; New York: St. Martin's, 1990), 1–4. Further details on many of the matters discussed in this essay will be found therein, hereafter cited as *EYP:AR*. *The Poems,* rev. ed., ed. Richard J. Finneran (New York: Macmillan, 1989), hereafter cited as *P.*

In fact, the process of canonizing *Poems* (1949) began well before the Prospectus. In *The House of Macmillan (1843–1943)* (London: Macmillan, 1943), Charles Morgan wrote of the unpublished Coole Edition—the Ur-text for the 1949 edition—that "all of it was seen and revised by Yeats" (*EYP:AR,* 2).

2. I quite favored Bradford's suggested order and contents for *Last Poems;* but until I discovered a letter from Mrs. Yeats (cited below), the possibility that Yeats had drafted a different plan for the Macmillan collection could not be discounted.

3. Jerome McGann, "Which Yeats edition?" *TLS* 11–17 May 1990, 494. Hereafter cited as McGann.

4. W. B. Yeats, *Collected Poems,* ed. Augustine Martin (London: Arena, 1990). Hereafter cited as Martin.

5. W. B. Yeats, *The Poems,* ed. Daniel Albright (London: Dent, 1990). Hereafter cited as Albright.

6. Jon Stallworthy, *Between the Lines: Yeats's Poetry in the Making* (Oxford: Clarendon, 1963), 68.

7. Yeats Archives, State University of New York at Stony Brook. Hereafter cited as SB. Using the original system of citation, the passage can be found at 24.1.006.

8. One would tend to think the earlier volume more likely, but the holograph omits line 25a ("Or those who need his bounty or his law,"), an omission first found in *The Tower.*

9. *Yeats's Poems,* ed. A. Norman Jeffares (London: Macmillan, 1989). Hereafter cited as Jeffares.

10. Although it is probably asking too much to expect these lists to be free from error, it is distressing to discover that Jeffares appears unable to grasp the apparatus in the *Variorum Poems.* His entries for "Politics" on p. 647 as well as three of the entries for "Man and the Echo" (ll. 20, 23, 45) on pp. 662–63, for instance, evidence his failure to realize that a citation such as "AM—95" in the collations includes all intermediate printings and is rather different from "AM, 95".

These lists include other kinds of mistakes as well. For example, the London edition of the *Collected Poems* (1933) does not read "cottages:" in l. 59 of "The Tower" (Jeffares, 646) but rather, correctly, "cottages." Here Jeffares replicates an error in *Variorum Poems* (411). Simply ignoring the information in *Variorum*

Poems (623) as corrected in *EYP:AR* (120), he overlooks the 4-4-2-4 spacing of "High Talk" in the *London Mercury,* an arrangement found on the last two typescripts (Jeffares, 647, 662). Misremembering *EYP:AR,* 54, he has Mrs. Yeats describing "Three Songs to the Same Tune" and "Three Marching Songs" as "on the whole, so similar" (Jeffares, 651) when in fact she wrote "on the whole, so different." And so on.

11. The scenario is easy enough to imagine: having received a typescript from Mrs. Yeats, Mark checks it against his copy of the *London Mercury;* he discovers "attention" and makes the "correction," with or without a query to Mrs. Yeats. In the spring of 1939 the contemporary documents are disorganized as well as scattered throughout England, Ireland, and America: "attention" carries the day (*EYP:AR,* 69–70).

12. The *OED* also cites T. Brown (1704) and Thackeray (1850). "To dance attention" is not attested.

13. Albright (359) offers "attendance," Martin (327) "attention."

14. Consistency would have called for the deletion of this date to be noted in the list of "Corrections of Misprints or Other Alterations Made to the Copy Text" (Jeffares, 647). And of course the date was "appended" to the poem a decade earlier than 1949.

15. The single correction on this typescript, the "e" in the title, could have been made by anyone. If an analysis were to disclose that the ink used was different from that in Yeats's corrections to the earlier typescript, further doubt would be cast on the contemporary status of this typescript, but the issue would still remain unresolved.

16. Martin (348) rejects "we shall sing" but accepts "notes"; his punctuation follows Jeffares except for the substitution of a colon at the end of l. 24. Albright (380) adopts the wording of Jeffares but the punctuation of *The Poems* (1989). Thus neither text corresponds to any previous edition.

17. Hugh Kenner, "Whose Yeats Is It?" *New York Times Book Review,* 27 May 1990, 12. Hereafter cited as Kenner.

18. So also in Albright (392) and Jeffares (469), though in the latter the proper title is listed as a "correction or emendation" to the copy-text (Jeffares, 647). Martin (360) retains the posthumous article.

19. The annotation is clearly *not* in Yeats's hand. Indeed, it could not possibly be, as the list was typed by Charles Kingsley, Scribner's London representative (or his secretary), not by Mrs. Yeats. As Kingsley explained in a letter of 24 June 1937 to John Hall Wheelock of Scribner's in New York, the previous day he had learned that H. Watt (Yeats's agent) had in his possession a list of contents for the Scribner Edition from Mrs. Yeats: "He hung on to it like grim death, and I have only just succeeded in getting the loan of it in order that I might make a copy for you" (Scribner Archive, Princeton University Library). It is this *copy* that contains Gould's quotation; Mrs. Yeats's list was duly returned to

Watt, as he had requested when loaning it to Kingsley on 23 June 1937 (Scribner Archive, Princeton University Library). Moreover, the annotation on the Kingsley copy is obviously not a subsection title. It is written vertically in the left margin, with lines drawn to bracket the poems from the volume; it is thus simply Kingsley's indication as to where Scribner's would find the relevant texts.

Mrs. Yeats produced three copies of her own list. Two of these survive in National Library of Ireland MS. 30,248—doubtless those sent to Watt (including "her own top copy" of the list for the poems) and to Yeats, who was in London when she prepared them. Both use simply "Poems 1933–37" and make no reference to "From 'A Full Moon in March.'" The copy sent to New York apparently does not survive, but a draft table of contents for the Scribner Edition demonstrates that the title thereon was again merely "Poems 1933–1937" (Harry Ransom Humanities Research Center, University of Texas). As Mrs. Yeats wrote to Watt on 22 June 1937, "I enclosed in each parcel of material for Scribners a complete list which was accurate" (Scribner Archive, Princeton University Library).

Gould is also mistaken when he argues that an earlier, January 1937 list of contents for the Scribner Edition calls for "a section to be entitled 'Poems from "A FULL MOON IN MARCH"'" (Jeffares, 723). Again, the point of the annotation is to tell Scribner's where to find the text of the additional poems; it follows after an instruction that the volume should "contain everything that is in the one-volume 'Collected Poems'" and is itself followed by a further annotation, "I have eighteen or nineteen new poems" (Scribner Archive, Princeton University Library). Obviously, it would be redundant to include in a volume entitled *Poems* a section called "Poems from 'A Full Moon in March'"!

Finally, both 1937 Scribner's lists derive from an October 1936 list for the Edition de Luxe. When Mrs. Yeats prepared the final list for Scribner's, she canceled the typed "Poems from 'A Full Moon in March'" and replaced it by "Poems 1933–1937" (MS. 30,248, National Library of Ireland).

20. Thus Albright (329) and Martin (289), though the latter offers "*'Parnell's Funeral' and other poems.*" Jeffares uses "From 'A Full Moon in March,'" with the 1935 title failing even to qualify as a "possible alternative" (Jeffares, 393, 651). So much for Martin's comment: "Scholarly consensus now decrees that the . . . volume be entitled *'Parnell's Funeral' and Other Poems* [sic]" (Martin, xxvii).

21. Although the letter to Mark is presently lost, and is known only from three sentences quoted by Jon Stallworthy (*Between the Lines,* 12), Gould is not deterred from offering the following commentary: "to Mark alone Yeats confided some of his 'metrical tricks': admiring Mark's suggested punctuation he evidently felt that his editor deserved an explanation of how he had arrived at his versification, presumably in part to help Mark in his work" (Jeffares, 708). Leaving aside Gould's characteristic "evidently" and "presumably," what of "to Mark

alone"? Not to Ezra Pound? to Mrs. Yeats? to Margot Ruddock? to Dorothy Wellesley? to . . . ? See also *EYP:AR*, 35.

22. In what from the perspective of both publishing and scholarly ethics can only be considered an extraordinary procedure, Gould was provided with a set of proofs (corrected? uncorrected?) of *Editing Yeats's Poems: A Reconsideration* without my knowledge or permission. Drawing in part on the new information found therein, he then proceeded to offer counterarguments in an essay that was published several months before the volume itself, an anomaly that has escaped all reviewers to date.

23. He went on to add, "I wish I had thought of it before." Gould offers an unlikely interpretation: "Yeats meant the comment to indicate that he wished he had thought of the two-part arrangement for *CP* when it was being planned" (Jeffares, 716). But when Yeats wrote, the *Collected Poems* was in the very *process* of being planned. The project had been agreed upon less than three weeks earlier; not a single character of the volume had been set into type; Yeats's letter would in fact prove to be the final document in the planning process. It would have been senseless to regret not having thought of the arrangement previously, since implementing it for the *Collected Poems* was to cause no trouble whatsoever to anyone.

Clearly, the most logical referent for "before" is the last time that a comprehensive edition of his poetry had been planned and set into type: that is, 1931, for the Edition de Luxe. Yeats may well have been hinting to Mark that he should ask the obvious question, "Should the new arrangement be applied to the Edition de Luxe?" But he did not, and Yeats did not press the point.

24. Of the various errors in Appendix 6 of *Yeats's Poems*, the most profound may occur in Gould's commentary on the 1956 American edition: "When George Yeats rearranged and provided corrections for *CP* (New York: Macmillan Company, 1956) to conform to the *P* (1949) arrangement, she did not admit 'The Hero, the Girl, and the Fool' but included 'The Fool by the Roadside'. This suggests that she accepted it as the later and preferable text. That edition was dubbed the 'definitive edition with the author's final corrections' (*Wade*, item 211A, 209)" (Jeffares, 741n.19).

Since Gould repeats Wade's misdescription—not "definitive edition with the author's final corrections" but "Definitive Edition, With the Author's Final Revisions," it is evident that he has committed the fundamental error of not examining important evidence at first hand, in this particular instance a volume used to justify a major emendation to the copy-text. In the 1956 *Collected Poems*, "The Fool by the Roadside" was in fact *replaced by* "The Hero, the Girl, and the Fool." Thus, invoking this edition to justify the choice of "The Fool by the Roadside" in *Yeats's Poems* is entirely erroneous.

More important for our purposes, there was absolutely no change in "arrangement" undertaken in 1956; other than the substitution of "The Hero, the Girl, and the Fool," the revisions are restricted to textual corrections. Since so much of Gould's argument is based on the presumed "delegation" of authority by Yeats to his wife, surely the imprimatur she gave to the format of the *Collected Poems* would have given him pause, had he ever seen the 1956 American edition.

25. Gould, in the *Times Literary Supplement,* 29 June 1984, 731; and in Jeffares, 714. Moreover, the *Collected Poems* was "a popular one-volume edition," "its new arrangement designed to win new readers," to reach a "new audience" (Jeffares, 706, 709, 735). Yet from the moment of its publication, the volume became the essential Yeats for *all* readers, old and new. Only therein, for example, could one find *The Tower* with a four-stanza "Two Songs from a Play" or with the entirety of "Fragments"; only therein could one find Yeats's latest textual revisions. Yeats's inscription of a copy of the *Collected Poems* to Sir John Squire with the Shakespearean accolade "the only begetter" (Jeffares, 714) suggests that he thought rather more highly of the volume than do the Edition de Luxeites.

26. Gould's "crucial sentence" (Jeffares, 715) hardly qualifies. Writing to Macmillan on 13 August 1933, Yeats noted that "The *Edition de Luxe* will not lack new work for I am constantly writing essays & poems & what I write will be added at the end of the various volumes." Gould comments that "to add new lyrics at the end of the 'Lyrical' section would have involved renumbering the pages of the rest of the book, not to mention the havoc it would cause with tables [sic] of contents and other necessary resetting" (Jeffares, 715). However, had Macmillan revised the Edition de Luxe to adopt the two-part arrangement, inserting new poems at the end of the first section and renumbering the remaining pages would hardly have been beyond the capabilities of either themselves or their printer, R. & R. Clark of Edinburgh, who were both more than accustomed to an author given to last-minute revisions on page proofs. Nor would there have been "havoc" with the table of contents, as there is no evidence that such had ever been set into type for the Edition de Luxe *Poems.* Likewise, as there is no evidence that any title or first-line indices had been prepared, it is difficult to envision the nature of the "other necessary resetting." Moreover, when in 1937 Macmillan agreed to an expanded edition of the *Collected Poems,* they were quite prepared to make all the required changes.

27. Albright and Jeffares use the quasi-chronological arrangement. Martin retains the two-part format except for his unique placement of "The Gift of Harun Al-Rashid."

28. McGann, 494; Kenner, 12.

29. Astonishingly, this interpretation is derived from Yeats's comment on the relationship between the Scribner Edition and the Edition de Luxe: "Of course if it is desirable to have the two editions completely different, I could make some rearrangement, though not much" (Jeffares, 721). Gould apparently finds that

the different arrangement of the poems qualifies as "not much" of a variation, writing that "it seems likely that Yeats was compelled by the advice of Watt to abide by the spirit of Macmillan's wish for 'divergence' between the two editions in order to preserve as one of its [i.e. the Edition de Luxe's] 'special features' the superior chronological arrangement of the poems" (Jeffares, 727). Further, although "Yeats had always intended to 'arrange the volumes to suit himself' . . . this wish was overtaken by the advice of Macmillan and Watt" (Jeffares, 745n.43).

30. See *EYP:AR*, 167n.18, for an instance of Yeats seeking Mark's advice about a matter previously discussed with his wife.

On the question of Yeats's "delegation" of authority to Mrs. Yeats. Gould makes an extremely surprising concession near the end of his essay. Having argued at length for the theory of delegation, he comments that "one must accept that Mrs. Yeats, with or without her husband's agreement, preferred the *Edition de Luxe* arrangement" (Jeffares, 730). Such a qualification, combined with his blunder about Mrs. Yeats and the 1956 American *Collected Poems* (see n. 24), seriously undermines a central tenet of his argument. Perhaps, as I have argued, "faced with ambiguous documents as well as posthumous statements by prejudiced parties . . . it is preferable to examine what Yeats in fact *did*" (*EYP:AR*, 167), rather than what he is thought by others to have wanted to do.

31. This copy, in the Pierpont Morgan Library, is that given by Mrs. Yeats to Mark in 1949 (cf. *EYP:AR*, 127–31, 174).

32. *Essays and Introductions* (New York: Macmillan, 1961), 519. Hereafter cited as *E&I*.

33. *Letters on Poetry from W. B. Yeats to Dorothy Wellesley*, intro. Kathleen Raine (London: Oxford University Press, 1964), 140; *Letters of W. B. Yeats*, ed. Allan Wade (London: Rupert Hart-Davis, 1954), 891.

34. Gould notes that in placing "Under Ben Bulben" at the end of the volume, "George Yeats and Thomas Mark were opting for a closure which was surely a convention for a memorial edition" (Jeffares, 737). But he rather neglects to mention the other revisions, for which a similar "convention" can scarcely be found.

35. Phillip L. Marcus, "Yeats's 'Last Poems': A Reconsideration," in *Yeats Annual No. 5* (London: Macmillan, 1987), 12. Gould considers this essay a "stout defence" of the posthumous rearrangement (Jeffares, 738).

36. Jeffares nearly follows *The Poems* (1989), using "[Last Poems] 1938–1939" (447). Albright gives the less accurate "Last Poems 1939" (373). Both place the three lyrics from *On the Boiler* in a preceding section. Martin, however, reinserts them into Yeats's order, in the process transferring "Three Marching Songs" to "'*Parnell's Funeral' and other poems*." Martin prefaces his unique order and contents with an equally inventive title, "*Final Poems* (1938–39)," thereby

"reserving the term *Last Poems* for reference to its use by the editors of the 1950 *Collected* [*Poems*]," by whom he apparently means Mrs. Yeats and Thomas Mark (Martin, xxviii, xxi).

37. I am indebted to Mary FitzGerald for this suggestion.

38. Albright includes this poem in his notes (555–56), Martin in *Michael Robartes and the Dancer* (180–81). However, both present not Yeats's final version but the earlier text reprinted in *Variorum Poems* (see *EYP:AR*, 147–51).

39. Albright (382) offers the proper text. Martin (294) and Jeffares (458) provide the correct first line but revert to the posthumous "men forgive" in the second. Martin offers no punctuation after "gain"—presumably a misprint; Jeffares offers the correct period, though both it and "We were" are listed as "corrections or emendations" to the copy-text (Jeffares, 647). Since it is not found in a printed source—that is, before 1983—Yeats's "man forgives" fails to qualify as a "possible alternative" (Jeffares, 660).

40. Jeffares offers the Scribner reading in his second list of "Possible Emendations" (664). Even to do so violates his statement that "Printed sources only are cited as authority for corrections or alterations in the copy text, or for suggested possible emendations of it" (Jeffares, 644; but the paragraph is garbled). Albright also gives the 1935 text but offers the revision in his notes (334, 760). Elsewhere he objects to my "obedience to authority," writing about the revision of "Brown Penny" for the Scribner Edition that "I doubt that Yeats would have allowed its printing—he frequently rejected experimental revisions" (Albright, xlix). Doubt is of course always possible, but by 1937 Yeats was rather beyond "experimenting" with revisions to his poetry. Martin (299) offers the 1935 text and makes no reference to the revision.

41. Gould questions my assumption that revisions that are "*later* must be *better*," finding it "illogical" (Jeffares, 745n.43). But where is the logic in the opposite assumption? With rare exception, readers of Yeats have agreed that the poet knew what he was doing, even at the very end of his career.

42. Martin (364) gives "meaning." Albright (395) and Jeffares (472) offer the correct reading, the latter claiming on no evidence that the Macmillan "meaning" was a "misprint" (Jeffares, 647).

43. Archibald MacLeish, "Public Speech and Private Speech in Poetry," *Yale Review* 27, no. 3 (March 1938): 545.

44. One might wonder if Yeats was familiar with Hemingway's *A Farewell to Arms* (1929), which invokes the same lyric both in its title and in the text, and which likewise treats the conflict between love and "war's alarms."

45. Martin (364) and Jeffares (472) retain the posthumous question mark, though for the latter Yeats's comma qualifies as a "possible alternative" (Jeffares, 663). Albright (395) offers a comma.

46. Martin (364) and Jeffares (472) offer "read and thought," though for the

latter "both read and thought" qualifies as a "possible alternative" (Jeffares, 663). Albright gives "both read and thought." All three retain Yeats's comma.

47. Martin (364) retains the exclamation point. Albright (395) and Jeffares (472) offer Yeats's period, though for the latter it is a "correction or emendation" of the copy text (Jeffares, 647).

48. D. C. Greetham, "Textual and Literary Theory: Redrawing the Matrix," *Studies in Bibiliography* 42 (1989): 13. Hereafter cited as Greetham.

49. Albright's text seems most closely derived from *The Poems* (1989). The dust-jacket claims that "The texts of the poems have been newly edited . . . ," but this was apparently accomplished without a detailed study of the archival evidence. Albright did not, for instance, undertake a firsthand examination of the Scribner Archive at the University of Texas (nor, for that matter, did Jeffares or Martin).

Editing William Carlos Williams

A. Walton Litz and Christopher MacGowan

I: *The Collected Poems*

A. WALTON LITZ

In editing *The Collected Poems of William Carlos Williams,* Christopher MacGowan and I had to make a number of fundamental decisions about the scope of Williams's poetic canon and the ordering of the poems. Throughout his long career Williams was obsessed with the relationship between prose and poetry. In *Spring and All* (1923) he stressed the radical differences between the two modes, using the prose to counterpoint the "purer" poems; but as his poetic developed this distinction gradually collapsed, and in *Paterson* "prose" and "poetry" are two complementary forms of the imagination at work. We decided to include in their entirety those works—such as *Spring and All* and *The Descent of Winter*—where Williams interwove prose and poetry in a single structure, but to exclude a work such as *Kora in Hell,* where the highly cadenced prose verges on "poetry" but never takes on, in lineation and cadence, the characteristics of even the most liberated *vers libre.* Some reviewers have challenged this decision, but we still believe that we followed a sensible method, making the sort of pragmatic judgment that must from time to time govern all editorial procedures. The alternative method would have involved establishing a theoretical borderline between poetry and prose that Williams himself could never define to his satisfaction.

Another basic question was the ordering of the poems. Writing to James Laughlin in February 1938 about his forthcoming *Complete Collected Poems* (1938), Williams said that he wanted the poems "to come out in subdivisions of the original books as they appeared, chronologically,"[1] and the 1938 volume did indeed follow this pattern for all but the longer poems, which are grouped together at the end. Initially Williams wished to organize *Collected Later Poems* (1950) and *Collected*

Earlier Poems (1951) in the same manner, but in the course of making the collections he adopted a thematic arrangement, which, especially in the case of *Collected Earlier Poems,* greatly obscured the order of publication and hence the record of his poetic development. "Portrait of a Lady," for example, is printed in *Collected Earlier Poems* as if it were a part of the 1913 volume *The Tempers,* although it was first published in August 1920. In making the new *Collected Poems* we decided to reject Williams's 1950–51 arrangements and to print the poems in chronological order, retaining (as Williams wished in 1938) the integrity of the individual volumes of poetry. This meant poems that appeared only in the collected volumes of 1934, 1938, 1950, and 1951, and all uncollected poems, were arranged by date of first publication and printed between the individual volumes. Among the exceptions to this rule are the relatively few poems published long after their dates of composition, which have been restored to their proper place in the chronology, and the sequence "Della Primavera Trasportata al Morale." This sequence was drafted in 1928, and a truncated version was published in 1930; but all the poems were not gathered together until 1938. We chose to preserve the integrity of the final sequence but to print it under 1930 to indicate the earlier composition. The result of our general policy, and of the pragmatic exceptions made in individual cases, is a comprehensive record of Williams's poetic achievement that seemed to us more valuable than any of his thematic arrangements, which reflected particular phases in his poetic life and can, in any event, be easily recognized from the tables of contents that we print as appendixes.

Once the order of the poetry had been fixed, we were faced with the question of which poems to include, realizing full well that the inclusion of many "minor" or ephemeral works might well change the appearance of the canon. Williams was often fastidious in the revisions of his poetry, but he seldom thought twice about allowing a poem to be published, knowing that he could always revise it in print or exclude it from a more permanent collection. He once told Louis Zukofsky that "most modern work is written to be printed and cannot be considered to exist until it is so."[2] On the other hand, in the course of his busy and sometimes chaotic life he occasionally lost track of poems that had been published, so his collected volumes do not carry the full authority of a rigorously selected canon. We therefore decided to include all of the poetry published within his lifetime that we could locate, but to exclude poems that remained in manuscript. There were, inevitably, exceptions to be made.

Williams told his publisher James Laughlin that his first volume of apprentice work, *Poems* (1909), was never to be reprinted, and we respected his wish, although we would have liked to include the poems both for the sake of completeness and as a testimony to Williams's remarkable "modernizing" of his poetry in the decade after 1909. Fortunately, several of the poems in *Poems* (1909) were reprinted during Williams's lifetime, and we were able to include these. We also decided to print any post-1909 poems that were still in manuscript at the time of Williams's death but had since been published.

We also decided to include all of Williams's translations, treating them in exactly the same way as the other poems. Like Pound, Williams thought of translation as a critical act, and like Pound he ranged beyond the languages he knew well (Spanish and French) to make his own versions based on the translations of others. The appearance of these translations and versions side by side with the poetry of the same period gives a new look to the Williams canon, especially in Volume II, where the proportion is much greater than in Volume I.

Once the order and scope of the collections had been established, we were faced with the choice of copy-text. We decided to rely on the 1951 *Collected Earlier Poems* and the 1950 *Collected Later Poems* for the poems printed in those volumes, since this was the last printing of these poems that Williams supervised, but we eliminated the errors in the two volumes caused by the complex circumstances of their preparation. (A detailed history of the making of the two collections, and the resulting textual confusion, is provided in the appendixes to our volumes.) This means that our text is essentially a hybrid one, with some poems appearing in their first published form and others in the form that resulted from later—sometimes radical—revision. To compensate for this mixed text we included in the annotations all verbal variants, so the reader can easily reconstruct the earlier versions of poems that appeared in the individual volumes and the 1950 and 1951 collections. We also printed in the main text two versions of a few poems, including several pairs that Williams produced for "demonstration" purposes.

Spring and All (1923) provides a good example of our method. The prose is that of the first (and during Williams's lifetime only) edition, but the poems—with one exception—are taken from the amended text of *Collected Earlier Poems*. The exception is poem IX, which we printed in its 1923 form because it differed substantially from the later text in spacing and format, and therefore illustrates his earlier use of typography (as Williams revised his poems they usually tended toward greater regularity and consolidation). We felt justified in this departure since the revised version of poem IX appears later in *An Early Martyr* (1935).

At the outset of our work on the *Collected Poems* we decided that our annotations would extend beyond textual matters, and would include as much explanatory material as we could locate. Williams has not been well served by his critics, and the type of annotation that is available in abundance for *The Waste Land* or *The Cantos* or *Ulysses* scarcely exists. Partly this is the result of the image of Williams received from the New Critics, who presented him as an anti-intellectual poet of concrete, immediate experience. We combed through unpublished letters, interviews, local histories, and standard sources, and were amazed to find how much annotation was needed. Some of it is similar to the information that the other modernists expect their readers to command, and this was the easiest to provide. In spite of his antagonism to international modernism Williams frequently trafficked in allusions to "high culture." Other annotations were demanded by Williams's frequent use of images from the visual arts, and by the local references that are part of his devotion to the American scene (it matters that "Park Avenue" is in Rutherford, not Manhattan). In making Volume I we were fortunate enough to discover John C. Thirwall's copy of *Collected Earlier Poems*, which he annotated in the 1950s during conversations with Williams; and in the case of Volume II much unpublished correspondence supplemented the more standard annotations. In general we confined the annotations to factual material and comments by Williams himself, avoiding critical opinions that would soon be outmoded.

In the course of our editorial work we had to resolve a number of problems that arose from Williams's special methods of composition and his frequent lack of attention to the details of printing and proofreading. As early as 1916 Williams made the decision to capitalize the initial letter of a poetic line only when it marked the opening of a grammatical unit; and soon after he began to free the line from the left-hand margin, allowing for a variety of indentations. This led to greater emphasis on format—the poem as an image on the page—and occasionally made it difficult to identify the poetic "line." Of all the major modern poets, Williams makes the most demands on our spatial as well as our aural imaginations. The pattern on the page often brings key words or images into alignment, and dictates the way in which the poem is said or performed. Similar uses of the visual pattern can be found in Pound or

Eliot—one thinks of the ending to Part III of *The Waste Land,* where the final word "burning" is set off to receive added emphasis—but Williams made the most systematic use of the poem as a pictorial unit. His deep interest in the modern visual arts probably contributed to this tendency, but it also resulted from his desire to find a flexible, nervous form that could embody the American idiom.

In addition, Williams often revised his poems—sometimes radically—when he reprinted them. The poem "Rain," for example, exists in seven printed versions that are very different in spacing, lineation, punctuation, and spelling. Many of these changes were made by Williams, but others were probably the result of differences in house-styling or careless proofreading. In recording these differences we were faced with the choice between an apparatus that would allow the reader to reconstruct the appearance of each printing (virtually copyediting or printer's directions for each poem) or the reprinting of entire poems to illustrate significant changes. We chose the latter approach, since any apparatus would have been inaccessible to the general reader; and we reprinted a number of alternate versions in the text and the annotations. Our work on the *Collected Poems* began before we had entered the world of the computer, and our collations were done in a conventional manner. If we were to begin the project today we would probably make a computerized record of all variant printings, and provide the interested scholar with copies of our disks, so that all versions of a particular poem could be printed out in variorum form.

Neither Williams nor his publishers gave much attention to line runovers or stanza breaks, and as a result many inconsistencies were introduced in successive printings. Lines in the early volumes were frequently run over, these books being small in format, while the larger page sizes of later volumes permitted longer line lengths. Through an examination of the various printings, earlier typescripts, and Williams's developing poetic practice, we were able to determine in most cases where he intended a new line or a stanza break.

These issues may sound minor, but they strike at the heart of Williams's poetic. Like so many modern writers, he composed on the typewriter, and could visualize the poem as a spatial construction. In addition, his decision—along with Pound and others—to "break the pentameter" and form a more flexible poetic line means that the editor is faced with problems different from those that confront the editor of a more traditional poet such as Yeats, whose lines are firmly anchored to the left-hand margin. Williams's harried life as a physician and poet often left him little time or inclination to oversee the printing of his poems in a careful manner. As editors we tried to fulfill his intentions, working from textual evidence where it was available but not hesitating to make choices based on our own sense of his changing poetic aims.

The textual authority for restoring Williams's original lineation is strong for most of the poems in *Collected Earlier Poems* and *Collected Later Poems*. However, the three-step poems that appeared in *The Desert Music* and *Journey to Love* presented a different set of problems when it came to runovers. In these poems, the additional fourth and sometimes fifth line in the otherwise consistent triadic arrangement appear in Williams's typescripts of the poems and in almost all of the periodical printings. Even if these additional lines are technically runovers, to print the double lines as one line would radically alter the appearance of the poem on the page, distracting from the predominant triadic pattern with a number of lines stretching to the extreme right of the page. In the earlier poems the restoration of Williams's original lineation usually has the effect of emphasizing a visual and organizational regularity in the poem's pattern, but in the case of the three-step poems of the 1950s an opposite effect would occur.

We discussed these "additional" lines with a number of Williams scholars, and found no consensus. Some felt that all of the lines were runovers and should be printed with the lines above. Others believed that some were runovers and some were additional lines, and that individual editorial decisions had to be made. A third group of scholars argued that the lines represented a deliberate introduction of variety into the triadic format. Christopher MacGowan, as sole editor of Volume II, finally decided to avoid individual (and often subjective) decisions and to leave the lines exactly as they appeared in *The Desert Music* or *Journey to Love*—and subsequently in *Pictures from Brueghel*. He did this on the strength of the visual considerations already mentioned; on the evidence that the matter was probably discussed with Williams; and on the stronger evidence of the original typescripts. It seemed to us that the most useful way to consider such lines was in the context of Williams's murky concept of the "variable foot." The poems as printed emphasize the variation and/or extension of the lines, and whether one reads them as runovers, as additional lines, or as an idiosyncratic combination of both depends upon one's personal interpretation of Williams's metrical theory and practice. This knotty issue and many others unique to the poem now confront Christopher MacGowan as he undertakes the editing of *Paterson*.

Looking back now on the completed *Collected Poems,* I realize that some of our editorial decisions resulted from first principles, others from our practical experience in gathering and ordering the materials. From the start we had the goal of presenting all of Williams's published poetry (excluding *Paterson*) in a form that would give the reader an accurate text and a comprehensive overview of his poetic development. The integrity of individual volumes was to be maintained insofar as possible, and the record of Williams's constant revisions was to be presented in a clear and consistent manner. Within this frame many minor adjustments had to be made to fit the exigencies of the existing materials and the changes over the years in Williams's poetic. Initial responses to the two volumes indicate that we succeeded in our general aims, although individual decisions can often be debated. It is now much easier to see the shape of Williams's career, and to identify the crucial transitional periods. Familiar poems take on a new significance in the context of the *Collected Poems,* and *Paterson* itself is more easily understood when seen against the background of the uncollected poems of the 1940s and 1950s. Above all else, the two volumes tell the story of a life lived through poetry.

II: *Paterson*

CHRISTOPHER MACGOWAN

In Williams's long poem *Paterson,* as in the two volumes of *Collected Poems,* the visual dimension of the text is central to the poet's concerns. On one level, reading any Williams poem is very much a spatial experience, and *Paterson* is arguably Williams's most developed treatment of that aspect of his poetics. But in large part because of *Paterson*'s printing history, textual corruption has compromised this feature of the poem to an even greater extent than with the shorter works. In addition, in the case of *Paterson*'s use of prose documents this printing history has led to the current (1963) text—particularly Book 5—being a text by several more hands than Williams intended, or than the reader of the current edition can realize.

The critical and editorial issues involved in trying to produce a text as close as possible to Williams's intentions raise difficult questions central to the work's themes and poetics. The social and economic factors behind many of the changes in the text are themselves part of the poem's themes, and these factors are incorporated into the poem in terms of process rather than as finished statement. *Paterson* is concerned with the economic forces behind the filling of space, be it a landscape or the page layout of a poem. And the poem actively incorporates the social and economic forces shaping the forces of history. The subsequent fame of a contributor to the poem, the incarceration and later release of another, the fame of the poem itself, the shifting authority of poet as editor and overseer of the typing and printing of his own work—all have contributed to the corruption of the present text, and yet all are issues shaping the central dynamics of the poem's meaning and structure. At a fundamental level this is a poem *about* the processes of economic, historical, and physical change.

Paterson is divided into five books, each book appearing individually from 1946 to 1958 in a limited edition. Once the first editions sold out, starting with Books 1 and 2 in 1949, each book was completely reset as the poem began to be reissued in a cheaper collected format, the "New Classics Series." The reset Books 1, 2, and 3 appeared in 1950, and Books 1–4 in late 1951. In 1963 New Directions completed the reset edition of the poem by adding Book 5 (and some fragments of an intended Book 6) to the first four books.

With the break-up of the first edition's page layout for the reset text, inevitably some of the spatial relationships of the poem were disturbed. Not all of the resultant spatial changes are the unavoidable consequences of changes in type size and pagination. This corruption of the text was compounded in 1969 when, to keep the retail price of the book down, for the fifth paperback printing the reset edition was submitted to a cut-and-paste job that added five more lines of type to each page and reduced the length of the poem by thirty-eight pages.

This textual history further complicates other difficulties confronting an editor of *Paterson* that stem from the serial nature of the work's issue. As noted above, Williams was rarely a careful proofreader of his work, but at least the typing, retyping, and checking of the 1950 and 1951 *Collected* volumes occurred within a short—albeit rushed—period. For *Paterson,* Williams proofread the typescripts and galleys of the individually issued books over a period of twelve years. As became clear in our editing of the collected poems, Williams seems to have only casually checked retyped scripts and galleys against originals—if at all—and further, the accuracy of his proofreading depended upon his state of health, the pressure of other demands, and his level of interest. In the case of *Paterson,* there is little evidence to suggest that Williams gave much attention to checking the resetting of the individual books.

A collation of the poem's typescripts and printed versions suggests that Williams gave the typescripts, first edition, and resetting of the earlier books a more careful reading than those of the later books. The first edition of Book 4 appeared in the midst of the same overload of commitments that produced his rushed examination of the *Collected Earlier* and *Collected Later* materials, and the reset text of Book 4 soon after a stroke and at a time of extreme anxiety and self-doubt. By 1958, the date of Book 5's first issue, Williams's sight was poor and his ability for sustained concentration impaired. The resetting of Book 5 for the collected format took place after Williams's death, and the more than sixty verbal changes between the two printings (changes not noted in the 1963 text except in one instance) were made largely on the basis of suggestions by a number of friends, scholars, and other concerned and well-intentioned readers.

The serial nature of the poem's composition and production, then, combined with Williams's erratic proofreading habits and the steady decline of his health in the last years of his life, oblige an editor to assign a different status to the author's supervisions of the poem's various typescripts, galleys, and printings over time. And the final version of Book 5, although a product of readers sensitive to the poem's and the poet's intent, has a different status again—as a kind of separate "edition" within the work. Thus while the collected reset format of Books 1 to 4, as the last printed version overseen by the poet, should serve as copy-text for those books, its value is compromised by the factors outlined above. And the first printing of Book 5, the only printing of that book overseen by Williams, has claims to be the copy-text of that part of the poem—but this printing contains many typographical errors, and since the motives behind the 1963 changes in the reset version were to restore the book to Williams's intentions, the result certainly deserves careful consideration, and perhaps priority.

This issue of problematic copy-texts creates more difficulties in dealing with the poem's prose than with its visual poetics, although the corrupt spacing of the current text, as noted above, has some of its origins in Williams's casual approval as well as in format changes. This corrupt spacing obscures a central aspect of the poem's expression, and the visual dimension of the poem parallels a number of its themes. The poem is concerned with both sight and sound—with *seeing* the role of the past and potential of the landscape, as much as with *hearing* the sounds and speech patterns around which the presentation of what is seen and heard must be shaped. The place that demands expression is both the local landscape and the space—on the page—of the poem. This duality is dramatized throughout the work. For example, in Book 1 the prose report of a 1737 earthquake 'releases' the hidden "father of all / speech"[3] revealed in the following lines of verse. Paterson's "walking" in Book 2 both records his searching push into the space of the park and (e.g., 52–53) set against the left-hand margin, serves as the visual equivalent of the setting down and push forward of the walking motion itself. In Book 3 Paterson sits within the confined space of a library while the momentary embodiment of the poem's central source—its "Beautiful thing"—becomes a scattering of butterflies or moths trapped within the spatial constraints, "battering against glass / at the high windows."[4] The "Beautiful thing" refrain, set within surrounding space on the page, itself opens up the poem's stanzaic clusters, the would-be confining structures that would limit and define the 'correct space' for the poem's language. "Let / me out!" demands one of the voices in Book 3's final stanza. In its movement through the space of the page, the text thus dramatizes the "dance" that is a central motif of the poem—and that concludes Book 5.

The first editions of each book carried no page numbers—an inconvenience to critics, annotators, and footnoters, of course, but a practice that allowed the poem's visual drama to be unimpeded by that particular convention. Thus in the first editions the space of the page and the poem is not defined through the linear progression of ascending numbers, but is shaped by the larger, looser framework of the poem's numbered sections and books, and the non-linear recording of dates—matching the multidirectional and cyclical themes that run counter to, e.g., the Passaic river's forward push. But an editor and publisher would rightly give pause before issuing an edition of a 250-page poem without page numbers!

The first, reset, and repaginated editions all inconsistently treat spaces that coincide with the bottom of the page—sometimes a space is left, sometimes not. Such decisions often appear to have been governed more by the requirements of the book's page design than by the poem's typescripts. In addition, the reset and repaginated editions print the spacing within the prose sections of the poem in an inconsistent format. For what are probably matters of economy, they do not reproduce the spacing of the typescripts or of the first edition.

These spatial changes in the poem have been dictated more by matters of format and economics than by the poet's intentions, although here, as in the *Collected Poems,* the problems are compounded by the unusual features of Williams's lineation and by the author's inconsistent guidance to typists and printers. Of course, the influence of economic and technological constraints upon the composition and production of texts has been an area of major interest in recent years. (Williams's own engagement with these forces would be an interesting study in itself—a study that would take in such matters as his early use of the typewriter, his subsidization of his first books, his necessary compromises with Harriet Monroe at *Poetry,* and his editing of his own magazines in the late 1910s, early 1920s, and 1930s.) Economic factors have clearly helped shape the present text of *Paterson,* but the editorial status these matters of format should be assigned is no easy matter to decide. For one thing, as noted earlier, the force of such economic pressures is itself a central theme of the poem, and to this degree of self-conscious implication acknowledged by the text must be added the fact that Williams himself apparently went along with the shifts and compromises in format. Indeed, a characteristic of Williams's thinking about his role as poet throughout his career is a constant dialectic between reaching out to the largest possible audience—and directing his poetics and his desires for the pricing and distribution of his books accordingly—and the modernist insistence upon refusing to compromise, and accepting the limitations imposed by reaching only an audience prepared to seek out, pay for, and read such work on its own terms.

At any rate, the net effect of these vagaries of format, as in the case of the 1950 and 1951 *Collected* volumes, is to make these visual aspects of the poem seem random, governed by no particular principle, whereas the first editions make clear this is not the case. Such randomness also goes against Williams's career-long comments on the nature of "free verse" as he saw it.

Another spatial feature of the poem's text that has been corrupted by the printing history is Williams's idiosyncratic use of periods following an extended space at the end of, or in the middle of, a line. Such use of space and the period, sometimes not followed by an uppercase letter, is a characteristic of Williams's poetics in the 1940s and early 1950s (see, for example, "Two Pendants: for the Ears" and "The Desert Music"). This use of the period in conjunction with space in effect extends the period's range, since it punctuates not just the syntactic unit before it, but rather the space and language surrounding itself. In keeping with the poem's larger thematic concerns, the effect is to qualify the period's signification of closure, and instead to emphasize balance. This usage provides a visual and syntactic equivalent of a central motif in Williams's work, the motif of an equilibrium of contending forces. The equilibrium at the edge of the Falls, for example, is a central place of discovery in *Paterson,* what the epigraph to the poem terms "an enforced pause." As the collation of texts for Volume II of the *Collected Poems* also revealed, this feature of Williams's poetics is not consistently reproduced in resettings and reprintings. Thus another level of the poem's spatial vocabulary loses coherence.

The text's resetting and the repagination have obscured some of the visual relationships within the poem that—as with the shorter poems—reinforce and complicate thematic connections. Some of these relationships involve the visual juxtaposition of two or more of the documents (letters, newspaper accounts, local histories, economic tracts, etc.) that Williams imports into the poem (pages 138–39 illustrate such a juxtaposition that was lost in the resetting and restored in the repagination: a reading list from Pound, and a repetitive drilling chart recording a failure to find water). But such relationships are also presented through the positioning of lines and stanzas, and some of these parallels are now approximate at best.

One fairly straightforward example is on page 173, where the call "Come to / Jesus" should be aligned on the right-hand margin with the line from the Billy Sunday hymn "Brighten / . . the corner where you / are!" (the hymn line itself echoed from page 128, where its visual elongation reinforces the poem's charge of the capitalist/protestant oppressive intent upon space). Another occurs in the final dozen lines of Book 5. The book's summary statement on measure (the measure of time, of the poetic line, of the dance, and of a number of associated motifs), "The measure intervenes, to measure is all we know," in the typescripts and first edition *does* 'intervene.' The line appears in the second, the *middle,* of the three-step line format used in the lines above—thus interrupting and varying the "measure." But this particular instance of a fused visual and thematic intervention is blurred in the current text because the key line is incorrectly spaced in relation to the left margin—

probably to avoid the otherwise awkward runover that would be imposed by the cramped format of the reset text.

A more complex example is the alignment—lost in the reset text—of "Persephone" and "Shaken" on page 125. Dr. Paterson comes to the abused woman in the basement who represents at this point one of the manifestations of "Beautiful thing." The moment of communication is itself silent, visual:

> —for I was overcome
> by amazement and could do nothing but admire
> and lean to care for you in your quietness—
>
> who looked at me, smiling, and we remained
> thus looking, each at the other . in silence .
>
> You lethargic, waiting upon me, waiting for
> the fire and I
> attendant upon you, shaken by your beauty
>
> Shaken by your beauty
> Shaken.

Syntactically, the poem associates "Shaken" first with Paterson's reaction to the figure, and then with the woman's abused beauty—but obscured in the present text is the exact visual alignment of "Shaken" with Persephone (the kidnapped goddess of Williams's 1920 *Kora in Hell*) twelve lines above—an association that reinforces the thematic parallel by visually returning the unsettling reaction and brutal treatment fused in "Shaken" to this 'eternal' source. In this third book of the poem, characterized by the destructive actions of wind, fire, and flood, in which Paterson's assumptions and the text itself are "shaken"—most visibly on page 137—the visual parallel anchored to a figure who for Williams served as a source of constant renewal represents in passing the promise of a fundamental stabilizing counterforce within both female figures, and within Paterson's own besieged imagination and the poetics that are embodying its expression.

The changes in the prose sections of the poem through the various printings stem from a number of causes. These causes include the request or insistence of the authors of the prose used and shifts in the poem's historical and cultural context (most notably Pound's release from St. Elizabeths, Allen Ginsberg's fame, and the correspondence of both becoming available in research archives). Book 5 has been the subject of most changes—more than sixty verbal changes between the first and the posthumous reset edition—and thus raises the most questions. The very fact that it has received a disproportionate amount of editorial attention reaches out, of course, to affect the whole poem, since as far as the prose sections are concerned, Books 1–4 have remained largely untouched. An underlying assumption behind many of the changes is that Williams or his typist unwittingly mistranscribed the sources—although as a number of scholars have demonstrated, Williams intentionally changes some of his source texts in Books 1–4 to point up thematic issues, and rightly these sections on the whole have not been 'corrected' against their source documents. (These matters surfaced in passing in the second volume of the *Collected Poems*—see the notes to "The Phoenix and the Tortoise" and "The Testament of Perpetual Change"—but become central issues in the editing of *Paterson.*)

A difficulty of editing the prose sections of the poem is evaluating the degree to which these posthumous 'corrections' should affect editorial decisions, a difficulty compounded by the presence of multiple authors and dual levels of authorial sanction. Thus some of the editorial questions raised by these sections of the poem are complicated by factors similar to those discussed above in connection with format and economics. Williams's thinking about the poem was clearly in the direction of not wanting a time-bound text, any more than he saw the imagination as time-bound. One of the poem's central characteristics, the hybrid of voices imported into the poem through documents and transcribed speech, acknowledges on one level that these documents and voices belong to their originators. And although assimilated into the voice of Paterson and *Paterson,* on another, practical level, they *do* belong to their sources—therefore, for example, e. e. cummings reasonably demanded payment for the use of his contribution in Book 5, while at least two authors included in earlier books expressed annoyance at the use of their letters.

The status to give these changes is further complicated by the unreliability of the first edition of Book 5 as a copy-text, and of the typescripts behind it, because of Williams's general poor health, and particularly his poor vision, in the late 1950s. On one measure of his difficulties in reading the typescripts and galleys, the first edition of Book 5 contains more obvious typographical errors than the other four first editions combined (most of these errors are corrected in the reset edition). But to conclude from this that Williams mistranscribed his source documents where they differ from the originals is to simplify some difficult issues.

One example of the posthumous changes made occurs in the final section of Book 5. Williams quotes Matthew 1:18. The language of the first edition differs from the King James version in a number of instances that modernize the language, although Mary is called by the Hebrew "Miriam." Is Williams mistranscribing the King James version? Using another biblical text? Or intentionally broadening the reach of the language? The Yale typescripts reveal that the final language of the first edition evolved through a number of retypings, but offer no clue as to whether the changes reflect compositional changes or typing errors not caught because drafts were not checked against each other or against originals (editing the *Collected Poems* revealed a number of instances of the latter). Nevertheless, in 1963 the reset text changed the first edition's language to the King James version (which Williams nowhere claims to be quoting) but leaves "Miriam" for "Mary" because, according to an editorial note, "Dr. Williams often referred to the mother of Jesus as Miriam."[5]

An assumption of mistranscription also lies behind the posthumous changes to the letters from Allen Ginsberg quoted in Books 4 and 5. Again the Yale typescripts are of limited help, although the publisher's file makes clear that the request for changing the poem's text did not come from Ginsberg but was suggested once the letters became part of the Beinecke Library holdings. Aside from the difficult question of mistranscription or intentional change, this aspect of the poem's textual history raises the issue noted above of the status of another's words when they are incorporated into the poem. Should the source document serve as copy-text here, or the typescripts that reflect the workings of the poet's imagination and—even if mistranscribed—his consent to the language as embodied in his poem?

Sometimes the changes in the reset text remove nuances of the poem, as well as creating new problems of inconsistency. The first of the Ginsberg letters was originally incorporated into *Paterson* over the initials "A.P."—diffusing and disguising the actual sender, and connecting the linguistic level of this new beginning—"A"—to Dr. P.'s search, and to Dr. P. The current text's identifying "A.G." is a posthumous change, as is the addition of the identifying initials to the second letter quoted in Book 4, which originally carried none. But the change is apparently sanctioned by the inclusion in Book 5's 1958 first edition of the by then well-known A.G.'s initials following another letter.[6] Nevertheless, the editorial imposition of consistency removes the narrative arc suggested by the earlier sequence of identifications—the birth, separation, and independent flowering of the poem's "A.P." to "A.G." In addition (ignoring for the moment the wishes of the persons involved) the retroactive identifications are inconsistent with retaining, for example, the anonymity and "*Paterson*" identity of the "Cress" letters, and of Book 1's 'T.' The result is to skew the text's editorial changes toward those letter writers who by the 1960s and early 1970s were well enough known for their correspondence to be catalogued, and also toward the source documents of the later books because these are more likely to have survived. (This particular issue does not in 1991 have to be conceded to the whims of time, since most of the prose documents have become available—nonfamous letter writers now accorded archival attention through their association with Williams and/or *Paterson.*)

An example from one of the Ginsberg letters in Book 4 illustrates the kind of changes that have been made in the text, and the difficulties involved in their evaluation.[7] The version of the letter in the 1963 reset edition contains six verbal changes from the first edition, changes that restore the text to the language of the letter itself, now at the Beinecke Library (although a definite article is added that is not in the source). In the third of the paragraphs Williams chose to use from the letter, Ginsberg is writing of Paterson's Mill and River Streets. The current text, and the letter itself, read: "I wonder if you have seen River Street most of all, because that is really at the heart of what is to be known." Williams's version in the first edition reads: "I wonder if you have seen River Street most of all, because that is really the heart of what is to be seen." Leaving aside the greater immediacy of the latter's more concise expression, the first edition's version emphasizes vision—"what is to be *seen*." Williams—or a typist—may have mistakenly picked up "seen" from the earlier part of the sentence, or "see" from the sentence before (noting a "taproom . . . window facing the river painted over so that the people can't see it"). On the other hand, since the whole thrust of the passage—and much of the poem—is on looking, seeing, Williams may be editing a document, as in earlier books, to emphasize a theme.

A final category of external changes imposed on the text of *Paterson* and complicating an editor's task stems from the authors of the poem's prose documents sometimes themselves editing their contributions to Williams's poem—Pound and e. e. cummings, for example. Where

Williams agreed to the changes this causes no serious editorial problems, but the textual status of some other external changes is more questionable. For example, Williams based his extract from Gilbert Sorrentino's "Bordertown" sketch in Book 5[8] on an early version Sorrentino sent him (now filed with the *Paterson 5* typescripts at the Beinecke). These typescripts show Williams himself editing the passage, making small verbal changes and deletions. But the current text reflects a later, slightly more polished version of the sketch, and the suggested changes to *Paterson* apparently came from "Bordertown"'s author *after* Williams's death. A different aspect of the problem is raised by the letter from Ginsberg in Book 5 thanking Williams for his introduction to *Howl and Other Poems.*[9] This passage contains sixteen verbal changes between the first edition and the posthumous reset text (changes made, again, to reflect the language of the source), yet the first edition is not only the version Williams himself oversaw, it is also the version Ginsberg was sent and approved.

Preparing an edition of *Paterson* is thus complicated by many of the factors involved in editing the *Collected Poems*—including Williams's innovative poetics, the difficulty of evaluating and recording spacing changes, the vagaries of format in reprintings, the multiple typescripts, and the different degrees of attention Williams granted to typescripts and galleys. The challenge such texts offer to an editor is compounded in the case of *Paterson* by its particular textual history and characteristics—its multiple copy-texts, authors, and levels of authorial sanction, and its thematic embrace of the very economic and cultural forces that have posthumously shaped it. In one summary moment, Dr. Paterson sits reading in Paterson library, while "Texts mount and complicate them- / selves, lead to further texts and those / to synopses, digests and emendations."[10] Dr. Williams anticipated something of his editor's dilemma. Yet with this poem that is in so many ways a poem *about* texts, to prepare an edition is to do more than merely consider further "synopses, digests and emendations"; it is to engage the shaping impulse of the poem itself.

NOTES

Paterson page numbers in the essay and notes refer to the 1969 repagination of the 1963 edition.

1. *William Carlos Williams and James Laughlin: Selected Letters,* ed. Hugh Witemeyer (New York: Norton, 1989), 31.

2. William Carlos Williams to Louis Zukofsky, 29 April 1931; Harry Ransom Humanities Research Center, University of Texas.

3. William Carlos Williams, *Paterson* (New York: New Directions, 1963), 39.

4. *Paterson,* 100.

5. *Paterson,* 228–29.

6. *Paterson,* 175, 194–95, 212–13.

7. *Paterson,* 194.

8. *Paterson,* 214–15.

9. *Paterson,* 212–13.

10. *Paterson,* 130.

Excavating the Ideological Faultlines of Modernism: Editing Ezra Pound's *Cantos*

Ronald Bush

During the last two decades, revisionary analysis of modernism has insisted on an essential connection between postsymbolist aesthetics and reactionary politics. Terry Eagleton, to take an influential instance, has argued that literature should be recognized as ideological practice, and that modernist literature's characteristic mythic and symbolic structures should be read in the light of "bourgeois ideology's growing dependence on [mystified] 'organicist' concepts of society."[1] Yet in an eagerness to clinch real arguments, this line of analysis sometimes commits the sin it associates with its target: for political purposes, it dehistoricizes and decontextualizes problematic works of poetry and fiction. This is true, I want to argue, even in commentary on Ezra Pound's *Cantos,* a text that has been called "the sacred poem of the Nazi-Fascist millennium."[2] Not that elements of Pound's poem do not substantiate the revisionists' claim. Rather, unless we credit the *Cantos* as a site of real ideological competition, a composite of real dialogue, we create an account of modernism as totalized as anything its apologists ever produced. Along with an inclination toward mythic closure, the *Cantos* sustain a genuine commitment to radical openness of a kind now commonly associated with postmodernism. More, a continuing and vigorous conflict between ideologies associated with openness and closure, the bohemian and the mandarin, epic and lyric, constitutes one of the sequence's identifying marks. True, Pound's own pronouncements and revisions in middle age helped construct his canon in a way that covered over its ideological inconsistencies. Yet, ironically, critics trained in poststructuralist suspicion have now replicated Pound by accepting his self-mystification on its own terms.

Frank Kermode, we might recall, was among the first to raise many of the same charges against Pound and modernism in *The Sense of an Ending,* but ended by rejecting them. The way the modernists qualified their myths by enclosing them in dialectic structures, Kermode thought, showed that their characteristic texts were self-conscious rather than naive. Even the modernists' most pernicious primitivism, he wrote, was in the best work "held in check" by a critical and pervasive "skepticism."[3] Kermode's point can be extended, however, to matters above and below the level of formal control. Both in their metapoetics and in their favorite stories, the modernists demonstrate ideological dissonance, not consistency. And nowhere is this clearer than in the twentieth century's archetypal poem-in-progress, the *Cantos.*

Had we genetic and variorum editions of the *Cantos,* all this would be transparent. As Christine Froula has shown in a study of Canto IV, "the authority that informs the *Cantos* is not monolithic, . . . [the poem's] finality is as contingent as death." But, she writes, to keep that in focus, editions of the *Cantos* must reflect the poem as "temporal process" and present a "fully and accurately documented text in all its historical changes."[4] Accordingly, the present essay offers a number of case studies to illustrate what the usefulness—and critical upshot—of a complete edition of the *Cantos* might be.

I

The most influential aspect of the revisionary critique of modernist writing has proved to be its analysis of the "organicism" of modernist aesthetic and social thinking. Behind the political application of Terry Eagleton stands the philosophical assertion of a critic like Paul de Man, who argues that modernism's reliance on symbol and myth to telescope the matter of different ages—what Eliot once called the mythic method—is in fact just an intensification of Romanticism's illegitimate aspiration to escape from history. For de Man, first Romantic and then modernist analogies between language and a mystified conception of nature point to an act of bad faith that ignores the characteristic discontinuities of human products. In de Man's words, symbolist and postsymbolist poetic structures, conceiving of form as a "well rounded shape" rather than as "a fragment in the incessant interpretation of Being that makes up our history," tend to surrender "the autonomy of the conscious mind to the unquestioned hegemony of the physical world."[5] Put more simply, the visionary structures of Romantic and modernist literature, once perceived as "organic" with the natural world, take on an authority beyond our provisional experience in time. And once that happens, the Marxists add, linguistic mystification becomes the basis of a political bad faith in which systems like fascism can be characterized as natural.

De Man's critique at first seems difficult to answer. Organicism of one kind or another does drive much of post-Romantic poetics, and early modernism owes a great deal to a resurgence of organicist metaphors. Certainly Ezra Pound's early writings lie within this tradition. Close to the heart of Pound's fundamental intuition of literature is his declaration that poetry associates itself with the phrase, "My words are the unspoken words of my body."[6] And an important element of his practice involved aspiring through organic structures to achieve the unmediated expression of sensibility. Asserting nothing and distrusting linguistic abstraction, his poems from at least the time of "The Seafarer" (1911) combine sensual particulars and conceptual thrust within symbolic forms, and return to the question of whether it is possible to dramatize thinking and feeling untainted by language.

In this respect the *Cantos* are no less mystified than the rest of Pound's writings, and the revealing directness of his drafts can make the case worse. So in an early draft of Canto XII we find Pound urging "A speech more real than speech, / the form cut into the stone."[7] The epigram formulates Pound's aspirations toward prelinguistic wholeness in the form of a medium in which words are at one with things, and it reveals in a nutshell a view of the world in which politics can be justified as inevitable and natural. If, after all, poetry is the unmediated expression of an enduring human nature, there must also be a political arrangement that is its natural complement. This would in the 1930s become the justification for Pound's fascist advocacy of the Confucian tradition, in which man as political animal stands to earth as what the *Cantos* call "two halves of the tally"[8]—that is, two halves of a broken tally stick, which when rejoined make a perfect fit.

And yet, though Pound's search for a form that would unite words with things seems to disclose the ideological orientation of his poetic project, at the same time he pursued another and (in our present understanding of the ideology of poetic forms) quite different ideal. The following *Cantos* fragment is also culled from early drafts, and no less than the phrase "a speech more real than speech" expresses a central Poundian imperative:

> What am I at?
>   You silly fool,
> How often must I stop the narrative to say
> That this is life. These things are life,
> Of which neither you nor I make head or tail:
> A maxim, pain, and half a sentence or two
> "It[']s low to try to coerce another person,
> Low to desire contro[l]
>   All we can do 's to set forth our own good
> within some other's reach.
>   not force it on him
> We have but few rights, the right of self protection.
> "Art's but integrity.[9]

This exhortation would generate Pound's search for a poetic form ample enough, as he put it in the first published version of Canto I, to meet the modern world's need for a "rag-bag to stuff all its thought in."[10] It is also intrinsic to the metrical revolution of the *Cantos,* in which breaking "the pentameter" was only "the first heave" (C81 / 532) against stifling poetic forms. As the fragment indicates, Pound here conceives his form as not totalizing but democratic: "It[']s low," he insists, "to coerce another person. . . . Art's but integrity." And in lines after the ones I have reproduced, he adds that art assures its "integrity" by a faithfulness to plurality and even messiness. Academic poetry, he maintains a few lines later, never comes near "the flow, the pulse, the surge, / the uproarious and outrageous, / The uncontrolled, indecorous, actual living."

There is a significant part of Pound's program, then, that belies the illusion of a homogeneous poetics linked to a consistent ideological stance. A desire for the "uncontrolled" counters Pound's yearning for "form cut into stone." Here Pound utilizes organic metaphors ("the pulse, the surge"), but uses them to attack rather than confirm totality. In the lines just quoted he articulates a programmatic openness and an antiformalist skepticism of the kind his fellow poets in the 1950s and 1960s assumed was his signature. For them, we may remember, Pound was a figure of the underground left, an iconoclast whose metrical experiments signified, in Allen Ginsberg's words, "no less than the whole alteration of human consciousness."[11] These poets also assumed (along with a more recent school of Pound's formalist critics) that the "pivotal . . . transformation of the Romantic (and Modernistic) lyric into what we now think of as postmodern poetry takes place in the *Cantos*."[12]

II

Nor are the *Cantos'* ideological inconsistencies confined to matters of poetics. They also pertain to the less sophisticated but more revealing matter of the tales Pound tells. For example, the conflict between openness and closure in the *Cantos* reappears in the poem's representations of gender relations. In passages written a few years later than the fragment just recalled, Pound entered the arena of sexual politics. And to a reader now opening the *Cantos,* the results were (to say the least) disturbing. Consider the opening and closing passages of Canto VI:

What you have done, Odysseus,
            We know what you have done . . .
        And that Guillaume sold out his ground rents
        (Seventh of Poitiers, Ninth of Aquitain).
    "Tant las fotei com auzirets
    "Cen e quatre vingt et veit vetz . . ."
The stone is alive in my hand, the crops
    will be thick in my death-year. . .
. . . .

E lo Sordels si fo di Mantovana,
Son of a poor knight, Sier Escort,
And he delighted himself in chançons
And mixed with the men of the court
And went to the court of Richard Saint Boniface
And was there taken with love for his wife
                Cunizza, da Romano,
That freed her slaves on a Wednesday
Masnatas et servos, witness
Picus de Farinatus
and Don Elinus and Don Lipus
        sons of Farinato de' Farinati
"free of person, free of will
"free to buy, witness, sell, testate."
A marito subtraxit ipsam . . .
    dictum Sordellum concubuisse:
    "Winter and Summer I sing of her grace,
    As the rose is fair, so fair is her face,

> Both Summer and Winter I sing of her,
> The snow makyth me to remember her."
>
> And Cairels was of Sarlat . . .
> Theseus from Troezene
> And they wd. have given him poison
> But for the shape of his sword-hilt.

One does not have to be a feminist to realize the complementary patriarchalism in these passages. Canto VI opens by linking the heroic figure of Odysseus with the only slightly less heroic seigneur and troubadour, Guillaume of Aquitaine. It then derives the latter's power from his sexual performance. The two verses of provençal give Guillaume's bawdy boast that he met a group of traveling gentlewomen and "fucked them, as you shall hear, 188 times." And as if that weren't bad enough, the following verse telescopes Guillaume's masculine prowess first with the organic vitality of the earth and then with the form-creating power of the architect and sculptor ("the stone is alive in my hand")—and by implication, the artist in general. The canto concludes by presenting the reverse side of this sexism in the story of the troubadour Sordello, who was born in Italy, where he courted Cunizza da Romano, whom Dante would place in the third heaven of Paradise. Cunizza's divinely inspired love, Pound implies here and elsewhere, generated the magnanimity with which she late in life freed her slaves. It was this Cunizza who facilitated the transmission of poetry from the troubadours to Dante and Guido Cavalcanti, the young attendants of Cunizza's last years. The canto concludes, in other words, with an idealization of erotic mysticism that is the predictable second face of its leering assertion.

Based on texts like these and worse, revisionist critics not uncommonly hold that Pound's activities are quintessentially misogynist. Thus, recalling Pound's efforts in the 1910s on the part of the London magazine that began life as *The Freewoman: A Weekly Feminist Review* and later, as *The Egoist: An Individualist Review,* published Joyce's *A Portrait of the Artist as a Young Man,* K. K. Ruthven speaks of sexism pure and simple. In Ruthven's words, Pound's machinations represent "a paradigmatic instance of the subordination of women by a male-dominated modernism." According to Ruthven, what happened was this: Rebecca West, the literary sub-editor of *The Freewoman* (which in June 1913 had been renamed *The New Freewoman*), was "aware of [Pound's] activities as literary talent scout for *Poetry*" and sought him out. "For Pound," Ruthven writes, "it was an opportune moment to use the *New Free-*

woman in the same way as he was using *Poetry* (Chicago), that is, as a base from which to campaign on behalf of the Imagist movement in general and the Pound version of it in particular." "He was willing to assume editorial duties," Ruthven says, "which . . . Rebecca West was in no fit state to take on," and in a very short time he and four other "self-styled men of letters" had changed the journal's name and changed its course. Thus "by a conjuncture of feminist insouciance [and] masculine opportunism . . . the gender-specific *New Freewoman* was erased from patriarchal memory" and "*The Egoist* consolidated its position in androcentric literary history."[13]

In Ruthven's account, a reified androcentric strain of modernism triumphs over an equally reified gynocentric one, much as the myths of organicism triumph over self-conscious allegory in the aesthetic story told by de Man. Considered historically, the facts were less neat. Dora Marsden started *The Freewoman* in reaction against the Pankhursts' singular concentration on the achievement of women's suffrage. According to one history, she began as "an energetic WSPU [Women's Social and Political Union] member," and was arrested several times in Manchester, "once for heckling Churchill from a glass roof." But having strategic and then philosophical differences with the WSPU, she started a revolutionary paper in which the issue of the vote was superceded by reflections on marriage, sexuality, and a new moral and political order. Most strikingly, in contrast to suffragist literature, which "took meticulous care to avoid any charges of immorality for fear of damaging the campaign for votes," *The Freewoman* encouraged articles reevaluating the "relationship between sexual morality and the oppression of women."[14] Describing herself as a "philosophical anarchist,"[15] Marsden immersed herself in a community of Nietzscheans, Fabians, Syndicalists, Theosophists, and Anarchists, and she more and more inclined toward the position of "individualism," a position in which men's and women's emotional and spiritual liberation counted for more than political reform. Thus she rehearsed what the historian Jonathan Rose has called the Edwardian obsession with Life, an obsession that "could mean the surrogate religion of vitalism, the worship of the life process as a spiritual force [or] an erotic impulse breaking out of Victorian constraints." "Life," Rose adds, "could also be a mysterious spiritual quality that endowed human beings with identity, consciousness, a moral sense, and free will—a vital spark very like the Christian concept of the soul."[16] According to Harriet Weaver's biographers, it was Dora Marsden herself who was responsible for subtitling *The New Freewoman* (the *first* reincarnation of *The Freewoman*) *An Individualist Review,* and it was she who proposed the journal's third name, *The Egoist.*[17]

Nor was Marsden alone in her circle to link the struggle of feminism to the goal of liberating the life principle. Pound's friend May Sinclair, in a now forgotten 1912 pamphlet entitled *Feminism,* wrote in response to the self-proclaimed "scientific" objections to feminism of a bacteriologist named Sir Almroth Wright that "the sublime enthusiasm and self-devotion and self-sacrifice of the suffragists spring from the same root"—the "stream of the Life-Force of which Woman is preeminently the reservoir" and which is associated with the "dawn of womanhood" and with sexual passion.[18] It was May Sinclair who introduced Pound to Ford Madox Ford and Ford's companion Violet Hunt, herself a suffragette.[19] During this period at their literary parties on Campden hill "les jeunes" met one another and breathed the air of a "new age." In the summer of 1913 Hunt introduced Pound to Rebecca West, and soon afterward West approached Pound about writing for *The New Freewoman.* Pound responded enthusiastically. Unquestionably, he helped reorient the journal toward literature, and (as he wrote to James Joyce) he thought the journal's title "unsuitable."[20] And yet the poetry and commentary he produced for the journal followed much of Rebecca West's own "programme"—which called for, in West's words, "the revolt of women, philosophic anarchism, and a general whip-round for ideas that would reform simultaneously life and art."[21]

In this context, one begins to see that alongside Pound's early fascination with masterful heroes exists an inclination toward early twentieth-century ideals of anarchism and vitalism genuinely affiliated with *The New Freewoman*'s feminist insistence on upsetting traditional sexual morality.[22] Further, much of his important early writing answers to such affiliation. A desire to effect the liberation of men and women is the theme of major essays as different as "Henry James" and "Psychology and the Troubadours."[23] It also informs poems as diverse as the near feminist "River Merchant's Wife," created out of more traditional Chinese materials in *Cathay,*[24] and Canto IV, whose conclusion affirms that natural energy can never be appropriated as political or sexual property ("No wind is the king's wind") (C4/16).

How then to explain the sweeping antifeminism apparent in the lines already quoted from Canto VI, a poem written in the same year (1919) as Canto IV? First, the opening and closing lines play a contrapuntal part in a larger literary structure: the central section of the full poem in which they appear concerns the futile enclosure of Eleanor of Aquitaine and appeals for the freedom of "My Lady of Ventadour" from a stifling and unnatural marriage. The core of the poem, that is to say, urges (exactly as *The New Freewoman* would) the liberating force of free love for women in a society of arranged marriages.

When a variorum edition of the *Cantos* is available, Canto VI's ideological cross purposes will be more obvious still. For such an edition would inform us that Pound's opening bravado and his concluding idealization were added a decade after the poem was written. The 1919 version that appeared in the *Dial* of 1921, in *Poems 1918–1921* and in *A Draft of XVI. Cantos* (1925) was a different poem. After brief allusions to the way Odysseus and Guillaume let their worlds get out of control, this canto tells the story of the machinations of Henry II at much greater length, adding the threatened political marriage of Richard to the two matches that constrained Eleanor. Much more than its successor, the 1919 version of Canto VI emphasizes Eleanor's energy, her entrapment in the venal and corrupt marriage conventions of late medieval society, and at the last her communications with the troubadour Bernart de Ventadour. Bernart's appeal to her on behalf of Lady Ventadour—a token of the energies of innovative art and free love—is in 1919 given the force of a peroration. And to readers informed about the relevance of Pound's bohemian life to the poem, the progressive associations of Bernart's story are inescapable (for the 1919/1925 text, see Appendix).

In 1919, Pound visited Castle Malemort in Corrèze with his wife Dorothy[25] precisely because he regarded the castle as a monument to a poetic martyr who had been divided from love by considerations of power and money. Dorothy was not Pound's first serious attachment, but their relationship was the first to survive serious resistance from the respectable world on his account. In 1908 Ezra had proposed marriage to the poet Hilda Doolittle. The two parted because her father, an eminent professor of astronomy, considered Pound "nothing but a nomad."[26] Then in the winter of 1909–10 in London Pound fell passionately in love with Bride Scratton, who returned Pound's ardor but refused to divorce because she was "too grounded in the comfortable present."[27] Finally, Pound's marriage was postponed for two years when Dorothy's lawyer-father, Henry Hope, objected to Pound's lack of a yearly income.[28]

The 1919 version of Canto VI, then, though not lacking Pound's temperamental machismo, takes its primary theme from his protest against the stifling situation of gifted men and women in Edwardian society. Ideologically it is as feminist as it is patriarchal, but without knowing the poem's textual history one would never know.

III

Related to the project of identifying ideological inconsistencies of the kind already examined, a genetic edition of the *Cantos* alive to the poem's historical development would also help focus the way Pound began to mute those inconsistencies after 1920. We would be able to see, for example, how he reorganized nearly ten years' work on the *Cantos* in late 1923 around the personal mask of Sigismundo Malatesta. This mask, as Lawrence Rainey has shown, had the potential to be inflected either toward anarchy or totality, but was finally annealed in the same forge as the triumphant Mussolini.[29] In the 1920s, Pound's interest shifted from London's bohemian mix of anarchism and feminism to a continental fixation with strong and patriarchal cultural forms. Pound moved to Paris in 1921, traveling extensively in France and Italy. In 1922, he translated Remy de Gourmont's *Physique de l'amour* into *The Natural Philosophy of Love* and began to champion Gourmont's biological explanation of the imagination in aggressively sexist terms. According to Gourmont, "the male of the human species . . . alone is capable of disinterested works, that is to say of aims unconnected with the physical conservation of the race, but without which civilization would be impossible."[30] From this Pound in his notorious postscript to the translation (protesting all the while that he was not "writing an anti-feminist tract") extrapolated the notion that "the power of the spermatozoide is precisely the power of exteriorizing a form" and therefore the form making "brain itself is, in origin and development, only a sort of great clot of genital fluid." Pound even went so far as to compare the acts of the imagination with the ejaculation of male sperm, adding "Even oneself has felt it, driving any new idea into the great passive vulva of London, a sensation analagous to the male feeling in copulation."[31]

After 1920, Pound's view of family life also changed, and he extrapolated from it an altered view of government. As Eva Hesse points out, in London he had espoused "a downright rejection of the bourgeois conception of family, [but] from his early forties to his early seventies he gradually went over to advocating [a patriarchalism that] passes for Confucianism."[32] By the 1930s Pound was condemning not just young lovers but also his first heroes. In *Guide to Kulchur* the *Odyssey* has become an "adventure story . . . preaching self-reliance" and Pound transfers his praise from "the maritime adventure morals of Odysseus or the loose talk of argumentative greeks" to Rome ("the responsible ruler") and "the need for coordination of individuals expressed in Kung's teaching."[33]

Inevitably the *Cantos,* Pound's poem of cultural values, absorbed these changes, and not just in new work. *A Draft of XVI. Cantos* (1925) introduced what a recent critic has called the "stereotypical male-writ-large" world of Sigusmundo Malatesta in Cantos VIII–XI.[34] Then in 1930 Pound went further. In *A Draft of XXX Cantos,* Canto XXIX versified his postscript to Gourmont ("the female / Is a chaos") and lionized Cunizza da Romano. As important, to smooth the way for it Pound made the already discussed changes in Canto VI, thus "anticipating" the poem's newly idealized view of women.

After 1930, then, it became possible to read out of "the poem as a whole" Pound's crypto-fascist emphasis on the organic structures of imagination and society. And between 1930 and 1969 such readings became easier still. In 1934 Pound published *Eleven New Cantos,* which draws parallels between Jefferson, Adams, and Mussolini. These cantos indirectly refer to Mussolini's "civilizing" invasion of Abyssinia in the story of Hanno's voyage to Africa, and they celebrate Cunizza da Romano in a context both mystical and sexist. (In Canto XXXVI, her words follow a translation of Guido Cavalcanti's "Donna mi pregha," and the two inspire a paean, "Sacrum, sacrum, inluminatio coitu"—a sacred thing, the light of coitus.)

By 1940, when *Cantos LII–LXXI* was published, Pound's organicist justification of patriarchal and political reaction had become virtually complete. In this volume, Pound links Mussolini with a mystified Neo-Confucianism and identifies the hierarchical state with the eternal verities of nature. With a small detour at Pisa this would be his position through 1959–60, when he gave the seventh book-length installment of the *Cantos* the title *Thrones* to assert his continuing belief in a hierarchical "order" beyond "egoism" "possible or at least conceivable on earth."[35]

IV

Yet through this thirty-year period when the ideological focus of the *Cantos* hardened, the poem maintained a programmatic openness that enabled and even encouraged antiauthoritarian currents to persist. And so we find on several occasions Pound repeated his pattern of 1915–30, composing ideologically ambiguous poetry and then revising it to suggest a hardened political stance. The history of *The Pisan Cantos* presents the first case in point.

Recently released archival materials push the beginnings of *The Pisan Cantos,* Pound's best and certainly his most controversial work, back to four months before he was imprisoned by the U.S. Army at Pisa, and perhaps several years before that.[36] These materials also cause us to think twice about the two prevailing ways of reading these cantos. In a 1948 review, Robert Fitzgerald suggested that *The Pisan Cantos* were the expression of "a personal desolation and a kind of repentance that is enormously moving,"[37] and inflected the poem away from epic and toward personal lyric. Fitzgerald's remark conditioned thirty years of criticism, until the revisionist consensus of the late 1980s declared that the sequence presented no sharp generic break and left Pound's "commitments to fascism almost completely intact."[38] Both readings, however, assume a demonstrably false consistency. The first highlights Pound's moments of sympathy for the other prisoners at the U.S. Army Disciplinary Training Center. The second focuses on Pound's defiant lament for Mussolini at the beginning of the sequence (Canto LXXIV), and on his melancholy farewell to several European collaborators at the end (Canto LXXXIV); and links the whole to Canto LXXXI's diatribe *against* the American Army ("half black half white / Nor knowst'ou wing from tail").

The textual history of *The Pisan Cantos* explains how such fundamental disagreement could arise. A set of holograph and typescript drafts in Italian at the Beinecke Library shows that Pound started a new sequence four months before his imprisonment. These drafts, following on the heels of the explicitly fascist Italian Cantos LXXII and LXXIII, were connected to the American destruction of Pound's beloved Renaissance sites, to the fascist resistance to the American war effort and to the figure of Cunizza da Romano through whom Pound once more invoked an earthly paradise of natural eros. Pound carried these Italian texts in his head during three weeks of incarceration in the elements before he broke down mentally and physically, and out of them he began a long poem in the center's medical compound. The new composition arrived at an opening that now appears as line eleven of Canto LXXIV: "The suave eyes, quiet, not scornful." The cantos that followed describe a visionary quest for the peace in these eyes, and several months later Pound believed he completed the sequence when he wrote Canto LXXXIII's affirmation of internalized peace: the eyes now "pass and look *from* mine."[39] This was the shape of Pound's polished typescript, and ideologically it resembles the cantos of the 1930s. Nature and eros had provided an equanimity couched in Confucian terms, and the shape of myth reinforced a hierarchical view of the universe.

Against this visionary and mystified symbolic structure, however, pulled another logic. Enhanced by the fragmentary movement of the *Cantos'* poetic and narrative idiom, and driven by a terror of having lost his memory (and, he feared, his identity), Pound filled out his quest with a combination of diary and reminiscence that his wife recognized as the substance of an autobiographical work they had talked about years before.[40] Significantly, his model here was not Dante's epic, construed as totalizing form, but the lyric and episodic *Testament* of Villon. He seemed especially to have in mind lines from stanza 29: "Where are those laughing comrades / that I was with in former days, / who sang so well, talked so well / and so excelled in word and deed? / Some are dead and stiff— / nothing now remains of them: / may they find peace in Paradise, / and may God save the rest."[41] Villon, with his scene set on the gallows, was important enough to be associated with the very beginning of Pound's holograph manuscript at Pisa—a line that identifies the hanging, on 2 July 1945, of Louis Till. Pound had used the *Testament* for an opera years before, and its open lyric progression proved ideal for recording the flow of his day-by-day memories, perceptions, and activities. An added bonus was the emotional catharsis he felt as he acknowledged the sometimes mortal suffering of the people and animals around him.

In the present context, though, Pound's Pisan imitations of Villon are most interesting for their ideological coordinates. Both Pound's matter and manner in these sections of the poem speak of an ideological affiliation with postmodernist openness. They return Pound to his early insistence on "the flow, the pulse, the surge, / the uproarious and outrageous, / The uncontrolled, indecorous, actual living." And they also identify the poem with the outcast instead of the governor, the renegade instead of the policeman, the bohemian instead of the courtier. Yet in the last stages of composition Pound did not associate the sequence with Villon, but rather with Dante and Confucius. As he had done in 1923, when he fashioned *A Draft of XVI. Cantos* around the most authoritarian possibilities of Malatesta, and again in 1930 when he covered over shadings of feminism in Canto VI, his revisions muted the ideological dissonance of his text. Only this time the process seemed instinctive and habitual.

Believing he had finished his poem and waiting to be transported to America, Pound heard from his wife that J. P. Angold, a poet and cherished friend, had died. In the same letter she also mentioned the pending deaths of several fascist collaborators.[42] Pound was moved by the former to begin another canto with a cry of grief, and before he knew it the new Canto (now LXXXIV) had turned into a bitter farewell to "il Capo [Mussolini],/Pierre [Laval], [and] Vidkun [Quisling]." He had begun to reframe the sequence, and he completed the job by taking lines he had put aside and affixing them to the beginning of the first canto he had written.[43] As difficult as it is to believe, the dramatic opening that gives *The Pisan Cantos* their shock and stroke was an afterthought. The new lines (with the now concluding Canto LXXXIV and a series of other small changes) begin a more political and a more programmatic poem than the one Pound drafted. I give them as they appear in manuscript:

> The enormous tragedy of the dream in the peasant's bent shoulders
> Manes / Manes was tanned and stuffed
> thus
> B[enito], and la C[lara], a Milano
> by the heels at Milano
>
> that magots shd / eat the dead bullock
> DIGENES, but the twice crucified
> where in history will you find it
>
> yet say this to the Possum, a bang, not a whimper
> with a bang not with a whimper
> To build the city of Dioce whose terraces are the colour of stars

However belated, Pound's last-minute revisions changed enough cues to make what remained vibrate in a different way, and made it more difficult to register the emotional and ideological contradictions of the rest of the text. The Mussolini lines send *The Pisan Cantos* on their way bristling with self-protective hostility and hurtling toward the new Canto LXXXIV. Tuning our ear to them, we hear not openness or generosity but only what one critic has called a "proud and intransigent . . . stoicism" that helps Pound "to control and order" his chaos and his despair.[44]

V

But the most interesting illustration of Pound's late textual and ideological transformations produced *Drafts & Fragments,* the final volume of *Cantos.* In this case, Pound's revisions enacted a double movement. First the bohemian themes of the early cantos regained a prominence they had lacked since the early 1920s, validating the reality of their continued persistence in the interim. As interesting, Pound's first revisions reemphasized some of the poem's original sense of questioning and openness. At that point, though, the values of thirty years reasserted themselves. Having composed eight striking new cantos, Pound balked at publishing them. And when a pirated edition made silence impossible, he or his publisher allowed one excised fragment to assume the importance of a finale that reinstated a strong Romantic organicism he had started to resist.

During the nearly thirteen years (from the autumn of 1945 until the early summer of 1958) that Pound was incarcerated in St. Elizabeths, he produced two volumes as insistent on authoritarian politics, natural order, and mystical perception as the cantos that had preceded Pisa. His ties to most of the world cut, and his defiance fueled by resentment at being unable to defend himself in court, he went about reworking old themes. In 1955 he published *Section: Rock-Drill, 85–95 de los cantares,* and the hammering in his title spoke volumes. Nor were the cantos he composed immediately afterward much different. By the time of his release on 18 April 1958, he had almost finished another volume, *Thrones: 96–109 de los cantares,* which he proofread that summer as a free man in Italy.

What Pound had not planned on was that life would grow more difficult. He returned with his wife and a young female admirer named Marcella Spann to Brunnenburg, the secluded castle in the Tyrol his daughter Mary de Rachewiltz had restored from ruin. And after over a decade of being shielded from problematic decisions, Pound now faced several. Though he appreciated his daughter's generosity, life at the castle bored him and the mountain air made it difficult for him to breathe. He also had somehow to negotiate the feelings of Mary, Dorothy, Marcella, and (in the background) Mary's mother, Olga Rudge. By that time his health had begun to fail. He tried to escape through travel, and on his trips he revisited the most important scenes of his adult life. But since he was usually accompanied by Mary, Dorothy, and/or Marcella, the trips were not always restful. There were rumors that in an overwrought moment he asked Marcella to marry him, causing Dorothy to engineer Marcella's return to America. Marcella denies this, but Dorothy's diaries at the Lilly Library testify to difficult moments. It was these moments and the trips that instigated them that form the personal background of *Drafts & Fragments.*

Pound's initial work on what would become Canto CX, the first canto of *Drafts & Fragments,* was done "while [he] was unsure exactly with what number *Thrones* would end."[45] After he finalized *Thrones* in the summer of 1958, he knew what he had left: a very short political canto and most of a long sequence internally dated (as if in a diary) "14 dec.[ember] '57" to "19th of June [1958]" and beyond. Both of these drafts are preserved in the Pound archives at the Beinecke Library at Yale, and both echo *Thrones'* tone of authoritative assertion. The first alludes to the historical importance of Pound's family history. The second announces "this part is for adults" and repeats the Dantesque insistence of *Thrones* that natural authority makes certain kinds of political arrangements "seats" for the gods.

Yet the second draft also expands allusions Pound had made in *Thrones'* Canto CIV to Joseph S. Rock's studies of the rituals of the Na Khi tribe of highland China. True, it assembles a varied but predictably unskeptical mosaic of the "reality" constituted by an eternal struggle of "cog against No-cog." But it also includes a startling personal interjection—the cry of a "beach bird" he had heard on 5 June [1958] in Virginia, probably in Marcella Spann's company, during the period between his release and the day he sailed to Italy. And what follows, though still inhabiting the world of *Thrones,* introduces what is to become the seed of *Drafts & Fragments:*

four four four four
        tullup tullup tullup
June 5, beach bird's opinion
yellow iris alone..
        the mauve field
Oaks on Mt Sumeru
        and with eyes of coral and turquoise,
can you see with such eyes on Mt Sumeru
        had queen Ash
                such eyes of turquoise
and will you walk with the oak's root
        yellow iris rise in that river bed

we have been here from the beginning
from her breath were the goddesses
^{2}La ^{2}-mun ^{3}-mi

without ^{2}ndaw ^{1}bpo, nothing solid
without ^{2}Muan ^{1}bpo, no reality
from the juniper is our agility
botanic beauty of shoulders
in fates tray are winnowed [pictograph]
ragion civile

The bird cry that opens the passage provides an occasion like the one T. S. Eliot records in *Burnt Norton.* In later revision it will become the focus of real self-questioning. Here it assimilates itself to the primal vision of the Na Khi. After a glance at the yellow iris that provides a setting for one of Pound's favorite Japanese Noh, we become aware of the eyes of the heroine of a central Na Khi romance about the suicide of a girl forced to give up her lover and marry a man chosen by her parents. (The Na Khi, a non-Confucian tribe, countenanced easy sexuality and free marital choice. When they were forced to emigrate to Confucian China, their old customs were condemned, and many young people chose to commit suicide rather than submit to the new ways. These tragedies were turned into romances, and the rituals that emerged from them concerned souls of the departed young women that were said to inhabit the wind.)

What rings false in this sequence from the perspective of what was eventually made of it is how quickly Pound moves from the somberness of the suicide romance ("will you walk with the earth's root") to another, more positive, ritual, the ^{2}Muan ^{1}bpo, which the Na Khi believe connects man to earth and heaven. The point of the suicide, apparently, is its illumination. And having registered that illumination, Pound immediately (as he had in most of the cantos after 1930) connects eros and ritual with *ragion civile*—political sense.

The interim drafts preserved in the Beinecke show this kernel turning into a very different poem, Canto CX, only with much difficulty. After composing a number of lyric passages for the following cantos and expanding the original historical and political material, Pound cut out the politics, displacing many lines about Florence and nineteenth-century America. What then remained began as does the published text: with an opening celebration of "exultance" followed hard by a revised version of the Na Khi tableau. By then, though, the emotional charge of the Na Khi material had been transformed by the addition of a somber prelude. I quote from the typescript (close to the text of *Drafts & Fragments*) that Pound sent Donald Hall on 7 April 1960. This is now preserved in the Houghton Library,[46] and begins with an allusion to Francesca and *Inferno V:*

> che poion' si al vent'
>
> ²har ²la ¹llu ³k'o
>
> of the wind-sway
>
> the 9 fates and the 7
>
> and the black tree was born dumb
> the water is blue and not turquoise
> When the stag drinks at the salt spring
> and sheep come down with the gentian sprout
>
> Can you see with eyes of coral or turquoise
> or walk with the oak's root

In this draft Pound shifts with real reluctance from the eyes of the suicide to the ceremony of heaven. The suicide, and not its illumination, takes center stage, and Pound's questions become more than perfunctory. "Do you know," he asks the girl in the story, "that the black tree on which you will hang yourself is dumb, and that your courage will be never spoken?" "Are you aware of the darkness and silence to come?" This version does not smooth over death, nor disconnect it from the forces of the surrounding wind.

But what is more remarkable than the passage's increased somberness is the kind of story it fleshes out. Thirty-some years after he altered the original version of Canto VI, Canto CX sympathetically invokes another young girl extinguished by custom and power. Once more we find ourselves in the world of turn-of-the-century bohemia, with its ideological resistance to patriarchal authority.

In a related and equally surprising development, Canto CX and the rest of *Drafts & Fragments* unfold a tentative progress that for the first time since *The Pisan Cantos* seems genuinely noncoercive. As Pound moves toward Canto CXVI's confession that "my errors and wrecks lie about me," his utterance regains some of the modesty of his Villon-related lines at Pisa. All the *Drafts & Fragments* cantos partake of this new tentativeness, but it is perhaps easiest to see in "From CXV." I give the New Directions text:

> The scientists are in terror
> and the European mind stops
> Wyndham Lewis chose blindness
> rather than his mind stop.
> Night under wind mid garofani,
> the petals are almost still
> Mozart, Linnaeus, Sulmona,
> When one's friends hate each other
> how can there be peace in the world?
> Their asperities diverted me in my green time.
> A blown husk that is finished
> but the light sings eternal
> a pale flare over marshes
> where the salt hay whispers to tide's change
> Time, space,
> neither life nor death is the answer.
> And of man seeking good,
> doing evil.
> In meiner Heimat
> where the dead walked
> and the living were made of cardboard.
>
> (CXV/808)

This is an elegy for Wyndham Lewis, who had died in 1957, and its opening celebrates his courage. Pound memorializes Lewis's 1951 decision to accept certain blindness rather than submit to an operation that might impair his mind. But, as Timothy Materer points out, "the tone of the elegy darkens" in the following lines[47] as Lewis's rebarbative resistance aligns with the night wind against the peaceful petals of the carnation ("garofani") and against the achieved serenity of the work of Mozart, Linnaeus, and especially Ovid, who was born at Sulmona. So what had started as Pound's affirmation of Lewis's energy turns into a questioning of Lewis's hate, and youth's diversions appear all the more wasteful from the perspective of "a blown husk that is finished." Lewis's disputations over time and space in *Time and Western Man* provided no answers, and Pound suggests his own categories were no more adequate ("And of man, seeking good, / doing evil. / In meiner Heimat / where the dead walked / and the living were made of cardboard"). Hauntingly, though, Lewis returns in the penultimate line, becoming one of the dead who continue to walk.

"From CXV" shows Pound's continued ability to mime the twisting stages of thought and feeling, and it looks even better compared to Pound's previous drafts. This is the beginning of "Canto 115" in a typescript now at the Beinecke Library:

> The scientists are in terror
>   and the european mind stops.
>   Su! corragio.
>   do not accept it.
> Tan [pictograph] the dawn
>   somewhere.
> Wyndham taking blindness, rather than risk having his mind stop.
> A bronze dawn, bright russet—but dawn of some sort
>   and some how.
>
> ---
>
> There is so much beauty.
>   How can we harden our hearts?
> A beautiful night under wind mid Garofani.
>   That wind wd be?
>   Apeliota.
> Do not move
>   let the wind speak
>   That is Paradise
> The petals are amost still.
>   [. . .]
> The beauty of my thought has not entered them.
>   That is, it has as but a flash in far darkness—
> I have tried to write Paradise—
>   let the Gods forgive what I have made.
>   Let] those I love try to forgive what I have made.
> Mozart, Linaeus—
>   Sulmona
>   out of dust—
>   out of dust

This passage's only twist is a belated, self-pitying turn against itself. It starts as does the New Directions text by affirming Lewis's courage, but proceeds to no second thoughts. Instead the lines move easily between the beauty of Lewis's act, the natural beauty of the dawn, and a (this time) benevolent wind, Apeliota. Then the sweetness of that wind comes to stand for a "Paradise" Pound unhesitatingly affirms, even as he is compelled to confess his own attempts "to write Paradise" (presumably in *Rock-Drill* and *Thrones*) require forgiveness. Suddenly disconsolate, he ends near despair, calling out to Mozart, Lin[n]aeus, and Ovid to help him arise "out of dust."

The way Pound revised "Canto 115" is of a piece with the way he revised "Canto CX"—toward something less sanguine and more exploratory. It was therefore a considerable surprise to open the 1972 New Directions *Cantos* and discover that six of the lines Pound omitted from "Canto 115" when he published "From CXV" in *Drafts & Fragments* (1969) had reappeared as "CXX," the last canto of the poem.

> I have tried to write Paradise
>
> Do not move
> Let the wind speak
> that is paradise.
>
> Let the Gods forgive what I
> have made
> Let those I love try to forgive
> what I have made.

As in their original setting, these lines, a recantation of sorts, more clearly represent an affirmation. Out of the dialectic, out of the search, they announce the natural site of wisdom. More, their authoritative tone seems to impose closure on a text that had begun to question its validity. One explanation is that Pound, in his very last intervention, succumbed to a thirty-year habit of resisting his poetry's antiauthoritarianism.

Nor is that explanation implausible. Donald Hall, we know, arranged to interview Pound for the *Paris Review* in 1960. Hall told Pound the *Review* did not pay for interviews but might be able to compensate him by buying other work (ideally, Hall suggested, new cantos).[48] Pound tentatively read some of his drafts to Hall, and Hall praised their less political texture and encouraged him to work them up. In other words, Pound's return toward a style closer to that of his youth was something he himself suspected. He pushed as far as he did due to the double encouragement of a financial reward and the praise of a young admirer. But by the time the *Paris Review* had printed its excerpts ("From Canto 115" and "Canto 116," in the Summer–Fall 1962 issue), Hall had done what he could do. He had enticed Pound into completing the best part of a polished manuscript, but the new poems did not look like *Thrones,* and Pound was unhappy. He allowed bits and pieces to appear separately as he had done with the volumes preceding *Drafts &*

Fragments, but he resisted efforts to publish what he had written until an imperfect piracy appeared in 1967. At that time, with James Laughlin's urging, he consented, and in 1969 New Directions brought out *Drafts & Fragments of Cantos CX–CXVII,* in 1970 incorporating them into the New Directions collected *Cantos.*

Pound's reluctance to publish *Drafts & Fragments,* then, as Peter Stoicheff points out, was in effect an analogue to the reappearance of Canto CXX. Both indicated how little Pound had come to terms with the submerged implications of his experimental style.[49]

There remains the complication, though, that we do not know for sure that Pound titled or authorized the publication of Canto CXX, either in its 1969 magazine appearance in *The Anonym Quarterly* or in the collected *Cantos* (1972). If he did not (and the evidence seems unclear[50]), we are confronted with an extremely intriguing situation. Canto CXX was greeted by friend and foe alike as a small miracle. As Pound released his grip on the poem, his readers—including not only the friends who thought they were helping to complete the poem as he would have wished, but also the detractors who were glad to have the *Cantos* end as they expected—instinctively supplied a reflex he may have outgrown. For thirty years, both groups had been led by Pound to see only one kind of truth in his poem, and it would appear they could not bear to see the poem end without it. Thus, as Stoicheff convincingly argues, the authority that confers significant form on the *Cantos* was irreversibly transferred into the community of its readers.[51]

But by now it should be clear that this process started long before 1972. The internal dispute between the *Cantos'* conflicting ideologies had been played out since the early 1920s, first in the text and then in the arena of Pound's audience, and it has continued to occupy his readers and his editors in the years since his death in 1972. The result is that we are certain to see not one but many future editions of the *Cantos,* each accompanied by sound and fury. But these editions, it is to be hoped, will also spur an increased appreciation of the complexities of modernist writing. And, if they do, we will benefit from a new sophistication about literary history, and about the connections between textual and interpretative work. For to hear the dialogue of ideologies in a text like the *Cantos* will require a critical literary history willing to eschew sympathetic and antagonistic totalizations—one that will tell not the story but the stories of a text.

NOTES

1. Terry Eagleton, *Criticism and Ideology* (1976; rpt. London: Verso, 1985), 103.

2. Massimo Bacigalupo, *The Formèd Trace: The Later Poetry of Ezra Pound* (New York: Columbia University Press, 1980), x. Studies that stress a link between Pound's aesthetic pronouncements and his fascist politics begin in 1980 with Bacigalupo and with Michael Andre Bernstein's more nuanced *The Tale of the Tribe: Ezra Pound and the Modern Verse Epic* (Princeton: Princeton University Press, 1980). More recent and more polemical accounts include Peter Nicholls, *Ezra Pound: Politics, Economics and Writing* (Atlantic Highlands, N.J.: Humanities Press, 1984); Maud Ellmann, *The Poetics of Impersonality: T. S. Eliot and Ezra Pound* (Cambridge, Mass.: Harvard University Press, 1987); and Robert Casillo, *The Genealogy of Demons: Anti-Semitism, Fascism, and the Myths of Ezra Pound* (Evanston, Ill.: Northwestern University Press, 1988).

3. Frank Kermode, *The Sense of an Ending: Studies in the Theory of Fiction* (1966; rpt. New York: Oxford University Press, 1968), 104.

4. Christine Froula, *To Write Paradise: Style and Error in Pound's Cantos* (New Haven: Yale University Press, 1984), 175–76.

5. Paul de Man, *Critical Writings 1953–1978*, ed. Lindsay Waters (Minneapolis: University of Minnesota Press, 1989), 114, 144. On de Man's equivocal relation to modernism, see my "Paul de Man, Modernist," in *Theoretical Issues in Literary History*, ed. David Perkins (Cambridge, Mass.: Harvard University Press, 1991).

6. Pound pointed to a phrase in Remy de Gourmont. See *Literary Essays of Ezra Pound*, ed. T. S. Eliot (New York: New Directions, 1954), 341.

7. Pound Archives, Beinecke Library, Yale University. The draft is reproduced in Peter D'Epiro, *A Touch of Rhetoric: Ezra Pound's Malatesta Cantos* (Ann Arbor: UMI Research Press, 1983), 56.

8. From Canto LXXXII, *The Cantos of Ezra Pound* (New York: New Directions, 1989), 540. Unless otherwise indicated, references to the *Cantos* will be to this edition and will be incorporated into the text in the form (C82/540).

9. From the draft of a very early and aborted Canto IV, circa 1915. The draft can be found in the Pound Archives, Beinecke Library. The draft and all previously unpublished material by Ezra Pound, copyright © 1991 by the Trustees of the Ezra Pound Literary Property Trust; used by permission of New Directions Publishing Corp., agents for the Trustees. All published material by Ezra Pound used by permission of New Directions Publishing Corp.

10. From the rejected first publications of Canto I, sometimes called Ur-canto 1, which appeared in *Poetry* magazine in 1917. Quoted from a recent reprinting of Ur-cantos 1, 2, and 3 in appendix 1 of *Personae: The Shorter Poems of Ezra*

Pound, ed. Lea Baechler and A. Walton Litz (New York: New Directions, 1990). See p. 229.

11. From an interview in *Allen Verbatim,* quoted in Marjorie Perloff's essay, "The Contemporary of Our Grandchildren: Pound's Influence," in *Ezra Pound among the Poets,* ed. George Bornstein (Chicago: University of Chicago Press, 1111985), 206.

12. Marjorie Perloff, *The Dance of the Intellect: Studies in the Poetry of the Pound Tradition* (Cambridge: Cambridge University Press, 1985), 181.

13. See K. K. Ruthven, "Ezra's Appropriations," *Times Literary Supplement,* 20–26 November 1987, 1278, 1300–1301. Ruthven's account depends upon Jane Lidderdale and Mary Nicholson, *Dear Miss Weaver* (New York: Viking, 1970), and upon Bonnie Scott, *Joyce and Feminism* (Bloomington: Indiana University Press, 1984). Ruthven distorts both, however, by relying on the interpretation advanced by Michael Levenson in *A Genealogy of Modernism: A Study of English Literary Doctrine 1908–1922* (Cambridge: Cambridge University Press, 1984).

14. Les Garner, *Stepping Stones to Women's Liberty: Feminist Ideas in the Women's Suffrage Movement 1900–1918* (Rutherford, N.J.: Fairleigh Dickinson University Press, 1984), 61, 67.

15. *Freewoman,* 19 August 1912, 295.

16. Jonathan Rose, *The Edwardian Temperament 1895–1919* (Athens, Ohio: Ohio University Press, 1986), 74.

17. See Lidderdale and Nicholson, *Dear Miss Weaver,* 75.

18. May Sinclair, *Feminism* (London: Women Writers' Suffrage League, 1912), 30–31, 32.

19. See Noel Stock, *The Life of Ezra Pound* (New York: Pantheon, 1970), 62, 68.

20. See *Pound/Joyce,* ed. Forrest Read (New York: New Directions, 1967), 17.

21. Quoted in Scott, *Joyce and Feminism,* 86.

22. For a more complete treatment of this material, see my introduction, "Ezra Pound," to *The Gender of Modernism,* ed., Bonnie Kime Scott (Bloomington: Indiana University Press, 1990).

23. For "Henry James" (1918), whose keynote is James's "hatred of tyranny," see *Literary Essays,* 295–338. "Psychology and the Troubadours" (written 1912) can be found in the expanded version of *The Spirit of Romance* (New York: New Directions, 1953), 87–100. The latter was written for the mystic G. R. S. Mead and in it, like Marsden or Sinclair, Pound argues that sexuality has an "educational" as well as a "reproductive" function, and that religions like Christianity have forgotten that their original object was "to stimulate a sort of confidence in the life-force" (94–95).

24. For a reading of Pound's poem against its original, see my "Pound and Li Po: What Becomes a Man," in Bornstein, *Pound among the Poets,* 35–62, esp. 40–42.

25. Carroll Terrell, *A Companion to the Cantos of Ezra Pound* (Berkeley: University of California Press, 1980), 1:26.

26. Humphrey Carpenter, *A Serious Character: The Life of Ezra Pound* (London: Faber and Faber, 1988), 82.

27. J. J. Wilhelm, *Ezra Pound in London and Paris 1908–1925* (University Park: Pennsylvania State Press, 1990), 48–51.

28. Wilhelm, *London and Paris,* 81 and passim.

29. See Lawrence Rainey, *Ezra Pound and the Monument of Culture* (Chicago: University of Chicago Press, 1991).

30. Remy de Gourmont, *The Natural Philosophy of Love,* trans. Ezra Pound (1922; rpt. New York: Collier, 1961), 52.

31. Ibid., 149–50.

32. Eva Hesse, "The End of *The Cantos,*" in *Ezra Pound,* ed. Harold Bloom (New York: Chelsea House, 1987), 32.

33. Ezra Pound, *Guide to Kulchur* (1938; rpt. New York: New Directions, 1952), 38.

34. Eli Goldblatt, "Gender Matters in Pound's *Cantos,*" *Journal of Modern Literature* 16, no. 1 (Summer 1988): 52.

35. Donald Hall, "Ezra Pound: An Interview," *Paris Review* 7, no. 28 (Summer–Fall 1962): 49.

36. For a fuller treatment of section IV, see my "'Quiet, not scornful'?: The Composition of *The Pisan Cantos,*" in *A Poem Including History: The Cantos of Ezra Pound,* ed. Lawrence S. Rainey (Ann Arbor: University of Michigan Press, forthcoming).

37. Robert Fitzgerald, "'What thou Lovest Well Remains,'" *New Republic,* 16 August 1948. Reprinted in *Ezra Pound: The Critical Heritage,* ed. Eric Homberger (London: Routledge and Kegan Paul, 1972), 363.

38. Jerome J. McGann, *Towards a Literature of Knowledge* (Chicago: University of Chicago Press, 1989), 113.

39. In a letter dated 2 October 1945 that is now at the Lilly Library, Indiana University, Bloomington, Indiana, Pound wrote his wife Dorothy that "I have done a Decad 74 / 83, which dont seem any worse than the first 70." He was definite that Canto LXXXIII would be the last, and in a letter of 4 October he instructed Dorothy to send "72 or 74 to 83" to T. S. Eliot.

40. On 25 September, Dorothy, still unsure that Pound would ever receive her message, wrote that "Should this reach you.—You may imagine that I am thinking of you all the time: but I do not worry all that time. I only hope captivity is not proving bad for your health, & that you are able to work at some writing or other. The moment perhaps for those 'memories'?" The word "memories" here has Dorothy's quotes around it, and points to the fact that the two of them have already discussed the possibility of a serious work about Pound's life. That explains why, on 13 October, having seen parts of Cantos

LXXIV, LXXV, and LXXVI, she writes with the delight of a prophet confirmed, and then with an uneasiness about private experience that mirrors Pound's own: "Of course," she exclaims, "all these last, apparently, scraps, for cantos, are your self, the memories that make up yr. person." But she adds: "Is one then only a bunch of memories? i.e. a bunch of remains of contacts with the other people?" (Lilly Library, Indiana University, Bloomington, Indiana).

41. *The Complete Works of François Villon,* trans. Anthony Bonner (New York: Bantam, 1960), 33.

42. Dorothy's letter, now at the Lilly Library, arrived sometime after 4 October, and on 8 October Pound began Canto LXXXIV.

43. The new opening was affixed to the beginning of an almost final typescript at a moment that can be precisely determined. Pound had written an "incipit" next to "Canto ?74" above the first page of what he intended as his setting typescript, which still began, "The suave eyes, quiet, not scornful." *After* that he affixed the page beginning "The enormous tragedy of the dream." And only then did he indicate that this extra page would be page "1" and renumber the next set of pages 2–9.

44. Peter D'Epiro, "Whose Vanity Must be Pulled Down," *Paideuma* 13, no. 2 (Fall 1984): 252.

45. Peter Stoicheff, "The Composition and Publication History of Ezra Pound's *Drafts & Fragments,*" *Twentieth-Century Literature* 32, no. 1 (Spring 1986): 80. Stoicheff's article initiated the textual study of *Drafts & Fragments,* and though I shall implicitly take issue with some of his findings, I want here to acknowledge my considerable debt to him.

46. Hall's letter acknowledging receipt is at the Beinecke. The story of his encounter with Pound is told below and fully recounted in Hall's *Remembering Poets: Reminiscences and Opinions* (New York: Harper and Row, 1978).

47. Timothy Materer, "A Reading of 'From Canto CXV,'" *Paideuma* 2, no. 2 (Fall 1973): 205.

48. For the story of Pound's interaction with Hall, see Stoicheff, "Composition," 81–91, and Hall, *Remembering Poets,* 111–94, esp. 158ff.

49. Peter Stoicheff, "The Interwoven Authority of a Drafts & Fragments Text," paper given at Yale in October 1990, to be published in Rainey, *A Poem Including History* (Ann Arbor: University of Michigan Press, forthcoming).

50. Ibid. With Stoicheff's discussion, see also Barbara Eastman's *Building the Temple* (Ph.D. diss., Oxford University, 1977), which alludes to a 1973 letter from William Cookson to James Laughlin asserting that the *Anonym* poem was pirated (p. 210). On the other hand, the *Anonym Quarterly* assigns the copyright of "Canto 120" to Ezra Pound.

51. Ibid.

APPENDIX

Text of 1919 / 1925 Version of Canto VI published in *A Draft of XVI. Cantos* (1925).

The tale of thy deeds, Odysseus!" and Tolosan
Ground rents, sold by Guillaume,
ninth duke of Aquitaine;
Till Louis is wed with Eleanor; the wheel . . .
("Conrad, the wheel turns
and in the end turns ill")
And Acre and boy's love . . . for her uncle was
Commandant at Acre, she was pleased with him;
And Louis, French King, was jealous
of days unshared
This pair had had together in years gone;
And he drives on for Zion, as "God wills"
To find, in six weeks time, the Queen's scarf is
Twisted atop the casque of Saladin.
"For Sandbrueil's ransom"
But the pouch-mouths add,
"She went out hunting there, the tuft-top palms
"Give spot of shade, she rode back rather late,
"Late, latish, yet perhaps it was not too late."
The France again, and to be rid of her
And brush his antlers: Aquitane, Poictiers!
Buckle off the lot! And Adelaide Castilla wears the crown.
Eleanor down water-butt, dethroned, debased, unqueen'd,
For five rare months.

Version of Canto VI, post- *A Draft of XXX Cantos* (1930). Text from *The Cantos* (New Directions, 1989). Material added in 1930 in bold.

What you have done, Odysseus,
We know what you have done . . .
And that Guillaume sold out his ground rents
(Seventh of Poitiers, Ninth of Aquitain).
"Tant las fotei com auzirets
"Cen e quatre vingt et veit vetz . . .
The stone is alive in my hand, the crops
will be thick in my death-year . . .
Till Louis is wed with Eleanor
And had (He, Guillaume) a son that had to wife
The Duchess of Normandia whose daughter
Was wife to King Henry e maire del rei jove . . .
Went over sea till day's end (he, Louis, with Eleanor)
Coming at last to Acre.
"Ongla, oncle" saith Arnaut
Her uncle commanded in Acre,
That had known her in girlhood
(Theseus, son of Aegeus)
And he, Louis, was not at ease in that town,
And was not at ease by Jordan
As she rode out to the palm-grove
Her scarf in Saladin's cimier.
Divorced her in that year, he Louis,
divorcing thus Aquitaine.
And that year Plantagenet married her
(that had dodged past 17 suitors)
Et quand lo reis Lois lo entendit

Frazzle-top, the sand-red face, the pitching
gait,
Harry Plantagenet, the sputter in place of
speech,
But King about to be, King Louis, takes a
queen.
"E quand li reis Louis lo entendit mout er
fasché."
And yet Gisors, in six years thence, was
Marguerite's. And Harry *joven*
In pledge for all his life and life of all his
heirs
Shall have Gisors and Vexis and Neauphal,
Neufchastel;
But if no issue, Gisors shall revert
And Vexis and Neufchastel and Neauphal
to the French crown.
A song: *Si tuit li dol el plor el marrimen*
Del mon were set together they would
seem but light
Against the death of the young English
King,
Harry the Young is dead and all men
mourn,
Mourn all good courtiers, fighters,
cantadors.
And still Old Harry keeps grip on Gisors
And Neufchastel and Neauphal and Vexis;
And two years war, and never two years go
by
but come new forays, and "The
wheel
"Turns, Conrad, turns, and in the end
toward ill."
And Richard and Alix span the gap,
Gisors,
And Eleanor and Richard face the King,
For the fourth family time Plantagenet
Faces his dam and whelps, . . . and holds
Gisors,

mout er fasché.
Nauphal, Vexis, Harry joven
In pledge for all his life and life of all his
heirs
Shall have Gisors, and Vexis, Neufchastel
But if no issue Gisors shall revert . . .

Now Alix' dowry, against Philippe-Auguste
(Louis' by Adelaide, wood-lost, then
crowned at Etampe)
And never two year sans war.
And Zion still
Bleating away to Eastward, the lost lamb,
Damned city (was only Frederic knew
The true worth, and patched with Malek
Kamel
The sane and sensible peace to bait the
world
And set all camps disgruntled with all
leaders.
"Damn'd atheists!" alike Mahomet growls,
And Christ grutches more sullen for
Sicilian sense
Than does Mahound on Malek.)
The bright coat
Is more to the era, and in Messina's
beach-way
Des Barres and Richard split the
reed-lances
And the coat is torn.
(Moving in heavy air: Henry and
Saladin.
The serpent coils in the crowd.)
The letters run: Tancred to Richard:
That the French King is
More against thee, than is his will to me
Good and in faith; and moves against
your safety.

Richard to Tancred:
That our pact stands firm,
And, for these slanders, that I think you
lie.

Proofs, and in writing:
And if Bourgogne say they were not
Deliver'd by hand and his,
Let him move sword against me and
my word.

Richard to Philip: silence, with a tone.
Richard to Flanders: the subjoined and
  precedent.
Philip a silence; and then, "Lies and turned
  lies
"For that he will fail Alix
"Affianced, and Sister to Ourself."
Richard: "My father's bed-piece! A
  Plantagenet
"Mewls on the covers, with a nose like his
  already."
Then:

In the Name
Of Father and of Son Triune and
  Indivisible
Philip of France by Goddes Grace

To all men presents that our noble brother
Richard of England engaged by our mutual
  oath
    (a sacred covenant applicable to
      both)
Need *not* wed Alix but whomso he choose
We cede him Gisors, Neauphal and Vexis
And to the heirs male of his house

Cahors and Querci Richard's   The abbeys
  ours
Of Figeac and Souillac And St. Gilles left
  still in peace
Alix returns to France.

      Made in Messina in
  The year 1190 of the Incarnation of the
    Word.

Reed lances broken, a cloak torn by Des
  Barres
Do turn King Richard from the holy wars.
      And "God aid Conrad
"For man's aid comes slow," Aye tarries
  upon the road,
En Bertraus cantat.

"Need not wed Alix . . . in the name
Trinity holy indivisible . . . Richard our
  brother
Need not wed Alix once his father's ward
  and . . .
But whomso he choose . . . for Alix, etc. .

And before all this
By Correze, Malemort
A young man walks, at church with
galleried porch
By river-marsh, a sad man, pacing
Come from Ventadorn; and Eleanor
turning on thirty years,
Domna jauzionda, and then Bernart
saying:
"My lady of Ventadorn
"Is shut by Eblis in, and will not hawk
nor hunt
"Nor get her free in the air,
nor watch fish rise to bait
"Nor the glare-wing'd flies alight in the
creek's edge
"Save in my absence, Madame
'Que la lauzeta mover,'
"Send word, I ask you, to Eblis,
you have seen that maker
"And finder of songs, so far afield as this
"That he may free her,
who sheds such light in the air."

Eleanor, domna jauzionda, mother of
Richard,
Turning on thirty years (wd. have been
years before this)
By river-marsh, by galleried church-porch,
Malemorte, Correze, to whom:
"My Lady of Ventadour
"Is shut by Eblis in
"And will not hawk nor hunt
nor get her free in the air
"Nor watch fish rise to bait
"Nor the glare-wing'd flies alight in the
creek's edge
"Save in my absence, Madame.
'Que la lauzeta mover'
"Send word I ask you to Eblis
you have seen that maker
"And finder of songs so far afield as this
"That he may free her,
who sheds such light in the air."

**E lo Sordels si fo di Mantovana,
Son of a poor knight, Sier Escort,
And he delighted himself in chançons
And mixed with the men of the court
And went to the court of Richard Saint
Boniface
And was there taken with love for his wife
Cunizza, da Romano,
That freed her slaves on a Wednesday
Masnatas et servos, witness
Picus de Farinatis
and Don Elinus and Don Lipus
sons of Farinato de' Farinati
"free of person, free of will
"free to buy, witness, sell, testate."**

A marito subtraxit ipsam . . .
  dictum Sordellum concubuisse:
  "Winter and Summer I sing of her
    grace,
  As the rose is fair, so fair is her face,
  Both Summer and Winter I sing of her,
  The snow makyth me to remember her."

And Cairels was of Sarlat . . .
      Theseus from Troezene
And they wd. have given him poison
But for the shape of his sword-hilt.

Canon, Gender, and Text: The Case of H.D.

Lawrence S. Rainey

the elixir of life, the philosopher's stone
is yours if you surrender

sterile logic, trivial reason

—H.D., *Trilogy*

I did not conceal from you that I think you overrate H.D.'s poetry. I do find it fatiguingly monotonous and lacking in the element of surprise. I mean that this last book [*Hymen*] is inferior to her earlier work; that many words should be expunged and many phrases amended; that the Hellenism lacks vitality; and also morally, I find a neurotic carnality which I dislike.

—T.S. Eliot to Richard Aldington, 17 November 1921[1]

When historians of the future seek to characterize the cultural life of the United States in the 1980s, they may just decide to name it "the decade of the canon-debate." One need only recall its salient moments. In 1981 Leslie Fiedler and Houston A. Baker inaugurated discussion with *Opening up the Canon;* in 1983 Robert von Hallberg edited a special issue of *Critical Inquiry* also devoted to *Canons,* lending the subject theoretical respectability and propelling it to the forefront of academic consciousness. Only a few years later the topic would attract still more attention when Allan Bloom published *The Closing of the American Mind,* a work that became a national best-seller and turned Bloom into a media celebrity. Shortly thereafter E. D. Hirsch issued prescriptions for "cultural literacy," a list of books and nuggets of information that he said were indispensable to participation in literate culture, and that critics charged with "Eurocentrism."[2] By 1988 Stanford University had announced that it was altering its required introductory course in the humanities in order to reflect more adequately the ethnic heterogeneity of its students, sparking new debate and a raft of proposals to emulate Stanford's experiment. By now the canon was an issue featured on the front page of national newspapers.

Any number of reasons could be cited to explain why discussion about the canon acquired such urgency in the 1980s. Inside the university, interest in the issue accompanied a broader shift in critical focus, a turn away from the systemic and linguistic paradigms of American deconstruction, and a renewed attention to issues of sociohistorical context that fueled the interest in New Historicism. But this development may only have been part of a wider change: in American society at large debate about the canon was part of a perceptible politicization of discussion about art and culture, a trend confirmed by bitter confrontations that have exploded throughout the last year. In April 1990 congressional leaders of the right, spurred by controversy over the Robert Mapplethorpe exhibition, threatened to cut the funding for the National Endowment for the Arts if it continued to support works that violated mainstream taste or mores; gay rights groups, in turn, charged that the conservative attack merely masked homophobia. In June the San Francisco Museum of Fine Arts, at a public meeting packed with antiapartheid protesters, decided that it would not permit Royal Dutch Petroleum company, which has a subsidiary in South Africa, to sponsor an exhibition of seventeenth-century Dutch painting. In August, the Actors' Equity Association in New York claimed that Asian-Americans would be offended if a Caucasian actor played the role of a Eurasian pimp in the New York production of the London musical "Miss Saigon," protest that resulted in the show's cancelation. As such events make clear, not only have cultural questions been sharply politicized, but their politicization is increasingly being shaped by a climate of heightened awareness about ethnicity, race, gender, and sexual orientation—a kind of awareness, it need hardly be said, that seems to conflict with basic notions of artistic quality that have been central to evaluative criticism as traditionally practiced.

While such issues attract media attention only when accompanied by sensational events or political repercussions, their effects for scholars are more typically felt at the local level of debate about canons in specific periods or generic traditions. And nowhere perhaps has this been quite so fierce as in the field of modernism, an area of study in which the canon of major poets—Yeats, Eliot, Stevens, Pound—had seemed the outcome of a substantial consensus that appeared relatively stable and difficult to dislodge.[3] However, that too has changed. The discourse of postmodernism has been fashioned partly by postulating an increasingly reductive view of the modernist moment and its achievements, often treated as little more than the sum of the most reactionary political or ideological positions that the modernists assumed at various points in the late 1920s or 1930s. Moreover, many of those positions were either unacceptable or repugnant to our contemporary consensus about ethics, politics, or religion—and consequently scholars have turned to neglected figures who better conform to ideological paradigms facilitating a revisionary account of the modernist achievement. For a growing number of critics, H.D. has become the writer who marked a difference. Virtually forgotten at the time of her death in 1961, her work, says one writer, "can finally assume its rightful place in the canon of the great modernist writers."[4] It has acquired, says another, "a central place in the history of twentieth century poetry."[5] Her long poem *Trilogy,* writes yet another, "must be ranked with *Four Quartets* and *The Pisan Cantos* as the major poems in English to come out of the war."[6] Indeed, H.D. should be considered "one of the most original poets . . . in our language."[7] Such claims, moreover, are often explicitly advanced against the background of the new awareness of ethnicity, race, gender, and sexual orientation: H.D. was a lesbian; she had an important relationship with a black artist, Paul Robeson; and she was responsive to the plight of Jews in the 1930s. As a consequence, it is claimed, H.D. developed a "particular modernism" that differed from that of her contemporaries: hers was "a modernism of the margins rather than the reactionary center [sic]".[8] H.D., it would seem, might almost have been made to meet all the criteria that potential critics could raise for entrance into the canon of the 1990s. What still remains to be established, though, is whether she was a great poet.

The answer to that question is neither easy nor straightforward. In part it is complicated by the genuine difficulties that attend all evaluation—the ineradicable tensions between cultural and aesthetic assessments, or between historical and transcendent values and evaluations—but also because the apparently simple pronoun *she,* as well as its antecedent, "*H.D.,*" can refer to a number of entities that are quite distinct and perhaps even incompatible. One "H.D.," for example, might be the poet who lived and wrote primarily between 1915 and 1960, who, exercising certain legal and proprietary rights, engaged in various arrangements for publishing the works that are ostensibly the subject of the current debate. Another "H.D.," however, might comprise a much looser and ill-defined entity: this "H.D.," created largely in the 1980s, has been instituted without the active participation of the earlier H.D., constructed through different legal, textual, and ideological conventions, fashioned through a canon of works unlike any that prevailed in the lifetime of the earlier H.D., and forged with the assistance of an apparatus of support literature issued by biographers and scholars offering new evaluations of her work. The identity of this "H.D.," in short, has been textually and culturally constituted by a much more recent array of agents, among them literary scholars, acting at a conjuncture of cultural, ideological, institutional interests—a complex individuality articulated within specific worlds of signification, worlds that are inevitably textual, even editorial, in character.

In a 1960 review of H.D.'s novel *Bid Me to Live,* which had recently been published, William Hogan, then book critic for the San Francisco *Chronicle,* confessed to his mistaken belief that H.D. had already died "years ago."[9] Hogan's remark, however cruel it seems in retrospect, testifies to how thoroughly H.D. had been forgotten by critics and literary historians. When, a year later in 1961, H.D. did die, the accessible canon of her work was exiguous.[10] Only four volumes were in print: the novel *Bid Me to Live,* a truncated version of her memoir *Tribute to Freud* (published in 1956), her long poem *Helen in Egypt* (published in 1961, only a few days before H.D.'s death), and a volume of *Selected Poems* (published in 1957). Taken together these represented but a fraction of her work in the three genres that she had favored, poetry, prose fiction, and autobiographical writing. The *Selected Poems,* for example, contained forty-two poems and four excerpts from longer works;[11] her *Collected Poems,* which had been published in 1925 and reissued in 1940, had already contained twice as many poems, and in the intervening years since 1925 many more had accumulated.[12] At best, readers could consult only a tiny portion of a canon far more extensive than anyone had dreamed.

Thirty years later, one is struck by the profound changes that have reshaped the accessible canon of H.D. More of her works are available today than was the case at any point in her lifetime. What has occurred is a wholesale transformation in the context for the study of her work and career. Consider briefly the poetry. In 1983, Louis Martz issued *The Collected Poems of H.D., 1912–1944,* a volume that contained almost two hundred pages of uncollected or unpublished material.[13] Aside from the long poem *Trilogy,* the volume contained 160 poems, almost double the number (84) of the earlier *Collected Poems* of 1925/1940. In addition, the other long poems, *Helen in Egypt* and *Hermetic Definition,* have been kept in print for almost twenty years running.

H.D.'s fiction and autobiographical prose have also proliferated. Between 1980 and 1990, thirteen books have been issued by the new "H.D.," of which nine were fiction or autobiographical writings. Six, it should be noted, had been out of print for more than half a century—no small amount of time in a period when a decade is an eon. Three others had never been published before.[14] More editions are also on the way: Robert Spoo's of the unpublished novel *Asphodel,* Susan Stanford Friedman's of the correspondence between H.D. and Bryher during the period of H.D.'s analysis with Freud, Caroline Zilboorg's of the letters of H.D. and Aldington, and Louis Silverstein's of the correspondence of H.D. and Norman Pearson. Still others, no doubt, have escaped my notice. Yet even this does not exhaust the extent of the H.D. phenomenon, for the outpouring of new materials by "H.D." was also accompanied by an apparatus of support literature issued in the form of popular biographies (Stevenson in 1982, Guest in 1984), critical monographs (Friedman in 1981, Blau Duplessis in 1986), new journals (the *H.D. Newsletter, Sagetrieb*), and more or less scholarly articles. The intertwining of these phenomena should not be underemphasized: the critical monographs repeatedly stressed that the unpublished works of H.D. were "deserving of publication" and suggested that H.D. had "suppresse[d] these books out of a pragmatic fear" of a climate hostile to their sexual or other concerns.[15] The unpublished works were a kind of sexual *samizdat* suppressed by a regime based on gender, and critics were urging "full disclosure." But to some degree the rhetoric of moralism merely obscured the institutional relations whose pressures were being brought to bear: the formal curriculum of the university is not only a canon, but also the gateway to a market, for more than anything the canon shapes what is now the principal market for works of poetry and literature, college class sales. Scholars, in effect, were assuming the task of market preparation and advance advertising for the commercial editions to follow. Behind the rhetoric of "the Other," in other words, scholars were working comfortably within the institution of mainstream publishing.

What ensued was the massive transmission of H.D.'s writings to a large new public commanded by the professoriate and the agency of university curricula—a readership quite alien to the world in which H.D.'s works had first been transmitted.

The smallness of the accessible canon of H.D.'s works at the time of her death was not entirely due to critical neglect. H.D. herself had published only one of her autobiographical writings, *Tribute to Freud,* during her lifetime. With regard to her novels, her output had been equally restrained, if not always by her own choice. Though she had written eleven novels and part of a twelfth, only one (*Bid Me to Live*) was in print at the time of her death. Only two others had been published during her lifetime: *Hedylus,* originally issued in 1928, and "Tatter," a section of an uncompleted novel, published in an anthology of 1931. Nor does it appear that H.D. had always been prohibited from publishing the others by malevolent forces. On the cover page of her novel *Asphodel,* for instance, she voiced her own injunction regarding its fate in no uncertain terms: *Destroy.* When this was written cannot be ascertained; but it says much about her own opinion of her work, which may have been prompted by shrewd self-assessment, and it raises important questions about possible editorial approaches to her canon. In 1934 H.D. submitted another novel, *Pilate's Wife,* to a mainstream publishing firm, which, after due consideration, decided that it lacked both quality and commercial promise. Another novel, *White Rose and the Red,* was also "probably rejected" in 1948.[16]

Her shorter fiction had endured much the same fate as her novels. *Palimpsest,* a collection of three novellas first published with Contact Editions and Houghton Mifflin in 1926, had never been reprinted. Three other collections of fiction had been privately published in 1934–35, issued in limited editions of one hundred copies that were addressed, in the words of the title page, to "the author's friends" (*Kora and Ka, The Usual Star,* and *Nights*). A fourth book, the delightful child's tale *The Hedgehog,* had been issued in London in 1936 by the Brendin Press, an operation owned by H.D.'s companion Bryher, which was effectively "their own privately subsidized firm."[17] It was a deluxe edition, ornamented with illustrations by the fashionable artist George Plank, limited to three hundred copies. None of the four had been submitted to a commercial press, and at the time of her death all had been out of print for a quarter of a century or more.

It is worth pausing over the four volumes of fiction issued between

1934 and 1936, if only because they epitomize key motifs in the evolution of H.D.'s career between roughly 1920 and 1940. Fine editions and small presses were, of course, typical venues of publication in the formation of modernism, playing a crucial role in its emergence and development. One need only recall a few salient names and dates of a phenomenon that has been extensively documented: the Dun Emer (later the Cuala Press), which Yeats dominated from its foundation in 1903 and through which, from that time on, he issued nearly all of his works in limited editions; the fine editions issued by Elkin Mathews from his famous shop in Vigo Street, which published Yeats, Joyce, Pound, and Williams; the Ovid Press of John Rodker, who issued deluxe editions of Eliot's *Ara Vos Prec* and Pound's *Hugh Selwyn Mauberley* in 1920; the lavish edition of *Ulysses* issued in 1922 by Sylvia Beach; the fine press edition of *The Waste Land* that Eliot originally planned with Maurice Firuski in February 1922, before he finalized his arrangements with Horace Liveright; or the deluxe editions of *The Cantos* that appeared in 1925, 1928, and 1930.[18] While the deluxe and limited editions responded to several conflicting imperatives, one important motive was economic. Authors, by restricting supply, could exploit the limited demand for modernist literature, turning each book into an *objet d'art* that acquired potential investment value for collectors. After 1930, however, this strategy no longer made sense: the onset of the Great Depression destroyed the economic climate that had sustained the market for fine editions, and in subsequent years the practice declined in importance.[19] Thus, the works published by H.D. between 1934 and 1936 were unusual in adopting a form of publication that was conspicuously outmoded. The 1936 publication of *The Hedgehog,* with its illustrations by Plank, was realized only because H.D.'s lifelong companion, Winifred Ellerman (better known by her pen name, Bryher), owned the publishing firm and was willing to underwrite the book's costs. The three other volumes were somewhat different. They were not, properly speaking, fine editions that appealed to a restricted market, but private editions that addressed a minute coterie, an audience that was explicitly described in their colophons, such as this one from *Kora and Ka:* "This edition of one hundred copies has been privately printed *for the author's friends.*" Or this one from *Nights:* "This edition, of 100 copies, has been printed by friends of the author *for private circulation.*" (All italics are mine.) Many of H.D.'s works, in other words, actively avoided contact with a wider public, not because H.D. was fearful of public reaction, but at least partly because she assumed that the public was unworthy of being addressed. Instead her works were circulated within a comfortable and "private" circle of well-to-do "friends." The same was true of the periodical publication of her poetry: of thirty-one new poems published between 1931 and 1950, twenty-three (74 percent) appeared in *Life and Letters Today,* the journal that Bryher purchased from Desmond McCarthy in 1931. Such publishing practices were an outcome of her personal and financial situation after 1920, when the combination of income from her inheritance and the patronage of Bryher insured that H.D. would live like the Victorian sages whom Robert Lowell once described as "breezing on their trust funds through the world."

The effects of this situation were not entirely happy. H.D.'s financial dependence on Bryher created an absorbing isolation that shaped much of her work. In the generic configuration of her canon, its effects are perceptible in the tiny quantity of her nonfiction or critical prose: from 1916 until her death in 1961, H.D. published only forty-three articles—less than one per year.[20] Compare this with the canon of other modernists: T. S. Eliot, in the course of a career that covered almost exactly the same period, published well over five hundred essays and reviews; Marianne Moore, more than four hundred; Ezra Pound more than fifteen hundred; W. B. Yeats, at least four hundred. An explanation for this is obvious enough: the income and hospitality furnished by Bryher meant that H.D. felt little pressure to engage in literary journalism. Yet the lack of critical prose is itself only symptomatic of another, more ambiguous result of Bryher's munificence. It is a commmonplace that literary modernism is distinguished by an unprecedented production of critical-theoretical writings that articulated the historical, formal, or ideological grounds for the modernist experiment, that sought to create or shape an audience receptive to modernist artworks. And yet one will search in vain for such writings within the minuscule corpus of nonfiction produced by H.D., for she felt little impetus to engage in an active or genuine dialogue with her contemporaries. For long years she could simply ignore them altogether: from 1918 through 1924 (seven years), from 1930 through 1936 (seven years), and from 1947 through 1960 (fourteen years), H.D. published no critical prose at all—twenty-eight years of silence, over half her career. And there is little doubt about why H.D.'s silence began precisely in 1918. As Bryher explained at the start of their relationship:

> I was glad of your letter and I hope if there is anything I can do for you, if another few pounds would be useful to you in a month or so, you will not hesitate to ask it.[21]

Isolated and lonely, H.D. divided her middle years between Bryher's palatial house in Territet and the furnished flats that Bryher leased for her in London, her journeys assisted by a retinue of bustling chauffeurs, her changes of trains calling forth an army of "porters at every stop."[22] In Territet H.D. was "isolated from the world," as her daughter recalls; "she was well-buffered" by "a staff" of servants that was "almost a bodyguard."[23] Her world, in short, was a cocoon, and she neither needed nor pursued the give and take of exchange with others. Nor did she need or seek an audience, be it small or large; her audience had already been acquired for her by the wealth of Bryher: "one hundred copies . . . privately printed *for the author's friends,*" or "100 copies . . . printed by friends of the author *for private circulation.*" Simply put, H.D. had little interest, and no reason to have an interest, in addressing anyone who stood outside the coterie that surrounded her and Bryher. Significantly, fourteen of her forty-three book essays and reviews (33 percent) are unsigned, while another four are pseudonymous, so that in some 41 percent of her nonfiction prose H.D. avoided a declaration of her own authorship. It is difficult to be more chary of public engagement. Likewise, ten of the reviews treat scholarly works on ancient Greek sculpture and art, topics that reflect her private interests, while scarcely any treat contemporary works issued by other poets or novelists, the kind of materials indicating a public dialogue with peers. After 1942, moreover, virtually all her nonfiction prose consists of her reminiscences about Freud, a kind of writing that suggests the solipsistic reverie that became her habitual state under Bryher's benevolent but narcotic care.

H.D.'s isolation after 1920 shaped not only the kinds of genres in which she worked, but the way in which she approached them. Not untypical is her practice in the novel, which she characteristically approaches via the *roman à clef,* a subgenre of the novel that originated among aristocratic circles of the seventeenth-century French salon and was later revived at various moments in both the French and English novel.[24] Yet whatever its permutations in the course of time, the *roman à clef* was always marked by its restricted appeal to certain social formations resembling or imitating an aristocracy, not least among them the aristocracy of sensibility that made up the wealthy bohemia surrounding H.D. and Bryher, an elite whose circulation among the "right" circles was itself the *clef* to a code of personal and autobiographical references. Which is why, no doubt, H.D. published only three of her twelve novels in the course of her lifetime: to anyone outside the inner circle, they were hardly of interest. Her prose fiction, as she herself may have realized, testified to "the peculiarly modern mix of the egotism of artistic ambitions and the vanity of upper-class leisure."[25]

Recent critics of H.D., however, have tended to view her use of the *roman à clef* differently. According to Susan Stanford Friedman, H.D. turned to the *roman à clef* because it was a "marginal prose genre."[26] Friedman is certainly accurate in characterizing the *roman à clef* as "marginal," insofar as its topical nature violates univeralist assumptions about the nature of aesthetic value; and yet however inadvertently, her use of the term also suggests that we view H.D.'s use of this genre within the context of Friedman's larger thesis that H.D. developed a "modernism of the margins," which she defines as "a modernism based on an identification with those left out of the cultural mainstream."[27] In broad terms, Friedman argues that H.D.'s work "expressed a progressive politics originating in an exploration of the power structures underlying the personal" (94). More particularly, this politics evolved in the course of her response to two kinds of cultural experience. "In the black experience . . . epitomized by [Paul] Robeson, she found an eloquent mirror for her own marginality, her sense of spiritual exile and alienation" (114–15). Further, "her involvement with psychoanalysis carried with it a profound identification with Jews" (115). H.D., in this account, consistently showed "sensitivity" and developed an "identification with Otherness" (115). Thus, we are left to assume, her choice of a "marginal prose genre" such as the *roman à clef* was only another aspect of her "identification with all the others who have been 'dispersed and scattered' by the forces of history: Blacks, Jews, Indians, homosexuals and lesbians, women, even artists" (116). Such an implication, while appealing to current moral concerns, is achieved largely through an abuse of literary terminology and history, an abuse that permits a quintessentially aristocratic genre to be conflated with the politics of egalitarianism implied throughout by the rhetoric of "marginality." It is a maneuver accomplished by an intellectual sleight of hand and a distortion of literary history. The *roman à clef* can be called a "marginal" genre only in a form of perverse logic that would enable us with equal justice to consider the palace of Versailles as "marginal housing."

The effort to revaluate the work of "H.D." by assimilating it to current interest in "the marginal" and "the other" has transformed not only the accessible canon of her own works, but how specific poems within that canon interact with others in the shaping of various larger canons, such as that of modern poetry or of American literature. Textbooks and anthologies, the mundane form of any canon, are both the principal agents and the registrars of these changes, and doubtless the weathervane of the anthology is the *Norton Anthology of American Literature*. Although not one poem by H.D. had been included in editions prior to 1985, more recently her work has been given relatively extensive representation, comprising six poems (seven in the third edition of 1989) and sixteen selections from *The Walls Do Not Fall*. The excerpts from a long poem are the editorial manifestation of recent claims that H.D.'s best work is found in the later "epics," while the selection of earlier poems follows the touchstones established by revisionist critics such as Friedman. Notable, for example, is the inclusion of the poem "Leda," a work omitted from the 1956 *Selected Poems*, which may have been chosen by H.D. herself, as well as the 1988 *Selected Poems*, selected by Louis Martz, yet a poem that has been highly praised by Susan Stanford Friedman for its "critique of classical tradition from a woman's perspective," and so accordingly included.[28] Accompanying the poems are introductory comments that furnish students with explicit instructions to read largely for contents: the "essential dilemma" explored in H.D.'s work is "how to be a woman poet speaking in a world where women were spoken for and about by men." Biographical information is presented in a similar vein: H.D.'s relationship with Bryher, we learn, "developed first as a love affair and then into a lifelong friendship," and "with Bryher's financial help she raised her daughter and cared for her ailing mother." What emerges is a sentimental portrait of solidarity based on gender, solidarity disturbed only by the occasional intrusions of men: "Freud and H.D.," the author notes, "had many arguments, especially over the destiny of women, for H.D. by this time had become a feminist." Bibliographical information, in contrast, is dispensed very sparingly. "During the thirties," we are informed, "H.D. worked mostly in prose forms and composed several autobiographical pieces (some of which remain unpublished)"; nothing is said about the private editions, the subsidized printing, or the publication of poems in journals owned and edited by Bryher. Subsequently, the reader learns, "the outbreak of World War II inspired three long related poems about the war . . . which appeared together as *Trilogy*." The claim is mistaken in a key respect: the three poems never "appeared together as *Trilogy*" during the lifetime of H.D., for no volume bearing that title was issued until 1973, twelve years after her death.[29]

In such remarks, the introductory comments replicate a certain one-sidedness perceptible in the recent surge of critical writing about H.D., a tendency to assess her poetry wholly in terms of its subject matter and contents, and to exclude questions of aesthetic value plainly relevant to a discussion of poetry. Typical in this regard is Susan Stanford Friedman's landmark essay "Who Buried H.D.? A Poet, Her Critics, and Her Place in 'The Literary Tradition,'" which issued the earliest and most significant call for a revisionary view of H.D.'s achievement.[30] Friedman's goal is to advance new evaluative claims about the quality of H.D.'s poetry: she urges that "her poetry is magnificent," adding that "her poems captivate, enchant, and enlighten me." But in explaining this evaluation, Friedman says only that her view is "single" and "necessarily subjective," pointedly resisting pressures for a more critical account of her captivation, enchantment, and enlightenment, and tartly dismissing "the thorny question of what makes literature 'great,' who determines the standards for greatness, or even whether the literary reputation of an author has much of anything to do with genuine genius" (803). When Friedman turns to specific works to substantiate her evaluation, she praises them wholly in terms of their contents: a passage from *Winter Love* is important because it portrays a "woman's anguish," while the long poems *Helen in Egypt* and *Hermetic Definition* are notable because they offer "poetic arguments for a belief . . . [that] the dominance of masculine values has brought destruction and suffering, like the catastrophe of the two world wars" (811).[31] And in a more recent discussion of H.D.'s earlier poems, Friedman pursues the same style of evaluation. The early poems are "brilliant" because they "reveal central conflicts in her identity as a woman poet"—note the same claim that appears in the *Norton Anthology*—and on this basis we can assess the individual works: the poem "Eurydice" deserves praise because it "present[s] a defiant Eurydice who angrily condemns her husband"; the poem "Helen" is noteworthy because it is "*about* the paralyzing misogyny at the heart of male worship of woman's beauty"; the poem "Cassandra" is praiseworthy for being "*about* gynophobia" (my italics); and the poem "Demeter" merits our attention because it "carries lesbian overtones." The crowning achievement is H.D.'s poem "Leda," published in 1919; it "reverses centuries of literary and artistic tradition" insofar as "there is no rape or violence in H.D.'s poem, in which the red swan and the gold lily commingle in the gold-red sunset, 'Where tide and river meet.'"[32]

Still, one may wonder whether such judgments do not privilege a constricted range of poetic and intellectual possibility. If H.D.'s "Leda" lacks the power of a poem such as Yeats's "Leda and the Swan," perhaps it is because the latter is so forthright in confronting the sheer otherness of violence, responding to a richer, more contradictory range of experience and thereby creating a more dialogical understanding of alterity. Consider, for example, the disparate tonalities articulated in the syntactic range of Yeats's poem: the omission of any verb in the famous opening phrase evokes an event with no discernible agent and places the reader in a dilemma analogous to that of Leda, who must decipher the source and meaning of an alien, overwhelming experience, while subsequently a magisterial sequence of verb tenses and temporal adverbs is unfolded to make the transient event reverberate in tragedy and beauty of unspeakable proportions.[33] A similar dissonance is encompassed by the poem's linguistic texture: no sooner does Yeats invoke the diction of conventional eroticism with the phrase, "her thighs caressed," than he transmutes it into an experience of alien ecstasy: "by the dark webs." His word choice emphasizes the encounter of the pathetically human and the indifferent other, probing discordant extremes of experience. H.D.'s poem, in contrast, explores a terrain of sensibility that is remarkably restricted: its verbs are all in the present or present perfect tense, emphasizing a flow of erotic pleasure that lingers into the poem's discursive present; and in her poem the verb "caress" serves only to reinforce this motif of prolonged languor, evoking little more than conventional tenderness: "the level ray of sun-beam / has caressed / the lily. . . ." And whereas Yeats depicts the swan in terms that signal its radical otherness, emphasizing the "bill" and "dark webs," H.D. uses a vocabulary that humanizes and softens its alterity, as in the lines, "the red swan . . . uncurls his coral feet." H.D.'s preference for a phrase such as "coral feet" rather than "dark webs" assimilates the alien beast to human prettiness, a tendency only accentuated by the adjective "coral," which decoratively echoes the unvoiced guttural (or hard "c") of "uncurled" and drapes the bestial with a thin veil of tintinnabulation. And while Yeats portrays "the great wings beating still / Above the staggering girl," as if to underscore the incongruity of human pathos and divine power, H.D. avoids this potential discordance by turning the woman into a "day-lily" that "rests / beneath soft fluttering of red swan wings." The emphasis on "soft fluttering," like the earlier "caressing" of the "sun-beam," reinforces a single note of tender eroticism—a monological texture that differs from the pluralism embraced by Yeats's poem, encompassing disparate and often powerfully opposed tonalities.

Friedman praises H.D.'s "Leda" because it lacks "rape or violence," a deliberate omission that "reverses centuries of literary and artistic tradition, which usually features Zeus in the shape of a swan raping Leda."[34] Doing so, she rehearses what is by now a familiar pattern of narrative in professional literary studies: "centuries of literary and artistic tradition" coalesce into a uniform motif of cultural oppression that is "reversed" at the stroke of a pen. The cultural tradition, however, is somewhat more complex than Friedman allows, and in some crucial respects it suggests a narrative antithetical to hers. As has long been known, the iconology depicting the story of Leda and the swan was produced in fairly distinct periods with corresponding styles of treatment. In late antiquity there are bas-reliefs, gems, terracottas, lamps, and scarabs that sometimes show Leda standing as she gently presses the swan in her thighs or caresses its neck, and sometimes show her reclining and clothed, pressing the swan to her bosom. It is the latter image that is recovered and reformulated during the Renaissance in a series of well-known paintings by Leonardo, Michelangelo, Correggio, Tintoretto, and Veronese. The setting is often a *locus amoenus;* the rape is aestheticized into seduction or, in Correggio's case, turned into a bathing party; Leda is elaborately coiffured and caresses the swan in graceful and stylized gestures. There is little indeed that suggests "rape and violence" in these works from the mainstream of the Western pictorial tradition, and even that little vanishes in later works such as the elegant sculpture of Jean Thierry or the graceful erotic bronze of Raymond Sabourand. In the mid–nineteenth century, when new interest in the Leda story arises, fear of its sexuality and bestiality ensure that visual and plastic representations of the tale stay firmly within decorative conventions. When the symbolist painter Gustave Moreau depicts the incident, in a work that Yeats probably knew well, he presents not bestial rape but sacred marriage, not violence but hieratic arabesque, not conflict but evasion. In short, as Ian Fletcher concludes his comprehensive survey of the iconological tradition surrounding the story: "Rape is found in the remoter myths and in Post-Yeatsian art, but not in the sources that were probably available to the poet."[35] It is Yeats, in other words, who "reverses centuries of literary and artistic tradition," not H.D. It is H.D., in fact, who continues the decorative aestheticizing of the story that has dominated both the pictorial and the literary heritage.

When Friedman praises H.D.'s "Leda" so highly for shunning "rape or violence" in its presentation, doubtless she intends to commend a poem for expressing attitudes that, in her view, are socially or didactically useful, *utile* in the most traditional formulation. Her aims emerge from a venerable tradition of criticism emphasizing the moral dimension of literary study and the ethical effects of specific works. Yet in pursuing this emphasis with provincial excess, Friedman loses sight of other truths no less important: that the aesthetic character of a literary work is not extraneous, but essential to questions of its social or ethical effects; that the morality of poetry is not exhausted in subject matter ("*about* gynophobia") or contents, but also resides in details of syntax, rhythm, diction, rhyme, and musicality, where an intangible yet perceptible integrity is also nurtured and sustained; and that much of the ethical character even of "contents" consists not in how these accord with political positions selected a priori, but in complex relations binding contents and style to audiences and occasions, to interpretive communities in contingent circumstances—settings registered precisely in the sociomaterial instance of the work.

If Friedman's assessment of H.D. diminishes the possibilities of poetic experience, constricting the range of values and traits that poetry can accommodate, in some important respects it may be doing no more than echoing a habit of H.D. herself. For when, in the poem "Leda," the speaker longs for "no more regret / nor old deep memories / to mar the bliss," most readers will not only sense a certain vacuity—no doubt exacerbated by the rhyme of "bliss" with "kiss"[36]—that recurs in H.D.'s poems early and late, but also detect the deeper intellectual limitations exposed by the wish itself. Those limitations, in turn, are inseparable from a more fundamental weakness that bears directly on the problems of audience and evaluation of her work: for H.D.'s is poetry that flatters its audience, that gratifies its readers' wish to believe that knowledge comes without pain, transcendence without suffering—that encounters with divinity can be as pleasant as "a kiss," and yet bring "no regret . . . to mar the bliss." This impulse to indulge her audience, to oblige it with comforting truths, is what lies at the heart of her early triumph as the poet of inwardness, the most popular of all the Imagists, and her subsequent success as a coterie writer, the kind of writer who thrives by gratifying an inner circle. And it is especially evident, I think, throughout the long poem *Trilogy,* a work currently "ranked with *Four Quartets* and *The Pisan Cantos* as the major poems in English to come out of the war," in H.D.'s ambivalent use of the pronoun "we," a usage that accommodates any potential reader or includes only the initiates who already share the poet's belief in a heady brew of astrology, Tarot cards, and seances:

> we [are the] authentic relic,
> bearers of the secret wisdom,
> living remnant
> of the inner band
> of the sanctuaries' initiate [.]

Readers, in other words, are encouraged to choose the most obliging interpretation, and to regard H.D. as the mystagogue who leads "us" to secret yet comfortable wisdom, insight that demands nothing and threatens no one; few readers, after all, will want to disagree that "we" are the "authentic relic" or "the living remnant / of the inner band." Yet as Robert von Hallberg has written: "Only poor poets flatter their audience interminably; only negligible ones play always to the reader's prejudices."[37]

Ultimately, H.D.'s confidence betrays the complacency of the coterie in its assurance that "we" can rest secure in the sense of our difference from "you others."

> So, in our secretive, sly way,
> we are proud and chary
> of companionship with you others[.]

This way of using pronouns stems, no doubt, from H.D.'s twenty years' participation in the coterie that surrounded her and Bryher. And its assurance is only echoed in the ease with which H.D. claims privileged access to unequivocal truth:

> so let us search the old highways
>
> for the true-rune, the right-spell,
> recover old values;

Or again:

let us entreat
that he, by his tau-cross,

invoke the true-magic,
lead us back to the one-truth[.]

H.D. never really doubts that "we" can find "the true-rune" or "the true-magic," or even "the one-truth," a realm of absolute verity signaled by the definite article. It is, again, the confidence of the coterie, assured that its privileged vision—at once portentous and yet accommodatingly vague—is also a vision of totality, "*the* one-truth."

Oddly, in spite of extensive evidence of this totalizing, if not totalitarian, vision, recent criticism of *Trilogy* has deftly converted the poem into a hymn to "a poetics, and a politics, of openness."[38] For Alicia Ostriker, this openness is articulated in H.D.'s description of a May-tree, in *Tribute to the Angels:*

yet no trick of the pen or the brush

could capture that impression;
music could do nothing with it,

nothing whatever; what I mean is—
but you have seen for yourself.

In Ostriker's view, the apostrophe to the reader ("but you have seen for yourself") constitutes a break "in the history of meditative poetry," for "no poet before H.D. invites us to trust not a still point outside of ourselves, transcending this world, but our own interiority."[39] And after citing the same passage, Cyrena Pondrom concludes that H.D. shapes "a new community" that "sweeps away" the "old hierarchies, linearities, and teleologies of male interpretation of experience," creating a brave new world in which "Divinity . . . is immanent in the experience of us all," one that differs radically from the "God [who] is outside or inaccessible to Eliot [in *Four Quartets*]."[40] Reading such claims, one wonders if libraries have been suddenly forced to close, rendering inaccessible the mystical poetry of the German baroque tradition, the great lyrics of the early Goethe, Wordsworth's "Intimations of Immortality" or *The Prelude,* as well as the collected poems of Emerson—surely works that "invite us to trust . . . our own interiority" and ponder the "Divinity . . . immanent in the experience of us all." Even so, one must concede that these claims do indeed describe an essential element of H.D.'s thought, merely endowing it with pseudo-historical importance. For H.D. really does believe in the nebulous and benevolent divinity of the self described by Ostriker and Pondrom; she really does believe, as Pondrom says, that the grace of vision is "free and joyous, and acceptance of the miracle certain, unavoidable";[41] she really does believe in a mix of bland notions from popular occultism and generalizations that denounce contemporary humanity in the abstract and yet promise everyone that he or she is assured of becoming a god. Yet are these ideas, even viewed only as "contents" apart from questions of aesthetic value, truly the best that have been thought and said in the poetry of this century? Many, I suspect, will find them neither sufficiently self-reflexive nor probing, neither important nor interesting. And yet if we assume that values are not intrinsic, but are constituted in relationship to specific interpretive communities in limiting historical circumstances, then the question of how these ideas have come to be so highly regarded becomes urgent.

The creation of the new "H.D." as the canonical figure for a poetics of political correctness is achieved largely by purifying the work of the material complexity in which it was formed, a task concretely accomplished through the neglect of bibliographical, textual, and editorial considerations in assessing her work's genesis and development. To date there is not a single critical edition of a work by H.D.; little awareness that the texts currently in circulation may differ in important ways from those that prevailed in her lifetime; and scarcely any discussion of the bibliographical codes embodied in the transmissive history of her work. Omitting such matters, criticism of the new H.D. erases from view the dynamics of coterie publishing that prevailed in the original setting of her work's production, dynamics that pose resistances to the ways in which recent criticism pursues its own forms of the imaginative reproduction of her work, exerting constraints on the ease with which "H.D." can be assimilated to the egalitarian tenor of the present. Recent criticism of H.D., in constituting the authority of its own interpreting self, must also construct a cultural other of textual and bibliographical criticism, whose resistances must be excluded from deliberations on the ideological and poetic values of H.D.'s work. Only then is such criticism free to construct its own accounts without hindrance, bypassing the sociomaterial instance of the work and the heterogeneous histories it encodes, bypassing too the communicative conditions informing the work's production and transmission. Only thus can a poet of the coterie be turned into the victim of malevolent neglect, the *roman à clef* be transformed into a "marginal" genre, a tradition of decorative aestheticizing become "centuries" of "rape and violence," or a commonplace of late and derivative Romanticism be called a novelty "in the history of meditative poetry." Subtly and yet surely, the rhetorical economy of such criticism insinuates its own form of flattery: only we, it suggests, have the acumen and understanding to appreciate truly the work of H.D., only "we" are the "authentic relic" and "the living remnant / of the inner band," a suggestion that gratifies our own pretensions to new insight even as it transforms us into members of the discursive coterie constructed around the new "H.D." Cognition of the Other turns out to be a mirror in which, dimly discernible at the margins, we also find its uncanny double, the Self of current criticism.

That the works of H.D. have recently been transmitted in ways inconsistent or incommensurable with the logic of their original production is a phenomenon to be neither lamented nor deplored. All works, in the course of time, must move from some specific sociohistorical matrix into others that are structured by different sets of values and concepts, different backgrounds of practice and knowledge in which those are integrated. Yet if our exchange with works from the past is not to be prematurely curtailed by the intellectual preoccupations and modes of the present, we must employ a wide range of critical stratagems to keep us aware of the tensions and discontinuities that are not merely obstacles and impediments to, but the preconditions of, our engagement with the past at all. Feminist criticism, to the degree that it has enabled us to reexamine the value structures that have grounded the production and reception of many works from the past, has performed a service for which no one of my generation, I think, will feel anything other than a deep sense of gratitude. But like any other form of criticism, it too is liable to unreflexive procedures that minimize, ignore, or even misrepresent those dimensions of the past that would most disquiet us, or that seem most foreign to us. The array of critical practices encompassed by philology, bibliography, and textual criticism, insofar as they address the productive apparatuses grounding the sociomaterial instantiations that link works to specific interpretive communities in limiting historical circumstances, can be useful in recalling such disquieting and forgotten dimensions, in reminding us that our own circumstances are no less limited and no less contingent, and in generating conditions of dialogical exchange that render our engagement with the past more self-reflexive and probing.

So how will critics of the future regard the new "H.D." and the evaluations of her work that have been advanced? No one can say for certain. But I suspect they may say something like this: that for a variety of reasons connected with the productive setting in which she worked, many of the works of H.D. were poorly known and, as a result, undervalued by critics of the 1960s and 1970s; that the massive publication of her works in the 1980s made it possible for critics to perceive that the range and variety of her writings were richer than had previously been supposed, and that among them were some minor classics such as *The Hedgehog* and her reminiscences of Freud; but that the new publications also made clear that previous evaluations of H.D.'s poetry were more or less fair in finding that early in her career she had written a few poems with astringent charms, while later she had written longer works whose limited perceptions and impoverished resources of diction, rhythm, and syntax made them little more than curiosity pieces. She was a figure interesting for the life of her times, but not a major force "in the history of twentieth century poetry," and certainly not "one of the most original poets . . . in our language."[42]

NOTES

1. *Letters of T. S. Eliot: Vol. 1, 1898–1922,* ed. Valerie Eliot (New York: Harcourt, Brace, Jovanovich, 1988), 488.

2. See Leslie Fiedler and Houston A. Baker, eds., *Opening up the Canon: Selected Papers from the English Institute* (Baltimore: Johns Hopkins University Press, 1981); Robert von Hallberg, ed., *Canons* (Chicago: University of Chicago Press, 1984); Allan Bloom, *The Closing of the American Mind* (New York: Simon and Schuster, 1987); E. D. Hirsch, *Cultural Literacy: What Every American Should Know* (Boston: Houghton Mifflin, 1987).

3. Inevitably this account oversimplifies the evolution of the modernist poetic canon, especially slighting asymmetries in the reception histories of Pound and Stevens. For fuller accounts see Hugh Kenner, "The Making of the Modernist Canon," in von Hallberg, *Canons,* 363–76, and Marjorie Perloff, "Pound / Stevens: Whose Era?," in *The Dance of the Intellect: Studies in the Poetry of the Pound Tradition* (Cambridge: Cambridge University Press, 1985), 1–32. Also slighted is the limited revival of interest in H.D. that occurred in the 1960s, perhaps best represented by the work of the late Robert Duncan; this revival owed much to H.D.'s association with Pound and Williams, poets whose work could be read as an alternative to the more canonical figures of Eliot and Yeats.

4. Michael King, Introduction to *H.D.: Woman and Poet,* ed. King (Orono,

Maine: National Poetry Foundation, 1986), 16. Further references to this volume are given by the editor's name.

5. Susan Stanford Friedman, "Hilda Doolittle (H.D.)," in *Dictionary of Literary Biography: Modern American Poets,* vol. 45 (Detroit: Gale Research, 1986), 144–45. Further citations to this essay are given by the abbreviation *DLB* 45, followed by a page reference.

6. Albert Gelpi, "Re-membering the Mother: A Reading of H.D.'s *Trilogy,*" in King, 174.

7. Alicia Ostriker, blurb on back cover of Louis Martz, ed., *H.D.: Selected Poems* (New York: New Directions, 1988).

8. Susan Stanford Friedman, "Modernism of the 'Scattered Remnant': Race and Politics in the Development of H.D.'s Modernist Fiction," in King, 116. It goes without saying that "the reactionary center" is a contradiction in terms. Elsewhere, Friedman also argues for "how important issues of racial discrimination and Afro-American culture were to the formation of her postwar modernist vision" (*DLB* 45, 132), as well as claiming that "H.D.'s particular emphasis grew out of her perspective as a woman . . ." (*DLB* 45, 117).

9. Quoted in Jackson R. Bryer, "H.D.: A Note on Her Critical Reputation," *Contemporary Literature* 10, no. 4 (Autumn 1969): 627.

10. The accessible canon refers to works that have been recently reprinted and so are available to a readership. I adopt the term from Alastair Fowler, *Kinds of Literature: An Introduction to the Theory of Genres and Modes* (Cambridge, Mass.: Harvard University Press, 1982), 214–15. Fowler goes on to distinguish this from "selective canons," which are an outcome of systematic preferences exercised within the accessible canon, and to argue that the "selective canons with [the] most institutional force" are "formal curricula."

11. Some of the texts that the *Selected Poems* printed as independent poems were actually portions of larger works wrested from their context. Thus "Heat" was actually the second part of a longer poem, "Garden," while the text titled "And Pergamos" was actually part of H.D.'s translation "From the *Iphigenia in Aulis* of Euripides."

12. There is no complete or reliable bibliography of H.D.'s works, though a very useful checklist was assembled in 1969; see Jackson R. Bryer and Pamela Roblyer, "H.D.: A Preliminary Checklist," *Contemporary Literature* 10, no. 4 (Autumn 1969): 632–75. More recently a useful supplement has appeared, which, although restricted to H.D.'s periodical publications, is intended as part of a complete bibliography in progress; see Michael Boughn, "The Bibliographic Record of H.D.'s Contributions to Periodicals," *Sagetrieb* 6, no. 2 (1987): 171–94. Hereafter this is cited by the author's name.

13. Friedman errs in reporting that all these were "unpublished" in *DLB* 45, 146; all but six or seven of the poems had been previously published in periodicals and were, therefore, uncollected rather than unpublished.

14. Works by H.D. published between 1980 and 1990 are: (1) *Hedylus* (Redding Ridge, Conn.: Black Swan, 1980), first published in 1928; (2) *Hermione* (New York: New Directions, 1981), not published during H.D.'s lifetime; (3) *The Gift* (New York: New Directions, 1982), not published during H.D.'s lifetime; (4) *Notes on Thought and Vision* (San Francisco: City Lights, 1982), not published during H.D.'s lifetime; (5) *Collected Poems 1912–1944,* ed. Louis Martz (New York: New Directions, 1983), with almost 200 pages of previously uncollected or unpublished poems; (6) *Bid Me to Live* (Redding Ridge, Conn.: Black Swan, 1983), first published in 1960; (7) *Euripedes' Ion* (Redding Ridge, Conn.: Black Swan, 1983), first published in 1937; (8) *Tribute to Freud* (New York: New Directions, 1984), published in 1956 and 1974; (9) *Hippolytus Temporizes* (Redding Ridge, Conn.: Black Swan, 1985), first published in 1927; (10) *Nights* (New York: New Directions, 1986), first published in 1935; (11) *The Hedgehog* (New York: New Directions, 1988), first published in 1936; (12) *Selected Poems,* ed. Louis Martz (New York: New Directions, 1988), not published during H.D.'s lifetime; (13) *By Avon River* (Redding Ridge, Conn.: Black Swan, 1990), first published in 1949.

15. Rachel Blau Duplessis, *H.D.: The Career of That Struggle* (Bloomington: Indiana University Press, 1986), 137; and Susan Stanford Friedman, *Psyche Reborn: The Emergence of H.D.* (Bloomington: Indiana University Press, 1981), 44.

16. For a brief overview of the publication of H.D.'s works, see Susan Stanford Friedman, "H.D. Chronology: Composition and Publication of Volumes," *Sagetrieb* 6, no. 2 (1987): 51–55. Bibliographically, these speculations on composition are lacking in methodological rigor, with no attention given to the extrinsic characteristics of H.D.'s manuscripts.

17. Perdita Schaffner, Introduction to *The Hedgehog,* by H.D. (New York: New Directions, 1988), ix.

18. On the Cuala Press see Liam Miller, *The Dun Emer Press, Later the Cuala Press* (Dublin: Dolmen Press, 1973), and on Elkin Mathews see the excellent study by James G. Nelson, *Elkin Mathews: Publisher to Yeats, Joyce, Pound* (Madison: University of Wisconsin Press, 1989). No comparable study exists for John Rodker. On the deluxe edition of *Ulysses* and its audience, see the fine study by J. Howard Woolmer, "*Ulysses* at Auction, with a Preliminary Census," *James Joyce Quarterly* 17 (1980): 141–48. On Eliot's plans for a deluxe edition of "The Waste Land," see Lawrence S. Rainey, "The Price of Modernism: Publishing *The Waste Land,*" in *T. S. Eliot: The Modernist in History,* ed. Ronald Bush (Cambridge: Cambridge University Press, 1990), 91–133; and on the deluxe editions of *The Cantos,* Lawrence S. Rainey, ed., *A Poem Including History: The Cantos of Ezra Pound* (Ann Arbor: University of Michigan Press, forthcoming).

19. A telling symptom of the change is the poor sales and profits of *A Draft*

of XXX Cantos issued by Nancy Cunard and her Hours Press in 1930. Relevant figures are given in Rainey, *A Poem Including History.*

20. The figure is from Boughn. In the category of nonfiction prose, Boughn adds seven items to the previous canon of thirty-seven items by H.D. listed by Bryer; Boughn's additions, using his reference numbers, are C96, C128 (conjectural), C129 (conjectural), C157, C159, C162, and C174. Boughn also removes one item given by Bryer, "[Review of] *On Being Creative,* by Irving Babbitt," *Criterion* 12 (1933): 714; most likely he is correct in supposing it to be the work of another author with the same initials, since it shows a lexical range and lucidity quite untypical of H.D. Also, it should be noted that the two bibliographies differ in reporting which articles by H.D. are actually signed by her. Boughn reports that C102, H.D.'s "[Review of] *Little Novels of Sicily* by Giovanni Verga," is signed, while Bryer reports that it is unsigned (655). Again, Boughn reports that C105, H.D.'s "[Review of] *The Polyglots,* by W. Gerhardi," is unsigned, while Bryer states the opposite. I mention these details in anticipation of the discussion on H.D.'s critical prose to follow.

21. Bryher to H.D., 23 December 1918; Beinecke Library, Yale University.

22. Schaffner, "Introduction," viii.

23. Perdita Schaffner, "The Egyptian Cat," in *Hedylus,* by H.D. (Redding Ridge, Conn.: Black Swan, 1980), 143.

24. Recent theory has largely ignored the *roman à clef* principally because its referential character violates the theoretical presuppositions of professional criticism. For a classic study emphasizing the formation of this tradition in the wake of Honoré d'Urfe's *L'Astrée,* published 1607–27, see Fernand Drujon, *Les Livres à clef* (Paris: E. Rouveyre, 1889), 2 vols. For a more recent survey, see Georg Schneider, *Die Schlüsselliterature* (Stuttgart: Hiersemann Verlag, 1951–53), 3 vols. For an extended theoretical discussion, see my forthcoming essay, "Some Clues to the Clef: the *Roman à Clef* in Literary History and Theory."

25. Charles Molesworth, *Marianne Moore: A Literary Life* (New York: Atheneum, 1990), xiv, describing Enid Bagnold.

26. *DLB* 45, 131.

27. Friedman, "Modernism of the 'Scattered Remnant,'" in King, 104. All further references to this essay are given in parentheses within the text.

28. *DLB* 45, 130.

29. The claim that *Trilogy* was "inspired" by "the outbreak of World War II" also conceals several complications. Janice S. Robinson, *H.D.: The Life and Work of an American Poet,* 305, reports that H.D. wrote *The Walls Do Not Fall,* which is the first part of *Trilogy,* only "in 1942," some three years after the war's outbreak. Yet even that claim requires qualification. It was in April 1942 that three sections (1, 21, 22) of what later became *The Flowering of the Rod,* the third part of *Trilogy,* were first published in *Life and Letters Today.* Six months later, in October 1942, one more section (ultimately section 4 of

The Flowering of the Rod) was issued, again in *Life and Letters Today,* and in November 1942 yet a fifth section was published (ultimately section 6 from *The Flowering of the Rod*), also in *Life and Letters Today.* In other words, only five sections from all 129 sections of *Trilogy* were published by November 1942. And other bibliographical information for the poem's composition and publication makes the *Norton Anthology*'s claim seem even less tenable. What is now the first poem of *Trilogy* was published only in April or May of 1944. What is now the second poem of *Trilogy* was not even composed until "the last two weeks of May" 1944, as H.D. explained to Norman Holmes Pearson (see Norman Holmes Pearson, Foreword to *Trilogy,* by H.D. [New York: New Directions, 1973, ix]), and remained unpublished in any form prior to being issued as a book in 1945. And what is now the third poem of *Trilogy* was composed, apart from the five sections published in 1942, largely between September and December 1944, and first published only in 1946. Still more important, H.D. herself described the second part, *Tribute to the Angels,* as "a sort of premature peace poem," suggesting that it was inspired not by "the outbreak" of the war, but by its opposite—the prospect of its end. (H.D.'s comment is quoted in Pearson's foreword, ix.) The same is probably true of most of the poem's last part, written when the conclusion of the war was but five months away and published in 1946. In short, the misrepresentation of bibliographical information directly bears on the field of interpretative possibilities advanced by the introductory comment of the *Norton Anthology.* And the commentary for individual poems also contains some oddities, though I shall omit discussion of the annotation that reports that Helen was "the wife of Agamemnon" and "the product" of Zeus's "union . . . with the moral [*sic*] woman Leda." Finally, one should compare the introductory comments in this edition with those in the 1985 *Norton Anthology of Literature by Women,* edited by Gilbert and Gubar, who report that H.D. "forge[d] a poetry dedicated to the daughter's excavation of the maternal principle."

30. Susan Stanford Friedman, "Who Buried H.D.? A Poet, Her Critics, and Her Place in 'The Literary Tradition,'" *College English* 36 (March 1975): 801–14. Subsequent references appear in the text in parentheses.

31. Perhaps it is unduly reductive to suggest that "the two world wars" were the outcome only of "the dominance of masculine values." Many historians have advanced other accounts of the origins of the war, most of them a bit more complex.

32. *DLB* 45, 130.

33. What is still the best close reading of the poem's syntax is given by Leo Spitzer, "On Yeats' Poem 'Leda and the Swan,'" *Modern Philology* 51 (1954): 271–76. For references to other studies, see note 35.

34. *DLB* 45, 130.

35. Ian Fletcher, "'Leda and the Swan' as Iconic Poem," in *Yeats Annual* 1

(1982), 85. See also his references to earlier discussions of both the poem and the iconic background, 110n.1 and 111n.13.

36. Keats, too, was fond of this rhyme when he was twenty-two, using it three times in *Endymion* (1:652–53; 2:807–8; and 4:663–64). But then, as he stated in his preface, he also recognized that "the reader" would "soon perceive great inexperience, immaturity, and every error denoting a feverish attempt rather than a deed accomplished" in this work, and he especially censured the "mawkishness" of the adolescent imagination that such rhymes epitomized.

37. Robert von Hallberg, *American Poetry and Culture, 1945–1980* (Cambridge, Mass.: Harvard University Press), 22.

38. Alicia Ostriker, "No Rule of Procedure: The Open Poetics of H.D.," *Agenda* 24, nos. 3, 4 (Autumn/Winter 1987–88): 151.

39. Ibid., 153.

40. Cyrena Pondrom, "*Trilogy* and *Four Quartets:* Contrapuntal Visions of Spiritual Quest," *Agenda* 24, nos. 3, 4 (Autumn/Winter 1987–88): 164. Such claims are curiously at odds with the historical sensibilities and refined scholarship that typically characterize Pondrom's work.

41. Ibid., 162.

42. In my own view, the major revision in the canon of modernist poets will involve not H.D., but Marianne Moore, and that criticism will see that issues of gender, among others, played a role in shaping the reception history of her work. For a representative step in this direction, see Molesworth, *Marianne Moore,* in particular his discussion of Eliot's major writings about Moore, 203–6 and 267–69.

Complete with Omissions: The Text of Marianne Moore's *Complete Poems*

Andrew J. Kappel

> To omit, says Stevenson, is the one art in literature: "If I knew how to omit, I should ask not other knowledge."
>
> —William James

At the moment and for the foreseeable future, the standard edition of Marianne Moore's verse is *The Complete Poems of Marianne Moore*, published jointly by Viking and Macmillan in 1981. It pronounces itself on its dust jacket as the "Definitive Edition, with the Author's Final Revisions," but as Moore's critics and scholars regularly point out, the volume is notoriously incomplete. We have no one to blame for this situation but Moore herself. The poetry missing from the 1981 *Complete Poems* is missing because she would have it so. That volume represents the culmination of a lifetime of editorial decisions on Moore's part; it incorporates the cumulative revisions she made to her work as the years went by, revisions that usually took the form of omissions. She made revisions, largely subtractive ones, at nearly every possible moment, for *Observations*, her first full-length book of poems, in 1924; for a *Selected Poems* in 1935; for a *Collected Poems* in 1951; for a *Complete Poems* in 1967; and at many points of lesser editorial moment along the way.[1] The 1967 *Complete Poems* is the last edition of her work Moore oversaw; she died in 1972. The 1981 *Complete Poems* is a reprint of the 1967 *Complete Poems*, with the addition of some poems Moore published in her very last years. It is a final gathering up of the successive volumes of her verse, complete with all the omissions she made as she went along.

Those omissions are a crucial part of the final volume, which would be incomplete without them.

It is not surprising that a history of the successive editions of a poet's verse would be largely the story of successive omissions. Such a process of winnowing is commonplace when poets collect and recollect their work. In Moore's case, however, the extent of the excisions is unusual. The initially innocuous impulse to delete became a striking habit as the years went by, and prompted Jerome McGann in his *Critique of Modern Textual Criticism* (1983) to call Moore's case a "notorious" one.[2] As the years went by and poem after poem dropped away and others were revised and revised again, and again, and reader after reader started to complain, Moore gradually became aware that she was, on this score, achieving notoriety. The matter came to a head when she was working on her 1967 *Complete Poems*. When Arthur Gregor, the editor at Macmillan responsible for the project, saw the extent of the cuts she proposed to make, he expressed some uneasiness and suggested that Moore include an explanatory note. She refused to do so, replying with a concision appropriate to the occasion: "omissions are not accidents."[3] Gregor, quick on his feet, suggested using that phrase. Moore did not reply, but when the volume came out, her clipped remark appeared, by itself, at the top of the page preceding the table of contents, more warning than explanation.

As a reviser by omission Moore stands out against some other modernists who tended to expand and elaborate when they revised. Anyone who has glanced at corrected proofs of *A la recherche du temps perdu* or *Ulysses* knows to what extent modern writers could be given to expansion and elaboration when revising. Where Proust and Joyce add and add, Moore cuts and cuts. Of course, perhaps we are seeing here a difference of temperament between novelists and poets, or a difference between the modernism of the novelists and the modernism of the poets, for the modernism of the poets was characterized by a commitment to concision. Pound was the foremost spokesman for this value, though he was not always its foremost practitioner. Its foremost practitioner was Moore and to the extent that concision is a central modernist trait, she is a model modernist. "Compression is the first grace of style," she wrote in her poetic homage "To a Snail" (*CP,* 85), and her editorial work bears witness to her unflagging, lifelong commitment to this tenet. "My own revisions," she explained in "Idiosyncrasy and Technique," "are usually the result of . . . an awareness that for most defects, to delete is the instantaneous cure."[4] To an editor protesting deletions, she replied "Anything is improved by omissions."[5]

The most famous instance of Moore's revision by omission is her radical reduction of her poem "Poetry." Jerome McGann was citing these ruthless revisions in particular when he referred to Moore's "notorious" case. These were the cuts that had struck Arthur Gregor so forcibly. They were only the latest in a long series of revisions to which that hapless poem had been subjected by Moore over the years; yet they are doubly significant, representing the culmination not only of her revising of that poem, but of her practice of revision generally. All previous cuts build up to them, the capstone of the tradition of revision by omission in Moore's verse which consolidates the tradition and certifies it.

The only revisions in modern poetry more famous than Moore's revisions of "Poetry" are Pound's and Eliot's revisions of *The Waste Land* manuscript. These are universally understood as the quintessential modernist revisions and are, like Moore's, revisions by omission. They vividly illustrate Pound's and Eliot's modernist commitment to concision. Pound's marginal comment next to the eventually deleted Fresca passage in the manuscript version of "The Fire Sermon" read: "Too loose, rhyme drags it out to diffuseness."[6] That passage and much other discursive, narrative, and connective material were cut away so that the hard-edged, compacted pieces might glint and glare out intensely. One effect of this editorial paring away, an effect not usually remarked, is to make what is already emotionally charged, even harrowing, all the more so. The early modernist cry for concision was a cry against emotional diffuseness, or "slither,"[7] to use Pound's word. One pared away in order to get to some emotionally charged essence. "The sort of thing I do," Pound wrote to Williams in 1908, "is the poetic part of a drama the rest of which . . . would bore me."[8]

Early in her career, Moore received a criticism to which other modernist poets were and sometimes still are subjected: that their verse is emotionally wanting, rather too intellectual. Eliot, himself called to task on this score, defended Moore against the charge in his introduction to her *Selected Poems,* where he pointed out that "for a mind of such agility" as Moore's, "and for a sensibility so reticent, the minor subject, such as a pleasant little sand-colored skipping animal, may be the best release for the major emotions" (*SP,* xi). Proposing the idea of Moore's affinity with the Imagists, Eliot suggested that her case illustrates his own sense that the aim of Imagism was, by means of a "peculiar concentration on something visual . . . to set in motion an expanding succession of concentric feelings" (*SP,* xi). Moore subscribed fully to this modernist sense of a direct relationship between stylistic concision and strong emotion. "The deepest feeling always shows itself in silence," she wrote in her poem "Silence," then corrected herself: "not in silence, but restraint" (*CP,* 91). This belief underlies Moore's lifelong editorial practice of revision by omission. She pared away and pared away in order to increase the emotional density of her work. Eventually the act of omission itself became expressive and toward the end, as we shall see, it became eloquent, finally more eloquent than the finest phrase could be, a moving last gesture of restraint testifying to her modernist loyalties.

The omissions of course were not always so momentous. At the beginning they were innocuous, an author's understandable jettisoning of forgettable juvenilia. The first volume listed in the table of contents for the 1981 *Complete Poems* is the 1935 *Selected Poems,* a fact that would suggest that the story of the publication of Moore's books of poetry starts there. Of course this is not the case. The 1935 *Selected Poems* was in fact the third book of poems Moore published; she was forty-eight when it appeared; and it incorporates much crucial editorial work done earlier for her first two volumes, *Poems* (1921)[9] and *Observations* (1924). That work consists primarily, as one would suspect in any case, of the deletion of earliest published verse. Moore had published ninety-nine poems at the time the *Selected Poems* was going to press, and she included fifty of those, or almost exactly half of her published verse to date. Her *Selected Poems* is indeed selected, but no more so than a cursory comparison with comparable cases suggests such volumes are. Also typical is Moore's tendency to retain a far higher percentage of later verse. She retained none of her earliest verse. None of the first eighteen poems she published were included. These may be thought of as her juvenilia, poems published between 1907 and 1913 in her college magazines, Bryn Mawr's *Tipyn O'Bob* and *The Lantern.* They have the interest juvenilia usually have—we can see the future poet we admire in the making. They also have the quality juvenilia generally have, and we can concur with Moore's decision to let them rest in peace.

Typical as it is to jettison juvenilia, Moore does it with a special thoroughness that, at least in hindsight, calls attention to itself. Pound, Eliot, Williams, Stevens, Frost—all of Moore's modernist poetic peers largely excluded their very earliest verses from their collections, but none so thoroughly as Moore. The others let a few stray pieces find their way in. Further, the earliest pieces of Moore's verse that she grants a place in her collections come from a rather later stage in her career than do the earliest poems in other poets' collections. Though she began publishing at the same time Pound and Eliot did, 1907 or so, she did not in her *Selected Poems* include any poems published before 1915. In Pound's *Personae* there are poems first published in 1908. In *Prufrock and Other Observations* there are poems from 1909. The earliest verses in Moore's collections catch her at a relatively more mature, more fully formed stage of development.

In his introduction to the *Selected Poems* Eliot confessed an inability in presenting Moore's work to "fill up his pages with the usual account of influences and development" (*SP,* ix). There is a detectable note of chagrin here, not with the explicitly stated inability to identify influences but with the implied convention of identifying influences and tracing from them lines of development. It is a chagrin Moore shared with Eliot and with other members of her poetic generation. Did poets of any other age lust so mightily after originality as did the moderns? Critics of the movement regularly singled out for criticism the technical innovation that characterized modernist verse. The reviewer for the London *Times,* commenting on Moore's 1921 *Poems,* lamented the presence there of many of the "latest devices for concealing a lack of inspiration by means of a superficial unconventionality." It was a criticism that Moore felt keenly. She copied it out in a letter to her brother Warner and admitted the cogency of the charge.[10] "Make it new" was the now familiar battle-cry, proclaimed most loudly by Pound, if not always heeded by him.

The characteristic modernist hankering after originality helps to explain Moore's especially thorough exclusion from her collected editions of any early poems that would not prompt a reader to observe that she and only she could have written them. Her reluctance to have a first book of poems published, when H.D. and Bryher proposed the idea to her in 1920, a reluctance Moore always presented as based on humility, probably had something to do with pride as well. She did not want to put herself forward until she could make the proper impression and as a good modernist she knew that she could make a proper impression only when she had something genuinely new and uniquely her own to offer.

The desire to be original, which is manifest in the pervasive experimentalism of modern poetry, was rooted in a belief in the significance of the individual, which was itself rooted in a collapse of faith in the old pieties. This complex of attitudes is a familiar one, and Pound put it neatly altogether in *Guide to Kulchur* (1937): "My generation," he wrote, was "a generation of experimenters" who were "unable to work out a code for action. We believed and disbelieved 'everything,' or to put it another way we believed in the individual case."[11] A belief in the individual case, however, can lead to contradictory behaviors. On the one hand, it may induce one to hanker after apparent originality, to cover one's tracks by excluding early derivative poems from the public record. On the other hand, it can persuade one that everything belongs in print, because what matters is the individual case, the record of which should be as comprehensive as possible. Certainly, this came to be Pound's view, however incompatible with a poetic of concision. Once he got well started on *The Cantos* everything he wrote became part of the poem, soon enough conceived of autobiographically as his "record of struggle."[12] After a while there could be no such thing as an omission. He was also at the end to allow his earliest verses to be resurrected, even the "stale creampuffs," as he called them, of *A Lume Spento*. "As to why a reprint?" he asked in a foreword—not because the poems were of any value in themselves but because they were part of the record of his development: "No lessons to be learned save the depth of ignorance. . . . Ignorance that didn't know the meaning of 'Wardour Street.'"[13]

Eliot was also to allow his earliest verse into print, though rather more reluctantly. In 1950 he supervised the publication of *Poems Written in Early Youth,* privately printed in Stockholm in a special edition limited to twelve copies. Of course he was merely preparing for the inevitable, which came in 1967, two years after his death, when these poems were published by Faber and Faber and became available for all the world to see. Reluctant to have them appear, but knowing they would, he controlled as best he could the damage he imagined they would do.

Moore's reluctance to collect her earliest verse in a book continued throughout her career. No collection of these poems now exists for the perusal of those interested in Moore's development. However, curiously, she did very late in her career resurrect two pieces of undergraduate juvenilia when putting together her 1959 volume *O To Be a Dragon.* There amid poems written during the late 1950s, when she was in her seventies, are two poems—"I May, I Might, I Must" and "A Jelly-Fish"—written during the first decade of the century, probably just as she was turning twenty-one. Her intention in resurrecting these verses was not Pound's, for she gave no indication of their anomalous status in that late volume. We are deceived into taking them as late work, and part of

Moore's intention here was to show that we could do so. Substantively and stylistically they are indistinguishable from other poems of the volume and the period. Rather than seeming to approve the conventional idea of poetic development, as Pound did, or acknowledging it with regret, as Eliot did, she sought to undermine it altogether. It was something of a cause célèbre for her, as her relentless revising and omitting of her poems would suggest.

Her revising, that is, should not be understood in the conventional terms memorably phrased by Yeats.

> The friends that have it I do wrong
> When ever I remake a song,
> Should know what issue is at stake:
> It is myself that I remake.[14]

Like Eliot, Moore sought to separate the person who suffers from the artist who creates. Her poems are not presented as personal acts of self-expression, and revisions of them are not to be taken as signs of a change of mind or heart. She conceived of her poems rather as Auden said a poet ought to, as if they were machines. Revisions are made in order that the machine might work better, might do what it has always done, only more effectively. The mechanic who repairs a jet engine may be sad and lonely, but he does not adjust the whine of the engine to match the pitch of his desolation.

❖

Moore's opposition to an autobiographical poetic helped to determine other oddities about her publications besides the nearly absolute omission of her earliest verse from the record and its mischievous inclusion among her latest. The table of contents of the 1981 *Complete Poems* lists the successive individual volumes of Moore's poetry and includes their dates of publication, emphasizing the chronological arrangement of the material. This is standard procedure, so the emphasis is not necessarily deliberate—indeed it may well have been largely a matter of adhering to a common practice, than which nothing better could be managed. Within volumes, however, much more could be done and there Moore set to work to reorganize her poems thoroughly out of chronological order. This rearrangement is most telling in the *Selected Poems,* but there we have Eliot and not Moore to hold accountable, though of course she implicitly endorsed his arrangement by permitting it and retaining it. It was left to him, he explained in his introduction, to "settle the order of the contents" (*SP*, xiv).

Eliot's rearrangement was elaborate and brilliant, and shaped forever the way Moore's work comes to her readers. There is insufficient space here to examine his work in all its cunning detail but its broader outlines can be quickly appreciated.[15] He began by putting later poems first; the first nine poems of the selection come from 1932–34. The remainder of the volume comprises poems published in *Observations* (1925). (Moore was working as editor of the *Dial* for most of the intervening years and that work consumed her energies; she did not publish any poems from 1926 to 1931.) In a letter to Eliot, Moore stated that the contents of *Observations* had been arranged chronologically.[16] This claim appears roughly true but breaks down in some particular cases. To cite just one oddity, her poem "Those Various Scalpels," first published in 1917, appears among poems first published in 1921. We know Moore disliked the autobiographical poetic that a chronological arrangement of poems would imply and promote. We also know that poets say things on these matters that they do not always entirely mean. And we know that even when they mean what they say they can be wrong—they are the poets, not the textual scholars. There is plenty of reason to doubt that the arrangement of *Observations* is strictly chronological.

But Eliot rendered all this speculation beside the point. He so thoroughly rearranged the poems of *Observations* when he brought them into the *Selected Poems* that all sense of chronology was obscured forever. Moore seemed not to have minded this in the least. The new arrangement proceeds along the lines Eliot followed in putting his own books together: poems related to one another in style and format are grouped together. This strategy presents Moore first and foremost as a poet given to longish descriptive-meditative poems in those patented, strictly controlled, elaborately patterned syllabic stanzas of hers. Eliot's decision to place "The Steeple-Jack," the most ambitious of such poems, at the head of the volume proved momentous. He recognized its status as an extended and deliberate statement of Moore's poetic vision, and he assured its appreciation as such by placing it in the first position. Over the years critics have followed his lead; no book on Moore is without a lengthy discussion of this poem.

The longish descriptive-meditative poems in syllabic stanzas give way in Eliot's arrangement to shorter efforts in syllabics, which give way in turn to a series of poems, rather longer again, in free verse. These testify to Moore's flirtation during the 1920s with *vers libre*. Then Eliot's arrangement reverts abruptly back to syllabic verse, suggesting, correctly, that Moore quickly reaffirmed her allegiance to her elaborate stanzaic contrivances, and implying, incorrectly, that she produced smaller and smaller, more and more concise poems until the process reached its inevitable conclusion in her poem "Silence," which Eliot shrewdly placed last in his rearrangement. In his introduction he quoted Moore's formulation in that poem, that "The deepest feeling always shows itself in silence; / not in silence, but restraint." The new order suggests that the smallness of Moore's poems as well as their elaborate forms are indications of her modernist commitment to concision, concision conceived of as emotional authenticity. His rearrangement makes the silence that follows the last poem speak feelingly. It was a brilliant editorial gesture that Moore was never to forget. She was to repeat it on her own, as we shall see, to even greater moment at the end of her career, when of course silence would perforce be more resounding.

By the time of the *Selected Poems* Moore's tendency to omit poems from collections was no longer innocuous. She was by 1935 beginning to develop a reputation, which was soon to solidify, as a ruthless exciser of her own verse. Eliot recognizes as much in his introduction, when he points out that his duties as editor amounted only to settling the order of the contents.

> The original suggestion was that I should make a selection, from both previously published and more recent poems. But Miss Moore exercised her own rights of proscription first, so drastically, that I have been concerned to preserve rather than abate. (*SP,* xiv)

Earlier, a few of the poems Moore failed to collect in *Observations* have an interest that goes beyond the interest of juvenilia or apprentice work. There is her homage to Gordon Craig, the set designer: "To a Man Working His Way Through a Crowd," which appeared in the 1 April 1915 issue of *The Egoist*. There is an odd little poem called "Holes Bored into a Workbag by the Scissors," which appeared in the 1 October 1916 issue of *Bruno's Weekly,* and which is of some interest here because it is an indictment of the excisive tendencies of her sensibility. As opposed to the constructive virtues of "craft, industry, resourcefulness" there are the holes bored in a workbag by the scissors, which "indicate the unfortunate, meek / Habitat / Of surgery thrust home to fabricate useless /

Voids." Moore recognizes here the surgical predilections of her sensibility, and disapproves of them. She did not yet see how expressive the results of that predilection could be; she did not see how useful voids could be as expressive textual features.

But if there is one poem of her early verse that Moore should not have allowed to drop from sight, it is her witty study of the philosophic mind, "An Ardent Platonist," which appeared in the June 1918 issue of *The Lantern.* This poem is rarely mentioned by Moore's critics; I know of no discussion of it. But its appeal is considerable. "He used to sit at the window," did the ardent platonist, "and smoke and / The mosquitos would come in; he was absolutely fearless." But "to be philosophical" as the ardent platonist is philosophical "is to be no longer mysterious; it is to be no / longer privileged, to say what one thinks in order to be understood." The poem is difficult, brilliant, an early modernist triumph.

But for the most part the poems excluded from *Observations* are not of this quality, and we do not miss them. With the omissions from *Selected Poems,* however, as Eliot himself seemed to feel, we have much more reason to be unhappy. We are sorry to lose the charming "To Be Liked by You Would Be a Calamity," a brief poem in which Moore observes that however difficult it is to have the person in question as an enemy, it would be far worse if he were to be a friend—not that he seeks such a thing. The poem is a jewel of crystallized complexities.[17] Critics have regularly expressed regret about losing two other, rather longer poems written during a period of creativity, 1919–20, that produced such minor masterpieces as "In the Days of Prismatic Color" and "England." One of these poems is "Radical," Moore's brilliant study of the carrot, that "wedge-shaped engine with the / secret of expansion, fused with intensive heat to / color of the set- / ting sun and / stiff."[18] As a poem about how an individual being uses its environment to become itself, the poem is recognizably central to Moore's concerns and to those of modernism generally. The other poem of this period whose omission critics have regretted is the rambunctious "Dock Rats," Moore's study of the New York harbor. The poem is flawed by a few slips beyond understatement into banality, but at moments it catches Moore at her modernist best, as when she keenly and wittily observes "a monkey / —tail and feet / in readiness for an over- / ture."[19]

The change in the omissions from *Observations* to *Selected Poems* is more than a change in the quality of what is omitted. With *Observations* the omissions were invisible. The dropped poems were neither good enough nor within the public domain long enough to be missed when they were gone. With *Selected Poems,* as Eliot's own remarks attest, Moore's omissions could not go by unnoticed any longer. They were now starting, paradoxically, to become part of the record, so many expressive voids. Their paradoxical visibility is especially apparent in the cases of a particular type of omission that Moore made dramatically here, had made before and would continue making, sometimes momentously, in her later work: the surgical—and conspicuous—removal of a poem from a sequence of poems.

From the very beginning Moore had constructed sequences of poems and subsequently dismantled them in later reprintings. She published a sequence of five poems entitled "Pouters and Fantails" in the May 1915 issue of *Poetry* magazine (incidentally her first appearance there); when gathering up her work for *Observations* some years later she dismantled the sequence, dropping the overarching title and two of the poems. She included the three others, one retitled, but with no indication that they had ever been part of a sequence. Of course, nobody noticed this. But when Moore did the same thing for *Selected Poems,* her omission was far more conspicuous, not only because of the greater popularity and quality of the poems in question, but also because she proceeded in a way that called attention to the fact that something had been omitted.

In the June 1932 issue of *Poetry* she had published a sequence of three long poems entitled "Part of a Novel, Part of a Poem, Part of a Play," which comprised "The Steeple-Jack," "The Student," and "The Hero," in that order. When Moore collected this sequence she dropped "The Student." Given that Eliot placed "The Steeple-Jack" and "The Hero" first and second in the *Selected Poems,* he most certainly would have noticed the omission, and indeed it may well have been one of those he had in mind when he spoke of his efforts to abate Moore's proclivity to omit. Significantly, though Moore dropped one of the poems of the sequence, she confusingly retained the tripartite overarching title. Earlier, when she dismantled her sequence "Pouters and Fantails," she dropped the title when she dropped out individual poems. Not so this time, and therefore we can tell—we cannot help but notice—that something is missing.

In the 1930s Moore put together what was to be her longest sequence. It was quickly dismantled. In *The Pangolin and Other Verse* (1936) she gathered four recent poems ("Virginia Britannia," "Bird-Witted," "Half-Deity," and "Smooth-Gnarled Crape Myrtle") under the title "Old Dominion." When she reprinted these poems in *What Are Years* in 1941 she dropped the title and changed the order of their appearance. When in 1951 she was putting together her *Collected Poems* she dropped one of these poems, "Half-Deity," altogether. (Incidentally, for *What Are Years* she resurrected "The Student" and printed it in a radically reduced version; positioned there, rather than with its original companions at the head of the *Selected Poems,* it is carried along in subsequent—but not all subsequent—collections of Moore's verse. Incidences like this, common in Moore's notorious case, test the patience of the textual scholar.)

This assembling and disassembling of poetic sequences—there are other examples—goes on with some regularity in Moore's career. It may best be understood as Moore's particular struggle with that well-known modernist problem, the long poem. The long poem was problematic for modernists, of course, because of their poetic of concision. Pound's solution to the problem was the ideogrammic method, which allowed him to compose *The Cantos* but did not convince everyone, not even, I suspect, Pound himself at times, that the aesthetic problem of the long modernist poem had been solved.[20] Among the modernists Moore was the one most temperamentally inclined toward the short poem, a fact that suggests her centrality in the movement, and she was also the one most consistently committed to it. Of course she had her ambitions—she is characteristically modernist there too—and toyed at times with a larger framework, as these efforts at composing poetic sequences indicate. The problem she thought she was facing here was the one all modernists thought they were facing, a problem of authority. They aspired to it but were leery of it. They believed and disbelieved everything, as Pound put it, but in the final analysis could trust only to individual experience. That experience was the only basis of authority, however much one might hanker after something less apparently limited.

The titles of Moore's sequences confirm the idea that she worried over the matter as a problem of authority. Conventionally, titling is an act in which some centralizing epistemological authority is asserted. Titles, such as *Astrophel and Stella* or *Paradise Lost* or *To the Lighthouse,* are conceptualizations that bring the diverse elements of the work at the head of which they stand into unity by identifying some essential and pervasive concern. The titles of Moore's sequences are very wary of asserting this titular authority and often undermine their authority as they, hesitantly, assert it. Moore had devised the title "Pouters and Fantails" when putting together five rather slight poems, as a way of giving them collectively a weightiness they did not have separately, but admitted in her title the ludicrousness of that effort as she made it. Pouters and fantails are types of pigeons given to ostentatious displays sorely inappropriate to their commonplace character. Soon enough, Moore dropped the title, dismantled the sequence, dropped some and then all of the poems from her collections. "Part of a Novel, Part of a Poem, Part of a Play" is another title that undermines its own authority as it assumes it. Moore did not title her sequence with a single overarching abstraction: "Literature." The title she devised does not subsume the identity of individual components but acknowledges them. It does not presume to have an overriding conceptual authority, some assured vision of the unity of the parts, of the whole they theoretically constitute. Further, the title admits that the components it would assemble toward a whole are not complete in themselves. Moore did not call her poem "Novel, Poem, Play." Her title is twice removed from the conventional titular position of absolute epistemological authority. What she modestly presents is an admittedly incomplete collection of parts of some pieces of a whole. She takes considerable pains in her title to emphasize that she is not presuming to present the total picture.

The crisis of authority played out in Moore's titling of her poetic sequences—as well as in her repeated dismantling of them nearly as soon as she put them together—is played out in Moore's practice of titling her poems generally. Evidently, she understood the act of titling a modern poem as a problem of authority. She frequently devised titles that also served as the first lines of her poems. "The Fish" is an early example. The text of the poem proper continues directly from the title: "The Fish," reads the title; "wade / through black jade" (*CP,* 32), continues the poetic text itself. Similarly, the poem entitled "The Monkeys" continues in its first line, "winked too much and were afraid of snakes" (*CP,* 40). In neither poem is the item named in the title a central item of attention, but only one of many items and indeed not the most important. Here Moore deliberately and emphatically eschews the opportunity afforded her by a title, indeed the duty conventionally expected of her, to assert a centralizing epistemological authority. Contrarily, she decenters the poem with her title, or rather refuses to center it conceptually.

Sometimes Moore's effort to undermine the notion of a title as an assertion of central authority is even more emphatic. In some poems the first lines of the poetic text proper, connected grammatically to the title, also directly contradict it. The poem entitled "The Mind is an Enchanting Thing" continues "the mind is an enchanted thing" (*CP,* 134). Here, furthermore, the crisis of authority is the very subject: the nature of mind, not exclusively controlling but also controlled.

The crisis of authority, the tension between unity and particularity, evident in Moore's titles and in her incessant assembling and disassembling of poetic sequences, pervades modern poetry, where it often manifests itself in the titles of poems, a natural sticking point for anyone alert to the issue. Stevens's title "Notes toward a Supreme Fiction" perfectly illustrates the tension, as does his alternate title for *Harmonium.* He thought of calling it *The Grand Poem: Preliminary Minutiae.*[21] The tension is also evident, less baldly perhaps, in Pound's title for *his* grand poem. To call it *The Cantos* displays some humility, for under that title the poem presents itself as so many individual songs, not the monolithic, absolutely authoritative Song, not the Tale of the Tribe but the different tales of the individual tribes. I stress this evidence of the modernist ambivalence about authority, not to say their downright suspiciousness, because at present modernism is under heavy attack from postmodernism—and postmodernist attacks can be heavy—on this very point. Postmodernists eager to find a banner under which to consolidate themselves and march forward beyond modernism should not forget that the words on the modernist banner—MAKE IT NEW—posed a direct challenge to authority. Postmodernists will have to devise something else if they want to distinguish themselves from their immediate forebears.

❖

In 1951 Moore undertook the task of bringing out a *Collected Poems.* No awareness of her predilection to pare her work away in reprinting could prepare one for the deep cuts she made at this point. Of course the preparation of a collected poems is an appropriate occasion for a thorough reassessment, and Moore was not one to miss such an opportunity. But the vehemence with which she obviously went about the task of revising at this point suggests that the time was ripe for her in a special way.

The late 1940s were for Moore a period of great personal suffering and turmoil. In 1947, after some years of fragile health, Moore's mother died, and the effect of the event on Moore was staggering. She had lived with her mother, a formidably intelligent, well-read, strong-minded, strong-willed, and devout Presbyterian, all her life. She had never married; she had never ventured forth on her own. The relationship was far and away the most important one of her life. It was only natural that after her mother was gone she should feel that nothing was the same.

All changed, changed utterly—what she had thought, what she had believed, what she had written.

Mrs. Moore was intimately involved in every aspect of her daughter's life, and that included her writing. Moore's poems contain many phrases of her mother's, and embody her influence in other, profounder ways that are harder to document. Moore's letters evidence the fact that her mother was always intimately involved in the act of composition, correcting, improving, chastising, commending. The publisher Monroe Wheeler tells of an occasion on which, while visiting the Moores, he witnessed what was clearly a typical occurrence. Moore observed that she had reached an impasse in the poem she was working on. "I don't know how to get out," she complained. Then, "quite calmly," Wheeler explains, as if it were the most natural thing in the world, Mrs. Moore turned to Marianne and said, "Give it to me and I'll show you how to get out." And, Wheeler continues, "she did, right then and there."[22] Very rarely did Moore explicitly acknowledge her mother's influence on her work, not out of pride but out of humility. There is a unique, momentous acknowledgment of the influence in a postscript to the *Selected Poems* (108).

> Dedications imply giving, and we do not care to make a gift of what is insufficient; but in my immediate family there is one who "thinks in a particular way;" and I should like to add that where there is an effect of thought or pith in these pages, the thinking and often the actual phrases are hers.
>
> M. C. M., 1934

Probably, the relationship between Moore and her mother is the single most important mother-daughter relationship in literary history.

So, it was inevitable that Mrs. Moore's death would have its effect on Moore's writing, in an especially profound and pervasive way. It made itself felt immediately as an utter inability to continue. There was no longer anyone there to help her when she "got stuck," and her production fell off dramatically during the years after her mother's death. Although she published two poems during this period which deal movingly but very obliquely with her mother's dying, "A Face" and "By Disposition of Angels," the sudden and enduring near-silence of these years is the greater tribute to her mother's memory. Of course Moore's friends and even her professional acquaintances were aware of her devastation and sought to do what they could. One of the most successful efforts to help was Auden's ingenious and feeling suggestion to his publisher, made in 1945 as Mrs. Moore's health was deteriorating rapidly, that Moore might be asked to try her hand at a translation of the fables of La Fontaine. It worked perfectly. Although the translating went slowly and arduously at first, especially during the period around her mother's death, eventually Moore was proceeding with her old commitment and energy and in the end produced one of the masterpieces of poetic translation of the century. Like the personal creative silence in which it was written, this work is another tribute to the memory of her mother. Committed throughout her life to making the most of every minute that her God, the God of the Protestant work-ethic, had given her, Mrs. Moore would have disapproved of Marianne's idleness. She would have thought it sinfully self-indulgent and would have been especially pleased to see her daughter overcome her incapacitation by devoting herself, like a good Christian, selflessly to the cause of another.

But perhaps Moore's greatest and most appropriate tribute to her mother's influence is the radical revision of her work she undertook when putting together her 1951 *Collected Poems.* Mrs. Moore's presence is inscribed deeply in those changes, which would have pleased her noted pithiness of thought and phrase and her Presbyterian disapproval of all but the plainest effects. Anything faintly extraneous could no longer be tolerated. After her mother's death Moore wrote in her Conversation Notebook, "I don't care for books not worked on by her."[23] Mrs. Moore "worked on" all the individual volumes that comprise the 1951 *Collected Poems*—and none thereafter, of course. For that volume, as if to reinforce her mother's presence, Moore assumes her missing mother's vacated role, cutting away superfluities with the requisite severity and rigor. She dedicated the volume: "To Mary Warner Moore 1862–1947."

Poems had been dropped in their entirety before—that is nothing new. But now for the first time Moore begins to cut out huge sections from within poems. The revisions to "The Student" for its inclusion in *What Are Years* (1941) were extensive, but they were anomalously so at that point in her career. Until the *Collected Poems* her tendency was to tinker when she revised material within poems, which was rarely. Now she leaves hardly a poem unaffected by her tendency to cut, and many of these cuts are deep and wide. She drew up for herself a working table of contents for the *Collected* volume, and it contained the following entries:

Camellia Sabina (revised)
The Plumet Basilisk (see memo of emendation)
The Frigate Pelican (abridged)
The Buffalo (emended)
Nine Nectarines (version of June 18)
An Octopus (with omission)
Injudicious Gardening (version of June 18)
He Digesteth Harde Yron (revised)
Virginia Britannia (revised)
Elephants (with omission)[24]

Significantly, the material Moore cuts from her poems when assembling them for her *Collected* is always material of the same sort. Again and again she cuts passages given over to the detailed presentation of particularities. She tends to leave intact the passages that consider the abstract issues that arise out of the amassed particularities, but whenever she perceives the possibility of cutting some of these she does so, slightly in some cases, dramatically in others but always more or less shifting the balance away from particularity and toward generalization.

For instance, she cuts from the middle of her long poem "An Octopus" a passage given over largely to the description of the flora on Mt. Rainier, the setting and subject of the poem.

Larkspur, blue pincushions, blue peas, and lupin;
white flowers with white, and red with red;
the blue ones 'growing close together
so that patches of them look like blue water in the distance';
this arrangement of colours
as in Persian designs of hard stones with enamel,
forms a pleasing equation—
a diamond outside, and inside, a white dot;
on the outside, a ruby; inside, a red dot;
black spots balanced with black
in the woodlands where fires have run over the ground—
separated by aspens, cat's paws, and woolly sunflowers,
fireweed, asters, and Goliath thistles
'flowering at all times as mutiplicitous as barley',
like pink sapphires in the pavement of the glistening plateau.
Inimical to 'bristling, puny, swearing men
equipped with saws and axes',
this treacherous glass mountain

> admires gentians, lady-slippers, harebells, mountain dyrads,
> and 'Calypso, the goat flower—
> that greenish orchid fond of snow'—
> anomalously nourished on shelving glacial ledges
> where climbers have not gone or have gone timidly
> 'the one resting his nerves while the other advanced',
> on this volcano with the blue jay, her principal companion.
> 'Hopping stiffly on sharp feet' like miniature ice-hacks—
> 'secretive, with a look of wisdom and distinction, but a villain,
> fond of human society or the crumbs that go with it',
> he knows no Greek,
> 'pride-producing language',
> in which 'rashness is rendered innocuous, and error exposed
> by the collision of knowledge with knowledge'.
>
> (*SP*, 86–87)

Toward the end of the passage, as Moore shifts her attention from the flora to the bluebird, a movement away from description occurs, interpretative and moral concerns begin to appear, and Moore stops her cutting.

Her cuts from "The Frigate Pelican" are of passages given over largely to description of the admired bird of the title. These lines from the dropped original third stanza are typical: "The toe / with slight web, air-boned body, and very long wings / with the spread of a swan's—duplicating a / bow-string as he floats overhead—feel / the changing V-shaped scissor swallow- / tail direct the rigid keel" (*SP*, 22). Similarly, almost all of the material cut from "Nine Nectarines" enumerates reiterative details out of which grow the poem's discussions of aesthetics and its conclusions. For its appearance in the *Collected Poems*, Moore pared down the poem's title from the original "Nine Nectarines and Other Porcelain" to merely "Nine Nectarines" in recognition of the fact that the passages describing the "other percelain" do not appear. These lines from the missing original sixth stanza of "Nine Nectarines" are typical. In them Moore describes in detail some of those other pieces of porcelain.

> Hunts and domestic scenes occur
>   in France on dinner-plates, signed on the
>   back with a two-finned fish; England
> has an officer
>   in jack-boots seated in a
> bosquet, the cow, the flock
> of sheep, the pheasant, the peacock

sweeping near with lifted claw; the
skilled peonian rose
and the rosebud that began

(*SP,* 30–31)

—and the poem continues in that vein. The cumulative effect of Moore's cuts in this poem, in "The Frigate Pelican," in "An Octopus," and in all the other revised poems of the volume, is to make her appear less our "foremost poet of the particular,"[25] as Randall Jarrell called her, and more a poet of argument and idea. This difference bears directly upon our assessment of her place among the modernists, who all more or less shared Williams's conviction that there ought to be no ideas but in things. Of course, that was not to say that there should be no ideas. And among her fellow modernists, Moore was one especially inclined to point that out. She was given to faulting Williams in particular for an excessive attention to "things" at the cost of more than occasional triviality.[26] A fear that at points her own work erred in this direction, that it failed to achieve the degree of pithiness that would have met with her rigorous mother's approval, motivated the radical cutting away of passages of detail and description as she put together her *Collected Poems.* For Moore, things were not an end in themselves, but the means to an end, which was some idea they served to express.

But there was a paradox here that she was keenly aware of, a paradox much of her writing is concerned with, a paradox at the heart of modernism. It is embodied innocuously in Williams's famous dictum. Pound's notion of the "luminous detail" was an effort to solve it; so was his ideogrammic method. The modernist program in all its commitment to eschewing absolutes and promoting individuality naturally called out loudly for particular details. But it soon became clear that not all details were equal. Some were more luminous than others. Practically speaking, this was a blessing, for if all details were equal, how was one to proceed? A prospect of pointless, undifferentiated proliferation spread out dishearteningly before one to the last syllable of recorded time. The notion of luminosity allowed for an escape from that fate and promoted the opposing poetic of concision. One pared away and pared away until the most luminous detail stood alone, expressive of what really mattered, privileged for its meaningfulness, positioned centrally in the place of authority.

Moore faced this confusion squarely from the beginning and did not hesitate to take her stand on the side of trenchancy over triviality, concision over proliferation. In her poem "The Web One Weaves of Italy" she complains of the abundance of diverse detail that confronts anyone who contemplates that country. The mental picture one draws—the web one weaves—"grows till it is not what but which, / blurred by too much" (*CP,* 164). But her position was not absolutist. She did not, for instance, succeed in writing a long poem—she tried to now and then but always thought better of it, and she did not always title her poems in the conventionally authoritative way. "The Web One Weaves of Italy," for instance, a poem calling for some centralizing principle of selection so that the truth of the luminous detail revealed by selection would shine forth, avoids the assertion of such a principle in its title, which leads directly into the first words of the text proper: "grows till it is not what but which." The title fails to do what titles conventionally do. It does not provide a "which," but contents itself with lamenting the need for one in the midst of so many "whats."

At least as telling as the substance of Moore's omitted material in her *Collected Poems* is her manner of excising it. Earlier she tended to close up the holes she created by cutting material. She worked to restore the seamlessness of her texts, thereby hiding the fact that anything had been cut. In *Collected Poems* she begins for the first time to let the seams show. She begins to make explicit in a consistent way the fact that omissions have been made.

Earlier she took delight in managing to extract a piece of a poem as neatly as possible, so as to upset the rest of the text minimally if at all. Usually a little rewriting at either end of the excision was required to restore the seamlessness of the poetic text. This earlier attitude is at work in the case of a momentous earlier instance of excision. When Moore moved "The Steeple-Jack" from its original appearance in the June 1932 issue of *Poetry* into her *Selected Poems* three years later, she omitted the sixth stanza, a telling omission in a prominent poem. In taking Eliot's lead and treating the poem as an especially significant, full-scale statement of Moore's poetic vision, her critics have recognized that the central issue of the poem is the nature of observation. It is a study of the dynamic of observer and observed, describer and described, with special attention to the issue of authority entailed in that dynamic. The exclusion of the sixth stanza bears directly upon this issue. The poem focuses its descriptive-meditative attention on a seaside town. Among the particular items Moore includes in her survey is the plant life. The sixth stanza is given over entirely to a simple listing of the different flora to be found in this town, which incidentally include some of the same specimens found on Mt. Rainier—sunflowers and asters. (The characteristically odd fragments of phrases at the very beginning and very end of the stanza are consequences of Moore's usual practice of breaking phrases across line and even stanza divisions).

> door; cat-tails, flags, blueberries and spiderwort,
>   striped grass, lichens, sunflowers, asters, daisies—the
> yellow and the crab-claw blue ones with green bracts—toad-plant,
> petunias, ferns; pink lilies, blue
>   ones, tigers; poppies; black sweet-peas.
> The climate

By omitting this stanza she tips the original balance in the poem away from mere presentation of particulars and toward consideration of the idea of their significance. She did not cut the stanzas in which their significance is considered. The web she would weave of that town was a matter of "not what but which" and she pared away some of the "what" so that the picture would not be "blurred by too much."

Typically, Moore was careful to excise this descriptive passage invisibly. Here are the fifth, sixth, and seventh stanzas of the original version.

> trees are favored by the fog so that you have
>   the tropics at first hand: the trumpet-vine,
> fox-glove, giant snap-dragon, a salpiglossis that has
> spots and stripes; morning-glories, gourds,
>   or moon-vines trained on fishing-twine
> at the back
>
> door; cat-tails, flags, blueberries and spiderwort,
>   striped grass, lichens, sunflowers, asters, daisies—
> the yellow and the crab-claw blue ones with green bracts—toad-plant,
> petunias, ferns; pink lilies, blue
>   ones, tigers; poppies; black sweet-peas.
> The climate
>
> is not right for the banyan, frangipan, the
>   jack-fruit tree; nor for exotic serpent
> life. Ring lizard and snake-skin for the foot if you see fit,
> but here they've cats not cobras to
>   keep down the rats. The diffident
> little newt

This is what we have in the *Selected Poems* when the sixth stanza is extracted.

trees are favored by the fog so that you have
  the tropics at first hand: the trumpet-vine,
fox-glove, giant snap-dragon, a salpiglossis that has
spots and stripes; morning-glories, gourds,
  or moon-vines trained on fishing-twine
at the back

door. There are no banyans, frangipani, nor
  jack-fruit trees; nor an exotic serpent
life. Ring lizard and snake-skin for the foot, or crocodile;
but here they've cats, not cobras, to
  keep down the rats. The diffident
little newt

(*SP,* 2)

Moore's careful restitching of the text over the excision preserved intact the proper syllabic counts for the lines in question (line one of each stanza, eleven; line two, ten). The change in line three—"if you see fit" is altered to "or crocodile"—is unrelated to the change necessitated by the omission, but we should note that in it as well, Moore carefully retained the proper syllabic length of the line. Clearly, she was committed to obscuring the fact that omissions and other revisions were made.

Some of the excisions made by Moore in 1951 when bringing her poems into the *Collected* volume were, like this earlier one, carefully hidden. For instance, she handled the excision of the flower passage from "An Octopus" in a way that obscured the fact that something had been excised. In its original printing the poem appeared as a long unbroken piece of free verse. In the *Selected Poems* a line space was introduced at the end of what was eventually to become the deleted passage, and the rest of the poem: between "by the collision of knowledge with knowledge" and "'Like happy souls in Hell', enjoyed mental difficulties" (*SP,* 87). The skipped line served to mark a plausible and expressive break at a point where the poem shifts in both focus and rhetorical character, from description of particularities to aesthetic and moral argument. In all printings after the excision of the flower passage, the skipped line was retained, but it does not serve to indicate that something has been taken out. It would appear to do so only if the revised version were set alongside the original. The skipped line indicates what it indicated before the flower passage preceding it was deleted: a rhetorical shift.

In another emendation made for the *Collected Poems* Moore again hid the fact that an omission had been made. She did not even list this omission—of a portion of her poem "The Jerboa"—in her makeshift table of contents. She cut out the fourth stanza of the second section of this long poem, the section entitled "Abundance." Again, as with the sixth stanza of "The Steeple-Jack," she extracted a formal unit, a stanza, which is easier to extract without disrupting things than half a stanza or some other portion of a formal unit would be, and she tinkered with the surrounding lines in order to heal the small peripheral tears created by the excision. She was also, again, unable to resist toying with passages close to but not directly affected by the excision and again she was careful to preserve as best she could her formal arrangements. Here are the third, fourth, and fifth stanzas of the poem as it appeared in *Selected Poems.*

hardship for one who
can rest and then do
  the opposite—launching
  as if on wings, from its match-thin hind legs, in
    daytime or at night; that departs with great
    speed, followed by, as a weight,

a double length, thin
tail furred like the skin;
  that curls round it when it
  sleeps 'round'—the nose rested in fur, a hind leg
    at each side of the head—or lies lengthwise,
    in view, when the body lies

flat. Seen by daylight,
the body is white
  in front; and on the back,
  buffy-brown like the breast of the fawn-breasted
    bower-bird. It hops like the fawn-breast, but has
    chipmunk contours—perceived as

(*SP,* 10)

Here is the version in the *Collected Poems.*

hardship for one who
can rest and then do
  the opposite—launching
  as if on wings, from its match-thin hind legs, in
    daytime or at night; with the tail as a weight,
    undulated out by speed, straight.

Looked at by daylight,
the underside's white,

though fur on the back
is buff-brown like the breast of the fawn-breasted
  bower-bird. It hops like the fawn-breast, but has
  chipmunk contours—perceived as

(*CollP,* 20–21)

Moore closed off the end of the third stanza, before the cut, rewriting the last two lines in a way that maintained her stanzaic rhyme scheme (aabcdd) and that kept nearly intact the syllable count. The last two lines of the stanza, which should be ten and seven syllables respectively, both run to an extra syllable, counting eleven and eight. Moore tinkered with the lines at the other end of the excision, but there carefully maintained both her rhyme scheme and her syllable count.

She handled the very deep cuts she made in her poem "The Frigate Pelican" with a similar commitment to hiding the omissions. Here she was brilliantly resourceful and shrewd. The cuts she made in this poem were huge, her deepest cuts to date. She reduced the poem from twelve stanzas to five and a half, from one hundred and eight lines to forty-seven. She cut away two chunks from different places in the middle of the poem, and a third chunk off the end. She cut half of the second, all of the third, and half of the fourth stanzas in one chunk; then she cut almost all of the seventh, all of the eighth, all of the ninth, and the very beginning of the tenth in another chunk; and lastly she cut away two-thirds of the eleventh and all of the twelfth and last stanza.[27]

Moore did make an effort to heal some of the gaping holes and glaring imperfections she created with these excisions, trying to maintain where possible the form of her stanzas. She attached the second half of the original fourth stanza directly onto the first half of the second, creating a hybrid stanza that is roughly the equivalent of what it should be to match the others. In the *Collected Poems* version (*CollP,* 31–32) the new second stanza, formed out of half of the original second and half of the original fourth, runs to eight lines, where it should run to nine, and the syllable count per line and the indentations roughly approximate the original stanza form. Similarly, at the other gaping hole in the middle of the poem she simply spliced together the phrases left hanging at either end of the excision. This is a crucial moment in the history of Moore's revisions. The phrase "of vigilance" was all that was left of the original seventh stanza. They were its first two words. The rest of that stanza is gone, and all of the eighth and ninth, as well as the opening four words of the first line of the original tenth, which were run over from the end of the ninth, completing a sentence begun there. Moore cut those opening four words away, leaving the last four words of the original line—"*Festina lente.* Be gay . . ."—to stand alone. Then she simply connected those words to the end of the truncated first line of the seventh stanza, thereby closing the gaping hole and creating a stanza of the prescribed form. However, she did not make the splicing process invisible. She inserted an ellipsis at the point of attachment, giving us the line: "of vigilance. . . . *Festina lente.* Be gay"—the first line of the new fifth stanza.

The impression, however, is not that material is missing but rather that a pause occurs in a continuous discourse. The effect here is the effect of what Richard Ellmann calls "the most important dots in English poetry," the ellipses in Pound's 1908 poem "La Fraisne": "Once there was a woman . . . / . . . but I forgot . . . she was . . . / . . . and I hope she will not come again." They are expressive of a "consciousness disjunct" as Pound was to name it years later in the case of Mauberley.[28] That Moore's ellipsis has this effect, and does not point to some extratextual omitted material, is due largely to the fact that, like Pound's, her ellipsis seems to be an integral part of the line. The poetic sensibility pauses plausibly after its formulation "an eagle / of vigilance." Then, as if musing, it continues with the foreign phrase that, we surmise, had been occupying its attention, going on to translate it and to query its validity: ". . . *Festina lente.* Be gay / civilly? How so?" The line length supports this reading. Were it the prescribed length, it would run to fifteen syllables; it has only nine and the ellipsis takes the place of the missing six. That is to say, paradoxically, the ellipsis, rather than indicating an omission, serves to hide the fact. *No* ellipsis would have better indicated an omission, for had Moore spliced the old line parts directly the new line would have run only to nine syllables, and therefore stood out as anomalously short, calling attention to itself and to the possibility of an omission.

Moore managed her last cut from this poem in a way that again obscured the fact that material was being omitted. After she cut away the last stanza and two-thirds of the preceding one, what remained, hanging at the end, was the first three lines of that penultimate stanza. Shrewdly, Moore allowed these to stand alone, as a new final stanza, different in form from the rest, but expressively different, plausibly serving as a kind of coda to what has come before. The anapests of the new concluding line ("the / weight of the python that crushes to powder"), once buried in the middle of the penultimate stanza, are a very unusual metrical feature in Moore's work, and serve here to give the feeling of finality to the line. We would never guess that material had been cut off from the end. So, Moore's handling of the three severe cuts in "The Frigate Pelican" bears witness to her lingering commitment to hiding omissions.

In other cases, momentously, Moore did not take these pains to heal the rifts she created. She did not hide the fact that omissions were being made. For instance, for the *Collected Poems* she made an even deeper cut in "The Steeple-Jack" than she had for its appearance in the *Selected Poems,* where the sixth stanza was dropped. For the *Collected* she maintained the omission of the sixth stanza and cut out as well chunks of material on either side of it: she omitted the last three lines of the fourth stanza, all of the fifth—the sixth is gone already—all of the seventh, all of the eighth, all of the ninth, and part of the first line of the tenth. The truncated fourth stanza is left to stand in its mutilated form, with only four of its original six lines. It stands in the midst of properly shaped stanzas, oddly incorrect, not at the end, where it might plausibly appear as a final stanza differently shaped for expressive purposes. Correspondingly, at the other end of the excision, she did not rewrite the affected first line of the tenth stanza so that it would have the proper number of syllables. Instead, she took positive steps to indicate its oddity by indenting it and thereby emphasizing the omission: the first lines of all other stanzas are flush left (*CollP,* 13–14).

But her most glaring disregard of the gaping holes she was creating occurred in her poems "The Buffalo" and "Nine Nectarines." She took deliberate steps to emphasize the holes: she inserted ellipses, but now in a way that prevents us from mistaking them for an integral part of a continuous poetic discourse. For the first time she was explicitly, programmatically indicating what had been the case all along, that she had made a cut; for the first time the act of omission is part of the explicit textual record. This change of heart—to note omissions explicitly rather than obscure them by reconstructing the damaged passages—is only explicit recognition of an expressive possibility of which she was aware from the start and with which she had been toying all along. She had been dropping poems and dismantling sequences from the start, more or less innocuously. With the *Selected Poems* in 1935 she began to proceed deliberately. She retained the title of a tripartite poetic sequence ("Part of a Novel, Part of a Poem, Part of a Play") but printed only two of the constituent poems. Some much remarked and admired poems disappeared. Eliot, among other readers no doubt, noticed and raised his voice to initiate what was to become the chorus of protest against the severity of her proscriptions. With *Collected Poems* she consolidated her commitment to proscription, and in 1967 with the teasingly incomplete *Complete Poems* she certified it with a flourish: "omissions are not accidents."

The momentous appearance of those ellipses that initiate the new openhanded approach toward omissions occurred first in "The Buffalo." Moore simply cut off the last three lines of the second stanza of the poem and part of the first line of the third. Here are the second and third stanzas as they originally appeared (in the November 1934 issue of *Poetry*):

> tail; what could that express?
> And John Steuart Curry's Ajax pulling
> grass—no ring
> in his nose—two birds standing on his back?
> though prints like this cannot
> show if they were black
> birds, nor the colour
>
> of the back. The modern
> ox does not look like the Augsburg ox's
> portrait. Yes,
> the great extinct wild Aurochs was a beast
> to paint, with stripe and six-
> foot horn-spread—decreased
> to Siamese-cat-

In *Collected Poems* we have the following:

> tail; what could that express?
> And John Steuart Curry's Ajax pulling
> grass—no ring
> in his nose—two birds standing on his back?
>
> . . . .
>
> The modern
> ox does not look like the Augsburg ox's
> portrait. Yes,
> the great extinct wild Aurochs was a beast
> to paint, with stripe and six-
> foot horn-spread—decreased
> to Siamese-cat-

(*CollP,* 33)

When Moore created a truncated stanza and permitted it to stand on its own in "The Steeple-Jack" she did not insert an ellipsis. That she did so here is a sign of the new desire to advertise rather than hide the omission. Here no one could take the shape of the stanza as somehow organically expressive—as the truncated last stanza of "The Frigate Pelican" might be taken (as a coda). Clearly, readers might have sought to do this with the truncated stanza in "The Steeple-Jack"; not wanting to mislead in that way, Moore here inserted the ellipsis and acknowledged the omission. It is no surprise that she did nothing to reconstruct the opening line of the third stanza here, which because of the cut is several telling syllables short.

The same procedure is at work in "Nine Nectarines," where the cuts are much wider. Moore cut out the second half of the fourth stanza, all of the fifth, all of the sixth, and all of the seventh—reducing the poem to approximately half its original length. She did not try to recast the truncated fourth stanza, but allowed it to stand in all its aberrant glory. Furthermore, at the other end of the excision, when she recast the first line of the tenth stanza in order to maintain sense she did not do so in a way that maintains the proper syllable count, though she did maintain the repeated pattern of indentation. But most important, there between the truncated end of the fourth stanza and what remains of the rest of the poem stands the ellipsis, attesting to the fact that something is definitely missing (*CollP,* 36).

❖

When in 1966 Moore was approached by Arthur Gregor and Ed Kennebeck, then editors at Macmillan and Viking respectively, with the idea of bringing out a *Complete Poems* the following year, in time for her eightieth birthday, she set about reviewing her work one last time. She no doubt realized that it would almost certainly be her last opportunity to separate the wheat from the chaff, and she did so with her now deliberate ruthlessness, playing out brilliantly the consequences of her new frankness in revision, most notably in her slashing cuts from her poem "Poetry," her most momentous, most notorious act of revision by omission.

At times during this last review of her work, however, she found herself in an oddly restorative mood. Given that she knew this would be her last chance to shape the record, the impulse to restore things is understandable. Though she worked with the 1951 *Collected Poems* as her base text, she often reached back to earlier volumes. For instance, she restored to "The Steeple-Jack," cut for its appearance in the *Selected Poems,* and cut again, drastically, for the *Collected Poems,* all of its lost material. It appears in the *Complete Poems* in its original thirteen-stanza form. Moore also restored "The Student," a poem with a particularly hapless history of publication. It was omitted from the *Selected* (1935), then was included in *What Are Years* (1941), then was dropped when the *Collected* (1951) was put together; now at the last it reappears, back in the *Complete* (1967), positioned among the contents of *What Are Years.* Moore also resurrected an early poem entitled "To a Prize Bird," an homage to George Bernard Shaw which had not been included in her collections since *Observations* in 1924. Its reappearance is part of that little series of gestures of recollection Moore made in her later years, when she included in her late volumes of verse some poems from her very earliest years.

Yet, though she added this and that here and there in her *Complete Poems,* the mood of her final revisions is subtractive with a vengeance. She did not want there to be any confusion on this matter any longer and looking around for an opportunity to make her point unmistakably she came upon "Poetry." It was a brilliant choice. Anything done to a poem with that title would have reverberations. Further, she would have recognized the poem as a familiar victim of her tendency to revise. The history of its different published versions is an especially checkered one, and that history has received a good deal of attention from critics,[29] an attention Moore at the end deliberately sought to provoke one last, stunning time.

The familiar poem first appeared in the July 1919 issue of *Others,* where it was composed of five carefully contrived, eight-line syllabic stanzas, with rhyme scheme abcddeef. When the poem next appeared, in *Observations* (1924), Moore was immersed in her momentary flirtation during the 1920s with free verse, and the poem was consequently recast into free verse, and radically shortened to thirteen lines (from the original forty). When the poem was next reprinted, in the *Selected Poems* of 1935 it appeared in its original stanzaic form, with some alterations. Again we had five syllabic stanzas, containing almost exactly the same material stanza by stanza as the original version, but the first and second, and third and fourth lines of each stanza had been combined, shortening the stanzas to six lines in overall length. Also, some rewriting had been done here and there that interfered with the rhyme schemes, now rendered sporadic. The version in the 1951 *Collected Poems* was a reprint of the version in *Selected Poems.* Then with the 1967 *Complete Poems* comes the notorious change. There on a page by itself in all its truncated glory is the final version of the poem, three terse lines:

> I, too, dislike it.
> Reading it, however, with a perfect contempt for it, one discovers in
> it, after all, a place for the genuine.

And there, where all those examples and illustrations and stunning formulations used to be, fastidiously devised in order to explain what she meant by "the genuine," marshaled together to define the essence of poetry, deployed in their carefully shaped patterns—where they had once ceremoniously unfolded themselves in admirable specificity and precision, we find a large white expanse of blank page. After so many revisions over the years she had finally realized that there was a better way to define the essence of poetry than by parading precept and example across the page. "When I am as complete as I like to be," she had finally learned about herself, "I seem unable to get an effect plain enough."[30] A plain Presbyterian effect was what she was after and so with one fell swipe she cleared away all those particularities she had so carefully amassed in answer to her misguided predilection for completeness. That bold erasive stroke was the act of a loyal modernist poet (and Presbyterian).[31] The blank page that resulted, as the record of her last and greatest act of excision, is meant to be understood as the essence of her poem and by extension of poetry generally. It is a textual void that paradoxically speaks volumes, a silence more eloquent than the finest phrases. The bold stroke that produced it was a faithful modernist's last excisive gesture, made in the enduring belief that art was a process of paring away the chaotic inessentials of experience to the passionate heart of the matter. That blank page cries out for life. We may dislike it, and all the other omissions that led up to it, but we can, after all, discover in it, and in each of the increasingly vivid omissions that made up Moore's long career as a ruthless reviser by excision, a splendidly devised place for the genuine.

NOTES

William James, *The Varieties of Religious Experience: A Study in Human Nature* (New York: Macmillan, 1961), 238.

1. Marianne Moore, *Observations* (New York: Dial, 1924); *Selected Poems* (New York: Macmillan, 1935), hereafter cited as *SP; Collected Poems* (New York: Macmillan, 1951), hereafter *CollP*; *The Complete Poems of Marianne Moore* (New York: Macmillan/Viking, 1967), hereafter *CP.*

2. Jerome J. McGann, *A Critique of Modern Textual Criticism* (Chicago: University of Chicago Press, 1983), 86.

3. Arthur Gregor, "Omissions Are Not Accidents," *Twentieth Century Literature* 30 (Summer/Fall 1984): 158.

4. *The Complete Prose of Marianne Moore,* ed. Patricia E. Willis (New York: Viking, 1986), 507.

5. Marianne Moore in a letter dated 8 May 1961 to Alice Morris, then Literary Editor at *Harper's Bazaar.* Harry Ransom Humanities Research Center, University of Texas at Austin.

6. T. S. Eliot, *The Waste Land, A Facsimile and Transcript of the Original Drafts,* ed. Valerie Eliot (New York: Harcourt Brace Jovanovich, 1971), 39.

7. *Literary Essays of Ezra Pound,* ed. T. S. Eliot (New York: New Directions, 1968), 21.

8. *The Selected Letters of Ezra Pound, 1907–1941,* ed. D. D. Paige (New York: New Directions, 1971), 3–4.

9. Marianne Moore, *Poems* (London: Egoist Press, 1921).

10. Patricia C. Willis, *Marianne Moore: Vision into Verse* (Philadelphia: Rosenbach Museum and Library, 1987), 17.

11. Ezra Pound, *Guide to Kulchur* (New York: New Directions, 1970), 291.

12. See Wendy Flory, *Ezra Pound and "The Cantos": A Record of Struggle* (New Haven: Yale University Press, 1980). "Record of struggle" is Pound's phrase; see *Guide to Kulchur,* 252.

13. Ezra Pound, *A Lume Spento and Other Early Poems* (New York: New Directions, 1965), 7.

14. *The Collected Works of W. B. Yeats, Volume I: The Poems,* ed. Richard J. Finneran (New York: Macmillan, 1989), 551.

15. For a full discussion see Andrew J. Kappel, "Presenting Miss Moore, Modernist: T. S. Eliot's Edition of Marianne Moore's *Selected Poems,*" forthcoming in 1992 in the *Journal of Modern Literature.*

16. Marianne Moore to T. S. Eliot, 2 July 1934: "The 1924 order was, as you infer, chronological." Marianne Moore Archive, Rosenbach Museum and Library, Philadelphia, file V:17:25.

17. The poem is available in *Observations;* in the July 1916 issue of *The Chimaera,* where it first appeared; and in Margaret Holley, *The Poetry of Marianne Moore: A Study in Voice and Value* (Cambridge: Cambridge University Press, 1987), 41, hereafter cited as Holley.

18. The poem is available in *Observations;* in the March 1919 issue of *Others,*

where it first appeared; and in Bonnie Costello, *Marianne Moore: Imaginary Possessions* (Cambridge, Mass.: Harvard University Press, 1981), 54, hereafter cited as Costello.

19. The poem is available in *Observations;* in *Others for 1919,* ed. Alfred Kreymborg (New York: Nicholas I. Brown, 1920), 127–28, where it first appeared; and in Costello, 75.

20. See Margaret Dickey, *On the Long Modernist Poem* (Iowa City: University of Iowa Press, 1986).

21. *Letters of Wallace Stevens,* ed. Holly Stevens (New York: Knopf, 1981), 237.

22. *Voices and Visions: Marianne Moore, In Her Own Image* (New York Center for Visual History Production, 1987).

23. Rosenbach Notebook, 1251 / 8, p. 69; quoted in Holley, 156.

24. Rosenbach III:01:05.

25. Randall Jarrell, "Her Shield," in *Poetry and the Age* by Jarrell (New York: Knopf, 1953), 137.

26. See Moore's review of Williams's *Collected Poems, 1921–1931,* in *Complete Prose,* 327.

27. "The Frigate Pelican" originally appeared in the *Criterion* 12 (July 1934): 557–60.

28. Richard Ellmann, *Eminent Domain: Yeats Among Wilde, Joyce, Pound, Eliot and Auden* (New York: Oxford University Press, 1967), 59–60. Pound may have declined this honor for his ellipses and awarded it to Browning whose dramatic verses, he well knew, regularly contained such punctuation.

29. See John M. Slatin, *The Savage's Romance: The Poetry of Marianne Moore* (University Park, Pa.: Pennsylvania State University Press, 1986), 55–58, for a recent discussion. Slatin considers the revisions of the poem unfortunate.

30. Marianne Moore, "Humility, Concentration, and Gusto," in *Complete Prose,* 420.

31. The religious dimensions of the act of omission are suggested by this passage from William James, *The Varieties of Religious Experience:* "To omit, says Stevenson, is the one art in literature: 'If I knew how to omit, I should ask not other knowledge.' And life, when full of disorder and slackness and vague superfluity, can no more have what we call character than literature can have it under similar circumstances. So monasteries and communities of sympathetic devotees open their doors, and in their changeless order, characterized by omissions quite as much as constituted of actions, the holy-minded person finds that inner smoothness and cleanness which it is torture to him to feel violated at every turn by the discordancy and brutality of secular existence" (238).

The Two Audens and the Claims of History

Edward Mendelson

There are at least two Audens, and the one you prefer to read reflects the person you think you are. One Auden is the body of work forged in the psychological and political heat of initial composition; the second consists of the work of the first after being reshaped and reworked in the cool light of later thought and mature experience. The editor who chooses between these two Audens is obliged to choose between two models of the act of authorship, two schemata of literary history, two ideas of truth.

In the early part of Auden's career, from 1927 (when, at the age of twenty, he wrote the first poem that he later wished to preserve) until 1939 (the year he moved from England to America) he wrote poems that he revised, often radically, between first periodical publication and first appearance in book form, and then revised again in later years for collected editions. These early years, especially 1932 through 1939, were also the period in which he experimented with immediate political commitments that were always complicated by his ethical and personal ambivalences. After 1939, alarmed by his own power to bring a political meeting roaring to its feet, Auden resolved never again to speak directly about politics. Partly as a consequence of this decision, he began in 1942 to plan a collected edition of his poems (published, after some delay, in 1945) with cuts and revisions that would drastically alter some of his most famous and most politically resonant poems.

Auden's turn away from the politics of many of his earlier poems was not a turn away from politics. It was a revulsion from his own earlier sense that he and those with whom he sympathized were the bearers of political and moral truth. Or, more precisely, it was a revulsion from his own willingness to pretend, for the pleasure of the resulting rhetorical effect, that he wrote as a bearer of political truths. He was perhaps shaken above all to find how many of his readers took him seriously as a potential leader during the public urgencies of the late 1930s. By the early 1940s he developed a new sense of a writer's powers and therefore of a writer's responsibilities; and his later versions of his early poems are the products of an altered sense of the relation of the world of language to the world of action. They are equally the product of Auden's realization that a poem, after being created in the privacy of its author's confrontation with the raw materials of language, is then recreated by its readers. As he wrote in his 1939 elegy for Yeats, the words of a poem "are modified in the guts of the living."

❖

The choice between Auden's earlier and later versions of his poems is a choice between axioms about literature. Both the editor and the reader of the poems are perhaps only half-conscious of which set of axioms they choose to believe. Every reader (to borrow a now-proverbial formula from Northrop Frye) is either an *Iliad* critic or an *Odyssey* critic—either a reader whose vision culminates in isolation and death or one whose vision culminates in community and renewal. In twentieth-century terms, one might say that every reader is either a *To the Lighthouse* critic or a *Mrs. Dalloway* critic. Corresponding to these preferences, every reader and every editor holds one of two models of the process of authorship: either the fading coal or the gothic tower.[1]

The most concise statement of the fading-coal model is Shelley's *Defence of Poetry:* "The mind in creation is as a fading coal, which some invisible influence, like an inconstant wind, awakens to transitory brightness. . . . Could this influence be durable in its original purity and force, it is impossible to predict the greatness of the results; but when composition begins, inspiration is already on the decline, and the most glorious poetry in the world is probably a feeble shadow of the original conception of the Poet." Much of modern criticism would rename Shelley's "invisible influence" in terms of language, psychoanalysis, or the social order, but the general argument remains the same: The initial conflagration or crisis is the most crucial moment in the composition of a poem, and the cooler moments that follow are more complex than the fading recollections postulated by Shelley but have the same effect—they are the moments of censoring, repression, and compromise that conceal the original conflict from which the poem emerged.

In its less sophisticated forms, this model is flattering to authors—although authors' naive admirers probably have far more faith in it than authors do. The fading-coal model implies that the faults of a completed work are faults of memory, not of inspiration. It is also flattering to editors. As they remove the encrusted errors deposited on the poet's pristine text by the typist and the publisher's reader and the compositor and proofreader, editors who work according to this model restore to their author the bright original conception that the author has long since forgotten—or, worse, has smoothed into insipidity through revision.[2]

The gothic-tower model is less gratifying but probably more realistic. According to this model, the original conception was merely a rough sketch, with none of the complexity or energy that the process of revision will provide. The finished work is the product of accumulated details, many of them chosen by a clearer-minded, more experienced artist than the one who started the work a few hours or months before. Some of these details result from chance events: a fax from Porlock interrupts one set of revisions and starts a train of thought that leads to another. Some details are the result of an unintended collaboration between the master-artist and practitioners of more mechanical crafts. A copyeditor capitalizes a word, and makes a character more pompous than the author intended; and the author, pleased with the new effect, adds a few more words to emphasize the pomposity. The compositor's eye skips over ten words in the typescript, and the author, when reading proof, realizes that a single word can fill the gap more effectively than ten. The finished work is an intentional as well as an unintentional product of collaboration. The author expects the typist to correct some (not all) of the author's lazy habits of spelling and punctuation, and expects copyeditors and friends to be alert to any details that might make the author look like a fool in public.

The fading-coal model, in its extreme form, seeks to recover the preverbal idea for a work, the idea that precedes its own crystallization into mere text. The gothic-tower model, in its extreme form, accepts every misprint and inkstain as part of the finished work. Whichever model an editor chooses, it is possible to satisfy at least some of the demands of the model without producing an absurdity. An edition of Auden's poems can make a compromise between the two models by choosing for the main text not the earliest moment of composition, but a point in the history of a work when it achieved a state suitable to be offered to readers.

Because Auden periodically published books of verse compiled from his work of the previous two to five years, a collected edition can conveniently use as its main text the contents of each of these books at the time of their first publication. This method admits the effects of early revision and collaboration, and presents between cloth covers a version originally intended for cloth covers. But it also presents each phase of Auden's work in the form that the work took at approximately the time of its initial composition. The 1930 text of Auden's 1930 *Poems,* and not the revised texts of 1933, 1945, or later, can be followed in such an edition by the 1932 text of Auden's 1932 *The Orators,* and then by the 1936 text of his 1936 *On this Island,* and so on. This, in outline, is the plan for the forthcoming volumes of poems in *The Complete Works of W. H. Auden,* published by Princeton University Press.

Like all compromises, this plan has its unsatisfactory aspects, but on the whole it is perhaps less unsatisfactory than any of the available alternatives. Its least satisfactory aspect is its banishment of Auden's later revisions to the notes and appendixes, a decision that seems to confirm the parenthetical observation in Auden's remark that "What every author hopes to receive from posterity—a hope usually disappointed—is justice."[3] This injustice to a dead author is diminished by the existence of an edition of his poems based largely on the gothic-tower model, and incorporating his last thoughts on his own work. The edition of Auden's *Collected Poems* published in 1976, three years after his death, is based on his retrospective collections from the 1960s; it omits all the poems that Auden rejected, among them some as famous as "Spain" and "September 1, 1939," and incorporates late revisions that alter other early poems almost beyond recognition.[4]

The decision to base an edition such as the Princeton *Complete Works* on the texts of Auden's books as they first appeared serves at least some of the needs of literary history, by presenting to anyone interested in the literature of the 1930s (for example) the texts that were available to readers in the 1930s. It also does justice to each phase of an author's work by presenting it on its own terms, rather than subjecting it to the author's own final judgment. The older poet may have been wiser than the younger one; the younger one still has a claim on posterity.

Yet the decision to compromise between the fading-coal and the gothic-tower model in the larger form of an edition scarcely resolves the question of which model to follow in preparing individual texts. Different types of writing call for different types of editions. The authors of lyric poems often claim, explicitly or implicitly, to regard their poems as private speech that the public overhears almost accidentally. In "Adam's Curse" Yeats wrote, "I had a thought for no one's but your ears," and proceeded to publish it for everyone's. More plausibly, Auden wrote in the preface to a book of essays: "All the poems I have written were written for love; naturally, when I have written one, I try to market it, but the prospect of a market played no role in its writing." He added, "On the other hand, I have never written a line of criticism except in response to a demand by others for a lecture, an introduction, a review, etc.; though I hope that some love went into their writing, I wrote them because I needed the money."[5]

But much of Auden's poetic work, like much of Yeats's and Eliot's, was in fact written to be performed on stage—and written not out of a lonely impulse of delight, but because someone else offered a commission. Auden's poetic drama was extensively rewritten during rehearsals, and the revisions were made sometimes at Auden's own instigation when he recognized problems on stage that were invisible in a printed book, and sometimes at the request of a director who wanted more or different verse to satisfy his own idea of the play.

In the case of *The Dance of Death,* a musical revue that Auden published in book form in 1933, dozens of lines of verse were added or substituted in rehearsals for its two productions in 1934 and 1935, but they never appeared in print because Auden either never wished or never bothered to add them to a printed edition, or because he knew that his publisher would balk at the expense of resetting.

Most of the revisions and additions in *The Dance of Death* fall into three categories. First, some new or revised lines underline points that may have been obvious to readers but that someone—either the author or the director—believed needed to be made explicit on stage. One simple example can stand for the rest. In the 1933 printed text the Announcer's opening speech began: "We present to you this evening a picture of the decline of a class, of how its members dream of a new life, but secretly desire the old, for there is death inside them." In the text as performed, the Chorus, behind the curtain, interjected "Middle Class" after the phrase "the decline of a class," in case any members of the audience were in any doubt that it was their own class (and that of the author, actors, and directors) whose decline would herald the coming revolution.

Second, Auden added some dialogue where needed to fill the time needed for stage action. At a point where members of the audience come up to the stage, he replaced four brief speeches in the printed text, each only a few words long, with eleven longer speeches in the text prepared for production. The longer speeches are more than filler: the "members of the audience" who speak them reveal their hidden psychological conditions.

Third, Auden—or perhaps the composer of the music for the play, Herbert Murrill—altered some of the printed verse to accommodate the meters of the musical settings.

An editor who prepares the work for publication must make a number of critical choices. Should *The Dance of Death* be understood primarily as a text for private reading or as a text for public performance? If the former, all the play's myriad editorial difficulties are swept away: the revisions belong only in the notes, and the 1933 printed text becomes the text of the new edition. But this decision, which keeps out of the text anything that could be regarded as an external imposition on Auden's original conception, ignores the fact that the original conception was not entirely Auden's. *The Dance of Death* came into existence because the director of the newly formed Group Theatre (the British Group, not the better-known American one) asked Auden to write a work for a dancer and suggested the medieval *danse macabre* as a theme.

The conventional modernist understanding of a literary text as the product of an author's personal choice, rather than as a response to the needs of others, normally endorses a decision to use the printed text. But that printed text is only one stage in the textual history that began with a commission and ended in additions and changes made in fulfillment of that commission. The printed text of 1933 is less political in content than the staged texts of 1934 and 1935, and correspondingly less public and less collective in its authorship.[6]

An editor who favors the production texts of the play faces a far more difficult task than one who chooses the printed texts. If an edition incorporates all the revisions made for production—metrical changes to accommodate the music, omissions and palliations made to satisfy British stage censorship—then the work becomes a document of stage history rather than a work of Auden's authorship. In a collection of stage documents such a text may be entirely desirable, but its appropriateness is more doubtful in an edition of an individual author.[7]

Problems like these make explicit a question that haunts all literary study: to whom does a text belong? If it belongs to its author, then the fading-coal model of editing has much to recommend it, and the task of editing is the recovery of the author's original text as the task of criticism is the recovery of the author's original meaning. If a text belongs to its readers, then the gothic-tower model is the one to follow; the task of editing is the presentation of the version known to the readers of a work, and the task of criticism is the reinterpretation of a work in the terms most significant to the critic. But this binary opposition disguises the complex conditions in which much literature is written. In the case of Auden's plays, the author made his work in part as a gift to those around him, and those who seek to recover authorial intention find, disconcertingly, that that intention explicitly accommodated and included the intentions of others.

And even if a work belongs in part to its audience, which of its many audiences has the greatest right to it? *The Dance of Death* was commissioned for an audience of subscribers to an experimental theater, but Auden also published the work for an audience of readers. An edition that excludes the changes required by the circumstances of production is true to the version known by those who read the printed book, but untrue to those who saw it performed on stage.

❖

The critical dilemmas created by the relation between Auden's plays and their audiences are at least easy to identify. The comparable dilemmas of Auden's nondramatic poetry take more subtle and less immediately visible forms. As with the plays, the problems concern Auden's revisions, but, with the poems, the revisions were those that Auden made after he perceived some of the ways that the poems were used by his readers—a more diffuse and difficult question than that of the ways in which his plays were altered on stage during rehearsals.

Auden's readers and critics have resisted, often angrily, the changes that he made in his lyric poems. Their resistance has a strong emotional justification: Auden made his revisions precisely because he was disturbed by the kind of approval those same readers and critics gave the poems when they were first published. One consequence of the changes that Auden made for this reason is a theoretical paradox. The version of a poem that first appeared in print—to wide approval—is generally the version closest to the private act of composition. The version in Auden's later collected editions—often to wide disapproval—is one that resulted in part from the approval that the poem received from its first critics and its first audience.

So, if an editor gives pride of place to the author's private version, the version that first appeared in print, the editor favors not the author but the critical audience that always preferred that version. The editor's decision, nominally in favor of the author's conception of the work, effectively denies the rights of the author, who came to prefer the later version. In effect, an editor who takes this course gives the author the right to revise his poem until the moment of publication—at which time the audience takes possession and the author's rights are annulled.[8]

The status of a work undoubtedly changes when it becomes available to the public, but the extent of the change is doubtful. Some of Auden's critics argued that once Auden published his poems, he was no longer to be trusted with them, because the later Auden was no longer in sympathy with his younger self. Even the most perceptive of all interpreters of modern British literature, Frank Kermode, wrote of Auden's "willful and, as I believe, imperceptive renunciation of his own work."[9] The editorial implication is that Auden's later revisions were, in effect, imposed on the work of the young poet by an older and uncomprehending editor who happened to bear the same name.

The fading-coal model assumes that the great "original conception" becomes increasingly inaccessible as the coal fades; therefore the more distant the poet grows from conception, the less well the poet comprehends it. The gothic-tower model, in contrast, assumes that any author competent enough to have brought the poem from its first conception to even a tentatively completed form deserves credit for understanding his own work. A later revision can be trusted to bring to light aspects of the earlier work that escaped the understanding of critics and readers rather than obscuring it.

Auden's chief discontent with the responses of his readers resulted, paradoxically, from the intensity of their approval. When he had (in the words he used in "New Year Letter" in 1940) "Adopted what I would disown, / The preacher's loose immodest tone"[10] it was disconcerting to him to find that tone admired. One of his most immediately celebrated and anthologized poems, "In Memory of W. B. Yeats" (1939), included these immodest lines about the dead poet:

Time that is intolerant
Of the brave and innocent,
And indifferent in a week
To a beautiful physique,

Worships language and forgives
Everyone by whom it lives;

Pardons cowardice, conceit,
Lays its honours at their feet.

Time that with this strange excuse
Pardoned Kipling and his views,
And will pardon Paul Claudel,
Pardons him for writing well.[11]

Immodest: because they assume the right-wing aristocratic views of Kipling, Claudel, and Yeats require the pardon of Time in order to survive, while the left-wing democratic views of Auden and those he admires implicitly do not. By the time Auden prepared a Penguin edition titled *W. H. Auden: A Selection by the Author* (published in 1958), he was less certain he wanted to put his name to that immodest assumption—less certain also that he wanted to republish a poem that would encourage the immodesty of a reader who shared Auden's political views—and so dropped these three stanzas entirely. The earlier version survived in anthologies, but Auden was no longer willing to endorse it or to profit from it.

Part of Auden's discomfort with the poem, and with other poems of the period, was its encouragement to self-satisfaction on the part of readers who shared the poem's views. Auden notoriously took an almost violent dislike to a poem written only a few months after his elegy for Yeats, "September 1, 1939."[12] In its initial versions, the poem included this famous stanza:

All I have is a voice
To undo the folded lie,
The romantic lie in the brain
Of the sensual man-in-the-street
And the lie of Authority
Whose buildings grope the sky:
There is no such thing as the State
And no one exists alone;
Hunger allows no choice
To the citizen or the police;
We must love one another or die.

In *The Collected Poetry of W. H. Auden* published in 1945, he omitted the stanza. In his *Collected Shorter Poems 1927–1957,* published in 1966, he omitted the whole poem. In the foreword to B. C. Bloomfield's *Bibliography,* Auden wrote that "The whole poem, I realised, was infected with an incurable dishonesty and must be scrapped."

Strikingly, Auden never rejected poems that held positions that he once held but later renounced; much of his early work, including the psychoanalytical speculations of his 1928 drama "Paid on Both Sides," took positions that he entirely disbelieved later. But he did reject work that held positions that, he said, he never believed. "A dishonest poem," he wrote in 1966, "is one which expresses, no matter how well, feelings or beliefs which its author never felt or entertained"; his motive for having expressed such a belief in the first place was generally that "it sounded to me rhetorically effective."[13]

Auden's revulsion against his "dishonest" poems arose as a consequence of his discovery of the effect his rhetoric could have on an audience. In the summer of 1939, he wrote to his friend A. E. Dodds that at a political meeting in New York a few months before, "I suddenly found that I could really do it, that I could make a fighting demagogic speech and have the audience roaring. And . . . it is so exciting but so absolutely degrading; I felt just covered with dirt afterwards."[14] Auden fully absorbed the significance of this realization a few years later when he renounced the poems that had the audience roaring over positions he had never believed.

Critics treat his decision as extravagantly overscrupulous, especially his rejection of so unobjectionable a sentiment as "We must love one another or die." But events proved that he was not merely imagining the effect of his poems or the use to which they could be put. In the 1964 presidential election a copywriter at Lyndon Johnson's advertising agency, who had apparently read "September 1, 1939" in a college anthology, prepared a television commercial that exploited public fears of Barry Goldwater's willingness to start an atomic war. A little girl appeared on screen, counting "One, two, three . . ." as she plucked petals from a flower; a male voice came in over hers, counting "Ten, nine, eight. . . ." When his countdown ended a mushroom cloud erupted on the screen, followed by the voice of Lyndon Johnson, who intoned: "These are the stakes: to make a world in which all of God's children can live, or go into the dark. We must either love each other or we must die."[15] Twenty-five years later another political speechwriter remembered different lines from the same poem:

> Yet, dotted everywhere,
> Ironic points of light
> Flash out wherever the Just
> Exchange their messages. . . .

And another president spoke of "A thousand points of light."

To print Auden's poems as they first appeared in print, without the benefit of their author's fullest understanding of their significance and their effect, is to deny their place in the personal history of their author while affirming their place in the public history of their times. An anthology of poetry of the 1930s may after all be the proper place to print Auden's 1930s poems in their 1930s versions. An edition that describes itself as an edition of Auden's poems may only be able to maintain theoretical coherence by printing the latest versions and omitting the poems that Auden abandoned. The procedures of the Princeton *Complete Works,* which attempt to mediate between the claims of history and the claims of the author, may not only deny justice to an author but obscure the nature of the author's claim for justice.

A central figure in Auden's poems from the early 1930s through the 1950s is the figure of the victim: the victim excluded by the injustice of the social order in general and of the poet and reader who have the luxury to read about that victim. The poems work to make it difficult for both poet and reader "To misrepresent, excuse, deny, / Mythify, use"[16] their own injustice. To the extent that Auden's fullest understanding of that injustice is excluded from an edition of his poems, that edition may add its own misrepresentation, excuses, and denials. The existence of the 1976 *Collected Poems* (now in paperback) as fullest possible expression of Auden's final understanding of his work does much to balance the effect of the *Complete Works,* but the conflict between the claims of the dead poet and those of his living readers remains incapable of resolution.

Recent theoretical criticism, with its emphasis on the ways in which literature is shaped by the microcosmic disorders of language and the macrocosmic disorders of society, has reduced the status of the author as person to its lowest ebb since the Romantic movement elevated the heroic individuality of the author to sublime heights. The Romantic artist-genius was a fantasy, and like all fantasies an evasion of responsibility on the part of those who believed it. Psychological, political, and linguistic criticism has produced clear intellectual and ethical gains by exposing that fantasy; and scholarly editing can increase those gains by its own increased understanding of the complexities of authorship. Yet the discredited author seems, after all, to be able to understand literary works in ways that the discrediting critic does not: no one but Auden anticipated the ways in which his own work has been used in the service of causes that the work itself opposed. And an author's knowledge has an ethical complexity and depth that criticism has largely renounced—although individual critics still try, often covertly, to achieve it in their lives. The unquestionable gains achieved by theoretical challenges to authors and authorship may have been attained only at the cost of something that exists only in the individuality of both authors and readers, something that used to be called, without embarrassment, wisdom.

NOTES

1. The argument of the next few paragraphs is based in part on two earlier essays: "The Fading Coal vs. the Gothic Cathedral, or, What to Do About an Author Both Forgetful and Deceased," *Text* 3 (1987): 409–16; and a "Diary" on the debate over the Gabler edition of *Ulysses, London Review of Books,* 27 October 1988, 29.

2. The fantasy that sustains the fading-coal model is the fantasy that scholarship can probe back to the lost origins of things. An especially subtle (or especially convoluted) version of that fantasy may be found in Hans Walter Gabler's theoretical justification for his corrected text of *Ulysses.* Gabler confidently distinguishes between two states of Joyce: one whom he calls "the author," the bearer of the inspired creative force who conceived *Ulysses;* the other whom he calls "the scribe," the mere drudge, who, while copying earlier drafts and correcting proofs, misremembered and generally botched the work of the author. The two worked together when Joyce copied earlier drafts: "the author composed and revised unceasingly," while "the scribe . . . was simultaneously prone to inattention and oversight" (*Ulysses: A Critical and Synoptic Edition,* prepared by Hans Walter Gabler [New York: Garland, 1984), 3:1864). Gabler's edition "restores text [*sic*] of Joyce, the author, that was impinged on by Joyce, the scribe"; it rescues the inspired artist from his bungling double, as well as from fellow-bunglers like typists and compositors. By clearing away the errors of the scribe, Gabler can offer his edition as "radically conservative: going to the roots of the text" (1:viii). Gabler describes the theory behind his edition as a sample of "Advanced thinking in textual scholarship" (3:1878), without, apparently, recognizing it as a romantic fantasy of the artist-hero overdressed in theoretical terms.

3. W. H. Auden, "Edgar Allan Poe," in *Forewords and Afterwords* (New York: Random House, 1973), 209. The essay was first published in Edgar Allan Poe, *Selected Prose and Poetry* (New York: Rinehart, 1950).

4. A reset edition of Auden's *Collected Poems,* published in 1991, restores

idiosyncratic spelling and punctuation that had been altered by over-enthusiastic American copyeditors of Auden's later books. Even a gothic-tower edition needs to make peace with the fading-coal model.

5. W. H. Auden, Foreword to *The Dyer's Hand* (New York: Random House, 1962), xi. Auden was virtually alone among twentieth-century poets in acknowledging *in his work* that he hoped to be paid for his work. His poem "The Cave of Making" calls poets' readers "our handful / of clients"—in the same way that lawyers would speak of their clients. The assumption here is that you go to a poet, prepared to pay, when you want poetry, as you go to a lawyer when you want legal advice. The poem appears in *About the House* (New York: Random House, 1965), 10.

6. Some distinguished scholarship of the modern period solves the problem of stage versions by ignoring them entirely. Donald Gallup's *T. S. Eliot: A Bibliography* (New York: Harcourt, Brace, 1969) omits all reference to the duplicated typescripts (mimeographed and otherwise) used in the productions of Eliot's plays.

7. The volume *Plays* in *The Complete Works of W. H. Auden* makes a somewhat uneasy compromise, but probably the least problematic one. It attempts to include in the main text all changes that were clearly made (or at least written out) by Auden himself. The metrical changes in the songs and the responses to censorship exist only in typescript or others' hands and are recorded or mentioned only in the notes.

8. An implicit contract between Yeats and his readers makes the editorial task far simpler for Yeats's editors. Virtually all critics prefer Yeats's later versions to his earlier ones; Harold Bloom, in his *Yeats* (New York: Oxford University Press, 1970), is a lonely champion of the unrevised texts. Now that Yeats's poems are out of copyright in the United Kingdom, anyone is free to publish an edition that reprints his separate books of verse as they first appeared. At least one scholar has tried to organize such an edition but has not yet aroused sufficient interest to convince a publisher.

9. Frank Kermode, *History and Value* (Oxford, Clarendon, 1988), 73. Kermode makes the same point two years later in *Poetry, Narrative, History* (Oxford: Basil Blackwell, 1990): "Not for the first time one feels that Auden willed himself into misunderstanding his own poems when he changed his politics and developed a new aesthetic" (65).

10. W. H. Auden, *The Double Man* (New York: Random House, 1941), 22.

11. W. H. Auden, *Another Time* (New York: Random House, 1940), 95.

12. One editorial dilemma raised by this poem is the problem of its title. In typescripts now in the Berg Collection, New York Public Library, and at the University of Tulsa, the title is "September: 1939"; this title was also used in the first periodical publication of the poem, in *The New Republic,* 18 October 1939. In the poem's first book publication in *Another Time* (98) the title is

"September 1, 1939," and this title persists in *The Collected Poetry of W. H. Auden* published in 1945. But a trial proof of the contents page of *Another Time,* now in the Random House archives at the Columbia University Library, lists the poem as "September 1st 1939." The absence of a comma between the date and year suggests that an American copyeditor may have transposed the first two terms of a date that appeared in British form, with the date preceding the month, in the lost typescript of the book. That is, Auden's title when preparing the poem for book form may have been "1st September 1939." A quarter-century later, in his foreword to B. C. Bloomfield's *W. H. Auden: A Bibliography* (Charlottesville: University Press of Virginia, 1964), Auden referred to "a poem of mine, *1st September, 1939*" (viii), a version that supports this conjecture, but complicates it with a comma. Of course, Auden may have preferred or even introduced the American form in 1940, not long after he had decided to remain permanently in America, but attention to this kind of detail is uncharacteristic of him.

13. W. H. Auden, Foreword to *Collected Shorter Poems 1927–1957* (London: Faber and Faber, 1966), 15.

14. W. H. Auden to A. E. Dodds [July 1939]; Bodleian Library, Oxford University (MS. Eng. Lett. c464).

15. The phrases about the children and the dark are also recollections of lines from Auden's poem: "Children afraid of the night / Who have never been happy or good," and "From the conservative dark / Into the ethical life / The dense commuters come." The commercial was shown only once as a paid political broadcast, but its notoriety caused it to be broadcast repeatedly as an example of the persuasive force of political advertising. The text of the commercial is quoted here from a transcript in *Time,* 25 September 1964, 16.

16. "Nones," from the sequence "Horae Canonicae"; the poem was first published in Auden's *Nones* (New York: Random House, 1951). The full sequence appeared in *The Shield of Achilles* (New York: Random House, 1955).

Intentional Error: The Paradox of Editing Joyce's *Ulysses*

Vicki Mahaffey

In the spring of 1990, I had an informal conference with a graduate student in architecture who was auditing my course in Yeats and Joyce. I asked him about his work, and he explained the project he was currently working on:

> I want to design a contemporary library, one that takes into account the change in the way readers are increasingly encountering the texts they read: on computer screens, with characters that are not inked, but which emit light. When you research the architecture of famous libraries, it becomes clear that throughout the era of the printed book, architects have had to factor in an awareness that light damages books. I am anticipating a situation in which we *read* light, and I'd like to design a library in which the architecture would express and reflect this startling reversal.

The student's comments crystallized for me some of the thoughts I'd been having about textual editing. Although I am not myself an editor, I started reading editorial theory in 1984, when I was reviewing Hans Walter Gabler's new edition of *Ulysses* for the Philadelphia *Inquirer.*[1] One thing that has emerged as incontrovertible is that editorial theory is inextricably bound to our conception of what a work of literature is and how it is authorized.[2] Our popular conception of the work of literature as fixed and monumental will increasingly be affected, perhaps eroded, not only by the substitution of lighted characters for inked ones, but by the fluidity, productiveness, and (as anyone who works on a computer knows) the potential for loss that computers bring to us.

Computers are subtly drawing power *from* the individual writing in isolation and bringing it *to* the overall system or network of interconnection, and this change in the material process of writing (which has become less laborious, more ephemeral) must, in time, silently but dramatically transform our assumptions about the authority and permanence of individual labor. Increasingly, computers are contributing to and may even eventually replace the printing of books in a way that will inevitably affect our theories of editing.

Given the dramatic transformation in the idea of the book that we are in the process of witnessing, in which the old contrast between black and white is being redrawn via different intensities of light, it is significant that one of the innovative features of Hans Walter Gabler's celebrated and maligned edition of *Ulysses* was his pioneering use of computers to help him assemble and edit his critical text.[3] Computers were not only pragmatically instrumental to the production of the edition (even the typesetting was done by computer), they also analogically reinforce the conception of writing (composition) as *process* rather than product, which is perhaps the single most important (and controversial) rationale behind Gabler's editorial methodology. My emphasis here is not on the future of editing in a world of revolutionary technological change, although such a future is relevant to what I want to suggest about editing Joyce. Instead, what I propose to do is to chart Gabler's editorial procedures against a broad background of continuity and change in the idea of the book, and especially Joyce's idea of the book as suggested by his methods of composing (and anticipating the decomposition of) both *Ulysses* and *Finnegans Wake*.[4] I will argue that Gabler is conservative (traditional) in the premium he sets on authorial intention at the expense of accident and circumstance, but radical in his decision to define authorial intention as multiple and changing; moreover, I hope to show that what is most crucial for the stability and reliability of the text is a balance of tendencies, and that Gabler achieves one such balance among many possibilities. What Gabler's methods allow us to perceive more sharply is the theory of text production encoded in *Ulysses* and expanded in *Finnegans Wake*, a theory licensed by the oxymoronic concept of "intentional error" as the basis of continued productivity and a stimulus for deeper and more complicated textual understandings.

Gabler's edition of *Ulysses* has stirred controversy that is unusual partly because it has been so public (much of it has been carried out in the popular press or in widely circulated literary newspapers, the *Wash-*

ington Post and especially the *New York Review of Books*). A brief summary of the edition's publication and reception is this: in June of 1984, Garland published Gabler's three-volume critical and synoptic edition of *Ulysses*. This edition, which ran to 1,919 pages, provided two "versions" or interpretations of the text on facing pages: a "synopsis" of different stages of the text's autograph composition (from final draft through the last set of proofs) on the versos, and a clear reading text on the corresponding rectos (which was the basis for the trade editions published by Random House, Bodley Head, and Penguin in 1986). The synoptic text, through the use of a complex set of diacritical marks, enables a reader in theory to reconstruct what Gabler calls the "continuous manuscript" of *Ulysses*, which he controversially assembled to use as the copy-text of his edition. This is the most unusual feature of the entire edition: Gabler's decision not to "correct" the most authoritative printed edition (in this case the 1922 first edition) or to choose one manuscript as his copy-text, but to assemble a compound "manuscript" out of the diverse fair copies, corrections, and additions in Joyce's hand (or dictated by him; a small portion of the Rosenbach manuscript was dictated by Joyce to Frank Budgen).

The publication of Gabler's edition was widely publicized and almost universally celebrated in the popular press when it appeared, and for good reason. Anyone who has worked closely with the 1961 Random House edition (*RH*) knows how appalling the state of that text was, and how many of its misprints gratuitously obscure the finer points of an already difficult text. When I taught the "Circe" episode out of the old Random House edition, I had to hand out lists of misprints that I had been able to ascertain as such, a strategy I devised when I realized how much unproductive trouble the misprints were causing in a text designed around verbal precision. In the stage directions that open "Circe," for example, it is difficult enough for students to recognize a nighttown reprise of a moment in "Wandering Rocks":

> *Round Rabaiotti's halted ice gondola stunted men and women squabble. They grab wafers between which are wedged lumps of coral and copper snow. Sucking, they scatter slowly, children. The swancomb of the gondola, highreared, forges on through the murk, white and blue under a lighthouse.* (*U*, 15.4–9)

In the 1961 edition, what was wedged between the wafers was "lumps of *coal* and copper snow" (emphasis added; *RH,* 429). In an early discussion of the implications of the Gabler edition at the first Philadelphia conference, Bonnie Kime Scott objected that this change from "coal" to "coral" made it seem as if the menu had changed from coal (which Scott saw as appropriately grotesque) to ice cream sandwiches; she used this change to support her claim that the new edition was responsible for a "loss of some interpretative possibilities."[5] Ironically, however, a closer look at the work shows that what we get in this instance (as in many others) is not a loss but a gain in interpretative clarity. The "stunted men and women" who open "Circe" *are* eating ice cream, a perception essential to the realization that this is a nightmarish reenactment of the scene in "Wandering Rocks" in which children are eating ice cream around Rabaiotti's ice cream car when a one-legged sailor passes by, growling "*For England . . . home and beauty*" for alms (10.228–56). The deaf-mute idiot that jerks past the children in "Circe," only to be imprisoned in a chain of their hands until he salutes and answers their question about the great light, *is* this one-legged sailor (it is because he's a sailor that the children order him to "salute"). The reader's ability to identify the ice cream provides a crucial link in the momentary connection between the two episodes, a connection that allows us to see at the outset how "Circe" works on the book as a whole; how the text of this episode, like Homer's sorceress, retrieves and grotesquely transforms bits of text that we as readers have half-forgotten into disgruntled stylistic equivalents. Joyce's Circean revisions, like dreams, offer us the opportunity to re-view what we passed by earlier as trivial, and to apprehend more vividly the sinister or troubling implications of what we may have glossed over as normative. Looking back, we can see that even in "Wandering Rocks" the one-legged sailor is presented as grotesque, a freak whom "barefoot urchins" halt to stare at, "gaping at his stump with their yellowslobbered mouths" (10.244–45). If we notice him at all in "Wandering Rocks," it is from the perspective of the children, or as the target of a coin thrown out the window by Molly's plump arm. When we see him again in "Circe," his role as semicoherent master of ceremonies in a red-light district makes his prostituted position—and our earlier blindness to it—troublingly unmistakable: despite his service to England (which presumably cost him his leg), he is forced to sing for his supper on the streets of Dublin. The red lights of nighttown signal *both* prostitution and British domination, and the one-legged sailor aptly appears to induct us into the district that represents Dublin under British rule, a self-betraying urban underworld.

The celebration of Gabler's edition as a superior replacement for the 1961 Random House edition still seems to me to be both understandable and warranted. But on 26 April 1985, nine months after the edition was published, it was challenged by John Kidd in a paper he delivered to the Society for Textual Scholarship in New York City.[6] Since that time, controversy has raged between those who call the validity (or, less damagingly, the sufficiency) of the edition into question (usually on Kidd's authority), and those who defend its integrity. The publicity escalated in June of 1988, when Kidd published another attack, this time in the *New York Review of Books,* called "The Scandal of *Ulysses.*"[7] There followed an exchange that appeared in six subsequent issues over the next year[8] in which eleven readers besides Kidd participated; the controversy was heightened by a similar exchange in the *Times Literary Supplement.*[9] In June of 1988, Random House announced that it was setting up a committee (chaired by G. Thomas Tanselle) to conduct an inquiry into the Gabler edition, and to advise them whether they should put the old Vintage (1961) copy back into print (which they have since done), and whether they should withdraw the Gabler edition from the market (which they have chosen not to do). The committee was dissolved before issuing a report in February of 1990, when Jacob Epstein of Random House dissociated himself from his own advisory committee.[10]

The controversy over the Gabler edition has unearthed some errors in the edition, many of which have been corrected (but not attributed—emendations seldom are). Although it has been valuable in its investigation of the accuracy of individual readings, the controversy has been damaging in another way: many of the most widely publicized attacks are based on premises about textual editing that the general reading public takes for granted, so when a critic proves that Gabler has violated these guidelines, his editorial competence is implicitly or explicitly called into question. It takes a reasonably specialized reader to realize that the weakness of such arguments, which seem logically convincing on their own terms, is at the level of the premise, since Gabler does not share many of the premises on which the critique is based. For example, when Robin Bates (taking his cue from Kidd) alleges that Gabler failed to collate an important edition of *Ulysses* (the 1935 edition illustrated by Matisse, which is demonstrably important in the history of the book's *transmission in print*), thereby violating conventional editorial guidelines, he makes Gabler seem irresponsible in a way that undermines the scholarship behind the edition.[11] However, what most general readers may not realize is that Gabler's decision not to collate a particular edition does not affect his edition at all; what it affects is his list of "Historical Collations" in the three-volume edition, which is for Gabler mainly an apparatus devised for the reader's convenience, to facilitate a comparison between Gabler's text and notable variants that have appeared in print.

Gabler's edition is not founded on printed editions (as many Anglo-American editions have been, either wholly or in part); instead, Gabler chose to edit the autograph documents up to but not including the first published edition in 1922. As he says in his first response to Kidd, "it makes little sense to hold against the edition that it does not do what it expressly sets out to avoid."[12] What Gabler tried to produce was an "ideal" record of the process of composition, an "authoritative text free of corruption [transmissional error]"[13]: "This edition's whole rationale is based on the assumption that the legal act of first publication did not validate the actual text thereby made public to the extent of lending authority to its high incidence of corruption. Instead, . . . the edition [presents] an ideal text freed of the errors with which *Ulysses* was first published" (Afterword, 1892). As Jerome McGann has explained most clearly, Gabler differentiates between "documents of composition and documents of transmission," giving preemptive authority to the former. Gabler's text, therefore, "represents the ultimate state of the work's composition (not its transmission)." This ultimately leads McGann to assert that "Gabler's is an imagination of Joyce's work and not its reconstitution. Gabler invents, by a process of brilliant editorial reconstruction, *Joyce's Ulysses* (as it were), a work that existed, if it ever existed at all in fact, for Joyce the writer rather than Joyce the author. Gabler's edition does not give us the work which Joyce wanted to present to the public; rather, he gives us a text in which we may observe Joyce at work, alone, before he turns to meet his public."[14]

McGann started a process of investigating the theoretical implications of the edition that the Kidd controversy aborted, or at least deflected, by measuring Gabler's scholarly competence against norms that Gabler had (rightly or wrongly) modified to suit the extraordinary circumstances of *Ulysses*'s composition and production. After five years of debate, it seems time to return to the theoretical axioms Gabler articulated as the basis of the edition in order to determine what exactly is at stake in his theoretical choices, what the implications of these choices are, how those implications are related to other poststructuralist theories of intentionality and text production (most notably deconstruction and new historicism), and what other choices might be possible.

The first question about the choices subtending Gabler's edition is not theoretical but practical: for what audience was the synoptic text intended? On one level, the answer to this is obvious: insofar as the layers of the continuous manuscript are designed to bring us by stages to the clear reading text, it is designed for all readers, and insofar as it represents a modification of the accepted practices of textual editing, it is addressed to editors. However, Gabler's article "The Synchrony and Diachrony of Texts" suggests a third audience, which may be the most important one of all for understanding the rationale behind the edition: critics. Here Gabler emphasizes the importance of access to authorial variants for a critical understanding of a work of literature, a point he illustrates through critically analyzing two authorial versions of a Faulkner story, "That Evening Sun." He argues that "the articulation of *critical understanding* . . . will reach its highest degree of definitiveness from a critical interpretation of the work's revisional variation," and he identifies the variations within an evolving manuscript as "stimuli to *interpretation*" (emphasis added). He then proceeds from the critical desirability of a genetic manuscript text to the fact that Anglo-American editing has no model for such texts: "we have currently no methodology or model for the constitution of critical texts, or of variance recording and presentation, that will answer sufficiently to the concepts of 'work' and 'text' as I have outlined them."[15] He goes on to rehearse the reason for this, a commonplace within textual studies that Gabler's editorial assistant Wolfhard Steppe explains most simply: the methodology of Anglo-American textual scholarship grows out of an engagement with "texts for which autograph sources are rare or lacking completely (e.g., for Elizabethan drama), so that printed sources—the second-best choice—have to be depended on."[16]

Given Gabler's editorial aim to make the process of authorial composition accessible to critical interpretation, one legitimate question is whether the synoptic text actually succeeds in stimulating such interpretations. The answer at this point in time seems to be "no," partly because the three-volume edition, being expensive, is not widely available, and partly because the system of diacritical marks used to designate the different levels of composition have proven difficult to interpret.[17]

This prompts me to ask whether the synoptic text should not be marketed separately, without the reading text, perhaps in a more readable format. (Could colors or different typefaces be used instead of half-brackets to indicate the most important levels?[18] Would it be practicable to print the fair copy on the verso and additions—at all subsequent levels—on the recto?) The question remains whether the synoptic text could be simplified and redistributed in such a way as to make it a more useful tool for the critical analyses it was (partly) designed to facilitate.

To move from practical questions to more theoretical ones, I propose to explore Gabler's response to major theoretical concerns in both editing and criticism—the status of the text as product (whether authorial, cultural, or both), the text as authorized by authorial intention, and the relevance of transmissional corruption—and to show where the Gabler edition positions itself in relation to each concept, with what implications.

Let us begin by positing a conceptual field for editing that ranges from the isolated author at one end to a heterogeneous group of well-intentioned but sometimes inaccurate "scribes" and an undifferentiated (and possibly uncomprehending or resistant) public at the other. One formulation of the editor's task is to restore the now-dead author's literary *product,* stripping it of the grime of history, the "impurities" occasioned by multiple transmissions. Conceived this way, editing seeks to produce a kind of literary monument.[19] An understanding of texts as monumental implicitly upholds a canonical view of literature, and it favors certain kinds of authority: the authority of the author over that of his or her readers, the authority of the individual over that of the public, the authority of genius over collaborative production and reproduction, the authority of preservation over decomposition, and the authority of the conscious will (intention) over the authority of unconscious need and desire (chance). It is important to defer judgment on these implicit preferences, since how we judge them should have an integral relationship to what we want an edition to accomplish under a specified set of circumstances.

The preferences outlined above might be said to describe a set of typical expectations about what an edition should do. The Gabler edition may be seen as subscribing to such a view of the editor's task only up to a point: Gabler does not challenge the authority of the individual author; if anything, he intensifies it by choosing to focus almost exclusively on what Joyce actually wrote (what McGann calls "documents of composition"), relegating the "documents of transmission" (the typescripts, proofs, and the editions of *Ulysses* actually published) to a "Historical Collation" (they are also mentioned in the footnotes at the bottom of the page in the synoptic text). With respect to authorial intention, then, Gabler is quite conservative; in this respect his edition is *not* the "postmodern text" that McGann labeled it. Gabler's synoptic text (and his editorial theory) *is* postmodern in another way, however—in his questioning of the privilege of an author's final intentions over the process of writing itself.

Gabler's edition might be envisioned as a kind of Scylla and Charybdis of editing: like Odysseus, in his first pass through the channel he hugs the rock of Scylla, which is roughly equivalent here to *what the author actually wrote.*[20] But when he is buffeted back into the channel to choose between extremes a second time, Gabler goes into the whirlpool, conceiving texts as "diachronous" as well as "synchronous." This puts him in a situation aptly described as "postmodern," since what he is attacking is nothing less than our assumptive falsification of writing as product rather than process. In "The Synchrony and Diachrony of Texts," Gabler presents his position almost in the form of a manifesto:

> *Ulysses* presents an amply documented case from which to work out the implications of the basic assumption that the object of scholarly and critical analysis and study—as opposed to an author's object of publication, and a general public's reading matter—is not the final product of the writer's art alone, but beyond this, the totality of the Work in Progress. It is an assumption that follows from the theoretical premise that the work of literature possesses in its material medium itself, in its text or texts, a diachronic as well as a synchronic dimension. The act of publication which confers upon it a synchronous structure does not at the same time have the power to obliterate the coexisting diachronous structure of the work, to which the discrete temporal states of its text coalesce by complex hierarchical interrelationship. The synchronous and diachronous structures combine to form the literary work in the totality of its real presence in the documents of its conception, transmission, and publication.[21]

Gabler suggests earlier in the essay that "the synoptic apparatus for *Ulysses* should encourage a reader to move . . . forwards and backwards along the axis of diachrony of the work's total text" ("Synchrony and Diachrony," 320); his Scylla and Charybdis, like Joyce's, turns out to be a way of making time a two-way street—Gabler's synoptic edition, in theory, clears the way for us to read backward as well as forward in narrative time.

Gabler's emphasis on the process over and above the product of writing is an approach particularly suitable to the works of Joyce, who continued to write *Ulysses* in the margins of anywhere from two to nine sets of proof per episode, right up until two days before its date of publication on his fortieth birthday. *Finnegans Wake* was known only as "Work in Progress" for years; its compositional process lasted seventeen years, and the progress it depicts is in a sense eternal (since the book itself is syntactically circular). An aspect of the edition that could be questioned is the apparent arbitrariness of where Gabler decided to begin and end his chart of Joyce's progress: why begin with the fair copy? Why not begin with notes and drafts? And why exclude other kinds of progress, including the progress of the book through different printings? There are good practical answers to such questions, but questions geared toward Gabler's theory are harder to answer. Gabler excludes all errors of transmission in the synopsis: why do this on *theoretical* grounds? Gabler's references to the public odyssey of *Ulysses* in print seem at times to suggest objections that are aesthetic and even moral: transmissional errors (in a usage commonly found in textual criticism) are referred to as "corruptions" and "impurities"; the implication is that the public text has been adulterated by the other hands through which it has passed. In contrast, what Gabler offers us is an "ideal" genetic approach that he describes as "essentially *virgin* land for criticism" ("Synchrony and Diachrony," 325, emphasis added). Gabler doesn't make a neutral distinction between documents of composition and those of transmission; he ranks them in a way that clearly privileges individual composition as potentially "pure," as opposed to transmitted texts that are presented as less desirable in their adulteration. Such an attitude seems sensible enough in a traditional editorial context, but it stands out conspicuously against the background of *Ulysses,* which takes adultery and adulteration (sexual and verbal "wanderings") as a primary subject and method. The privileging of "purity" and the dismissal of scribal departures is what Fritz Senn objects to in the edition; evoking Joyce's characteristic emphases on sin and chance, he writes that the synoptic text "refines corruptions out of visible existence. . . . It pretends that no accident ever intervened. The documents (typescripts, placards, page proofs, etc.) that Joyce actually had in front of him, naturally, were not immaculate but showed all those corruptions."[22]

Since Gabler clearly advocates the presumptive authority of authorial intention as it progresses, it makes sense to test his preference for the "pure" (conscious and intentional) over the adulterated (unconscious and accidental) in terms of what Joyce has to say about these categories in both *Ulysses* and *Finnegans Wake.* First of all, we can point to Stephen's famous celebration of error in his disquisition on Shakespeare, which clearly runs counter to an ethic of ideal purity: "A man of genius makes no mistakes. His errors are volitional and are the portals of discovery" (*U,* 9.228–29). Stephen here suggests that error can be volitional, even (in a sense) intentional. He implies that Shakespeare refuses to label his errors "mis-takes"; instead of closing the door on alternative, unexpected possibilities, he perceives them as openings, as "portals of discovery" through which he can proceed. In *Finnegans Wake,* Joyce fleshes out the view of mistakes as tantalizing and potentially productive possibilities by personifying them as women, "misses in prints," punningly identified with misprints: "For that (the rapt one warns) is what papyr is meed of, made of, hides and hints and misses in prints. Till ye finally (though not yet endlike) meet with the acquaintance of Mister Typus, Mistress Tope and all the little typtopies."[23] Joyce suggests that misprints become the occasion for future productivity, producing a "tiptop" family of type.

Finnegans Wake also challenges the privileged view of the author as an individual writing in isolation: in the letter chapter, the "objective" narrator insists that the idea of an individual author is a fiction, that what we call the "writer" is an illusion born of reading with our eyes closed to an entire palimpsest of historical conflicts: "Closer inspection of the *bordereau* would reveal a multiplicity of personalities inflicted on the document or documents. . . . In fact, under the closed eyes of the inspectors the traits featuring the *chiaroscuro* coalesce, their contrarieties eliminated, in one stable somebody" (*FW,* 107.23–30). A few pages later the narrator attributes literature not to an author but to "the writer complexus (for if the hand was one, the minds of active and agitated were more than so)" (*FW,* 114.32–35). If we look to Joyce's texts for evidence of his intentions, we discover him minimizing the importance of authorial intentions by stressing the ways in which they are modified and reframed by the variable processes of writing, transmission, and reception. Joyce, then, uses his authority to recontextualize that authority against the broader backgrounds of history and production, insisting upon the irreducible oscillation between intention and circumstance.

Ulysses and, to an even greater extent, *Finnegans Wake* welcome adulteration, chance, the transmigration of written characters through time. Joyce's most emphatic presentation of writing as a process involving many hands and instruments is found in an editor's description of writing in the *Wake:*

> every person, place and thing in the chaosmos of Alle anyway connected with the gobblydumped turkery was moving and changing every part of the time: the travelling inkhorn (possibly pot), the hare and turtle pen and paper, the continually more and less intermisunderstanding minds of the anticollaborators, the as time went on as it will variously inflected, differently pronounced, otherwise spelled, changeably meaning vocable scriptsigns. (*FW,* 118.21–119.1).[24]

Ironically, although the Gabler text does not register the obliterations that time and usage have worked on *Ulysses* historically (it seeks to obliterate them), although it resists the way that coincidence has operated *on Ulysses,* its "ideality" has sharpened the representation of the way that coincidental misprints work *within* the text, thereby stimulating the very critique I just articulated. One of the most famous examples of the several typos that the Gabler edition has restored is in the telegram Stephen recalls having received from his father recalling him from Paris. We find from Gabler's Historical Collation that all the editions he collated from 1922 through 1961 read

> a blue French telegram, curiosity to show:
> —Mother dying come home father.

As several people have pointed out, this telegram isn't much of a "curiosity," but Gabler identifies "Mother" as a scribal error on the last (fifth) set of proofs for "Nother," so that the telegram in his edition reads "Nother dying come home father" (*U,* 3.199). This is indeed a "curiosity to show," one that reveals the chance significance of scribal error within the fiction that the scribal "correction" to the fiction had inadvertently obscured. The unreliability of print—"the line of botched type" and the misspelling of Bloom's name as "L. Boom" in the *Telegraph*—nettles Bloom "not a little" in "Eumaeus," along with "the usual crop of nonsensical howlers of misprints" (*U,* 16.1262–67); one of the difficulties of editing *Ulysses* involves preserving the misprints that Bloom and Stephen register without allowing the misprints in *Ulysses* itself to upstage the inculcated awareness that, as the narrative shows, print itself can "tell a graphic lie" (*U,* 16.1232). The difference between the tolerant, even opportunistic attitude the book encourages its readers to take toward the vagaries of print and the precise, scholarly attitude an editor must take to allow the narrative to convey this message is something that should be explicitly stated: the book's theory is necessarily and meaningfully at odds with editorial *and* critical practice.

In *Finnegans Wake,* one of the substitutions for "Ireland" is "Errorland" (as Yeats punned on "Eire" and "air" in *The Wind Among the Reeds,* Joyce puns on "Eire" and "err" in *Finnegans Wake*). Errancy (modeled on odyssey) provides the very structure of *Ulysses* ("Longest way round is the shortest way home"; *U,* 13.1110–11), and the texture of language in "Penelope" and the *Wake* is saturated with apparent "errors." The main task of the editor is to eliminate error,[25] which if literally carried out in the editing of Joyce would obscure his *modus operandi* in *Ulysses* and eliminate *Finnegans Wake* almost entirely. (Many of the erroneous "corrections" made by typists and compositors of *Ulysses* resulted from just such an attempt to eliminate error, but in eliminating Joyce's intentional errors they homogenized the interplay between intention and chance that is such an important part of Joyce's subject.) What editors need in the case of Joyce is an oxymoronic category of "volitional error," but how can an editor determine which errors are "volitional" without relying solely on individual critical judgment? Gabler's controversial and not altogether unproblematic strategy was to follow the authorial inscriptions whenever possible, thereby construing *Ulysses* less as a commodity given to the public in 1922 than as a representation of one man's thought as it grew under his hand. Gabler has made a judgment: that Joyce's critical choices as he constructed his text are more precise and meaningful than corrections and accidents introduced later by other hands, that Joyce's work is more "his" than "ours." What makes Gabler's verdict interesting is that when he chooses the act of authorial composition as the basis for his copy text, he not only privileges active over passive authorization, individual and private determinations over more public and social ones, and the author's labor over that of others involved in the process, but his choice also has the unexpected and paradoxical effect of amplifying the author's critique of authorial intention. In effect, Gabler focuses his attention as editor on what Roland Barthes has called the work as opposed to the Text, which has the effect of emphasizing Joyce's investment in Text. Barthes argues that "the work is held in the hand, the text is held in language . . . *the Text is experienced only in an activity, in a production.*"[26] One of the main differences between Barthes's "work" and "text" is in what authorizes each: he argues that the work is something that we attribute to an author, who "is reputed to be the father and owner of his work," whereas "the Text . . . is read without the Father's inscription"; the metaphor of the work is the image of a growing *organism,* whereas "the metaphor of the Text is that of the *network* . . . no vital "respect" is therefore due to the Text." In Barthes's terms, Joyce uses his works to draw the reader's attention to what Barthes calls "text," the dynamic process of reading/writing, theory/practice. By enhancing Joyce's authority, Gabler therefore promotes Joyce's miniaturization of such authority. As Barthes explains, the author does not necessarily disappear from the Text, but when he returns, "he does so, one might say, as a guest; if he is a novelist, he inscribes himself there as one of his characters, drawn as a figure in the carpet; his inscription is no longer privileged, paternal, alethic, but ludic: he becomes, one can say, a paper author."

Joyce's use of "volitional errors" may be the most far-reaching of his many innovations: it is one of the guiding principles behind the evolution of Joyce's style, and it also provided him with a way of intertwining conscious and unconscious awareness, intentional and unintentional expression, individual purpose and an almost providential appreciation of chance and coincidence. Joyce's exploration of error began with the epiphanies, which he defined as records of inadvertent "slips" by which people unintentionally gave away what they cared most to conceal. Error in *Dubliners* is offered as a point of entry for the reader, a threshold through which we can see that what the characters don't know *does* hurt them. A dramatized moment of willed ignorance or arrogance, a punctiliously recorded "mistake" that no one points out—these are given to us as the vortices of the narrative, where we can begin to see a character's intention unraveling into its opposite, paralysis. Most critics would now agree that the "meaning" of *Dubliners* is found in its gaps, "between the acts"—not in the narratives that the characters construct about themselves, but in the errors that show us, as readers, how to deconstruct those narratives.[27] In *Ulysses* error takes many forms—of errancy, excess, gleeful self-parody. Characters suffer themselves to be transposed and transformed, but willful obscurity increasingly infiltrates the narrative, and in the obscurity of the later episodes the real novelty of the book's transgressive language begins to work its dark magic. *Finnegans Wake* leaves us largely in the dark; it could be described as a book composed entirely of misprints—"volitional errors"—carefully selected to show that when meaning is obscured, we find ourselves inventing new principles of interconnection, or rediscovering a host of old ones. What we find when we turn away from enlightenment is what the "light" of conscious reason and intention has whited out, as the sun outshines the stars: what Stephen in *Ulysses* calls the "darkness shining in brightness which brightness could not comprehend" (2.160). Stephen always knows that "Darkly they [the stars] are there behind this light, darkness shining in the brightness, delta of Cassiopeia, worlds" (3.409–10). One of the narratives of *Ulysses* is a search for the stars behind the sun, for the Greek constellations behind the Christian concentration on the one son / sun, for the "heaventree of stars hung with humid nightblue fruit" (17.1039) that is the book's Ithaca. That hidden tree of light with its dark fruits, always with us somewhere beyond the light of reason and the fire of individual purpose, is what all Joyce's works try to lead us toward.

Editing is an enlightenment activity; the word comes from "edere," to bring forth, and it means "to publish" (*OED*), to bring to light. Webster's is even more specific: to edit is "to alter, adapt, or refine esp. to bring about conformity to a standard or to suit a particular purpose." Joyce poses a particular problem for the editor because he situates many of his characters' thoughts and utterances on the line between wanting to "bring forth" a word or idea and wanting to suppress it. This conflict produces meaningful error (a "Freudian slip"), which should not be regularized or brought into conformity with a standard. What this error has the power to represent in miniature is the conflict between an individual's "ideal purpose" and its incompatibility with historical contingency—our inability to ensure the realization of that purpose in exactly the form in which it was conceived. To edit *Ulysses* with reference to texts that have already been intentionally "corrected" *and* accidentally corrupted is to see history at work on print in exactly the ways Joyce described, but it is to obscure that description itself. Anyone who has had occasion to use the title *Finnegans Wake* in his or her own writing has experienced in miniature the challenges and frustrations of editing Joyce, of preserving Joyce's solecisms against the almost universal impulse to standardize a familiar usage. If you write *"Finnegans Wake"* nine people out of ten will transcribe it as *"Finnegan's Wake"*; one of the functions of Joyce's title is to inculcate an awareness that we are all editors, that reading is itself a transitory editorial practice. It is unconscious editing that produces transmissional errors, and it takes a different, more self-aware and responsible kind of editing to delete them.

Other editions of *Ulysses* are certainly possible. We can imagine editions with a textual apparatus that is easier to use, or a historical collation of *all* the extant printings of *Ulysses* (which would be invaluable for a detailed assessment of how accident has operated on Gabler's "ideal" text). But given what we know about the 1922 edition, and how it was prepared, it is hard to imagine a better strategy for preserving Joyce's volitional errors than the one Gabler devised. Gabler has recovered *Joyce's* garbles, and most importantly, he has done so in a way that makes public his own procedures and assumptions. He has given up the anonymity, the veil of editorial authority (invisibility) that is the editor's traditional privilege, presenting it instead as grounded in specific (if controversial) historical and textual contingencies. In the process, he has done more to make public the difficulties of textual editing than any other editor of the last twenty-five years. In a sense, his explicit representation of his editorial procedures has invited readers to collaborate in the recreation of the edition, as an almost unprecedented number of readers, led by John Kidd, have tried their hand at doing.[28]

By editing *Ulysses* in the way that he has, Gabler has done two things, then: first, he has challenged the fetishizing of texts as the product rather than the process of composition. Second, by questioning the definitiveness of the fact of publication, he has transformed the role of the editor: in some ways, he has amplified that role, assuming for his own construction of Joyce's "continuous manuscript" the authority that he had disallowed in the first edition of 1922 (just as he amplified the voice of the author by multiplying its articulations as they evolve through time). Although his methodology has enhanced the editor's authority to select individual readings (from among authorized variants), it has diminished the apparent absoluteness of that authority, its invisibility to the general public.

Gabler unveils his editorial authority to be as provisional, dynamic, and contingent on judgment and accuracy as Joyce's, although his eyesight and "memory," aided by documents not available to Joyce and by computerized collations of those documents, are better; moreover, like Joyce, Gabler invites his reader to participate in the process of reconstructing (or constructing) the text.

Gabler's edition—in conjunction with Joyce's text—has the effect (if not the intention) of advertising the insufficiency of any one edition of a book with so many previous lives. We could perhaps fault Gabler for his intention of producing an "ideal," private text rather than an actual public one, for his apparent preference for individual intentions (conceived severally) instead of multiple realizations (integrated through "correction"). What makes the debate exciting is the new possibilities it engenders, but what validates the theory behind Gabler's edition, making it successful on its own terms (if necessarily insufficient), is the way that its effects counterbalance its published intentions. If it once hoped to present itself as definitive (the impossibility of such a hope was not acknowledged until the second impression of the Garland edition), its effect is to call definitiveness into question; if it intends to give us ideal perfection, it allows us a surer glimpse into Joyce's depictions of the operations of the real. Gabler chose to reconstruct Joyce's process of composition, replicating in his edition even the number of years it took Joyce to complete the book (seven); interestingly, his effort reproduced the controversy that followed publication as well. John Kidd has emerged as a contemporary avatar of Wyndham Lewis, attacking the assumptions that subtend the edition as Lewis attacked the world view reflected in *Ulysses.* What Joyce's script would seem to demand is that we put the antagonists together, as warring twins, to produce a new and much-needed edition of *Finnegans Wake.*

Interestingly, despite its productive (and modernist) contradiction between intention and effect, the ideology behind Gabler's edition is nevertheless harmonious with many of the most recent (postmodern) tendencies in literary theory. Its implicit critique of the overwhelming product-orientation of a writer's labor, the traces of which are erased in the publication of a cleaned-up printed book to be sold to the public, has a distinctively materialist overtone. Gabler presents *Ulysses* not as a sacred book, but as a labor-intensive process the intricacies of which are (theoretically if not always practically) recoverable. Similarly, Gabler's privileging of authorial intentions, which paradoxically highlights both the power and the limitations of conscious and intentional uses of language, amounts to a restaging of a "deconstructive" insight attributable to Joyce. Intentionality (as an ideal) versus the production of the real; the corrosive power of a communally authored, metaphorically suggestive, sensual language to undermine and complicate individual intent;

laborious production as it invisibly underwrites idealized and sanctified (i.e., privileged) "creation"—these are the issues of our time. Gabler's edition of *Ulysses* has revitalized these debates, not as they affect the abstract realm of ideas, but as they destabilize our notion of what constitutes and authorizes literary "work"—from the author to print, from an apparently transcendent "origin" of a work to its most immanent "ends"—and what connects them: those "variously inflected, differently pronounced, otherwise spelled, changeably meaning vocable scriptsigns" (*FW,* 118.26–28), the "radiooscillating epiepistle" in black and white (or electricity and light) to which "we must ceaselessly return" (*FW,* 108.24, 26).

NOTES

1. James Joyce, *Ulysses. A Critical and Synoptic Edition,* prepared by Hans Walter Gabler with Wolfhard Steppe and Claus Melchior (New York: Garland, 1984), 3 vols. Hereafter cited as *U,* followed by episode and line numbers. My review appeared on Sunday, 9 September 1984, 7.

2. See, for just one example, David F. Hult's excellent article, "Reading it Right: The Ideology of Text Editing," *Romanic Review* 79 (January 1988): 88: "What is crucial about the editor's craft is its direct placement at that spot where modern concerns meet medieval ones in the very conception of the literary object."

3. Cf. Gabler's afterword 1905–7 for a description of how his editorial team used TUSTEP, "an autonomous system of computer programs for text data processing developed at the computing center of the University of Tubingen," and also Gabler, "Computer-Aided Critical Edition of *Ulysses,*" *AALC* (Association of Literary and Linguistic Computing) *Bulletin* 8 (1981): 232–48. The clearest account of the way the edition was put together (and the role played by computers in that process) is Michael Groden's "Editing Joyce's *Ulysses:* An International Effort," *Scholarly Publishing* 12 (October 1980): 37–54. Some of the criticism leveled at the edition has suggested that the use of computers made the process of editing too mechanical, a protest I see as being directed not so much at Gabler as at technological change in general.

4. There is some disagreement over whether the theories of writing and reading found in *Finnegans Wake* are applicable to a discussion of *Ulysses,* whether it is legitimate to "read backwards." I am taking the position that *Finnegans Wake* is directly relevant to *Ulysses,* that it is (among other things) an elaborate response to the ways in which *Ulysses* was printed and received (or misconceived). Joyce frequently used critical responses to a previous work (including his own criticisms) to help him design its successors, and the emphasis on problems of textual transmission in *Finnegans Wake* lends itself to an analysis of comparable problems with (and in) *Ulysses.*

5. See Jane Ford, Bonnie Kime Scott, Jean Kimball, and Fritz Senn, "The New Edition of *Ulysses:* An Assessment of its Usefulness One Year Later," in *New Alliances in Joyce Studies,* ed. Bonnie Kime Scott (Newark, Del.: University of Delaware Press, 1988), 221.

6. John Kidd, "Errors of Execution in the 1984 *Ulysses,*" printed together with Gabler's reply in the special issue on editing *Ulysses* edited by Charles Rossman, *Studies in the Novel* 22 (Summer 1990): 243–49 and 250–56. This issue also concludes with an annotated bibliography of what has been written on the Gabler edition (257–69). Kidd's attack on Gabler was effectively advertised before the fact by an article in the *Washington Post* by David Remnick called "The War over 'Ulysses,'" 2 April 1985), B1–4, in which a picture of Kidd bears the caption, "I think what I have to say is going to blow the whole Joyce establishment wide open."

7. Kidd, "The Scandal of *Ulysses,*" *New York Review of Books* 35 (30 June 1988): 32–39. See Peter du Sautoy (one of the trustees of the James Joyce Estate), "Editing *Ulysses:* A Personal Account," *James Joyce Quarterly* 27 (Fall 1989): 76, for a reasonable objection to the hyperbole of the headline: "I must conclude by saying that I am surprised the *New York Review of Books,* a reputable journal though little known in Britain, should indulge in a scare headline, 'The Scandal of *Ulysses,*' thus turning what is essentially a dispute between scholars into a sort of prize fight."

8. The issues concerned are those of 18 August 1988; 29 September 1988; 8 December 1988; 19 January 1989; 30 March 1990; and 1 June 1989. My thanks to John Crowther for assembling copies of these articles for me.

9. The *Times Literary Supplement* (*TLS*) exchange was sparked by a review of new editions of Proust by Roger Shattuck and Douglas Alden, "Searching for the True Text," *TLS,* 10–16 June 1988, 640–41; Gabler responded with a letter, 1–7 July 1988, 733; followed by Peter du Sautoy, 8–14 July 1988, 755. John Kidd replied to Gabler, 22–28 July 1988, 907, who countered in the issue of 12–18 August 1988, 733. Charles Rossman then entered the fray with "Editing *Ulysses,*" *TLS* 2–8 September 1988, 963; and Peter du Sautoy answered on 9–15 September 1988, 989. In the same issue (and on the same page) Stephen Joyce responded to Alden, Shattuck, and Rossman. Michael Groden replied to Kidd in *TLS,* 7–13 October 1988, 1109; and Kidd answered in *TLS* 21–27 October 1988, 1175. Ian Gunn's response to Kidd appeared in the issue of 4–10 November 1988, 1227; and Gabler finished off the exchange in *TLS,* 16–22 December 1988, 1395.

10. For an account of why Epstein might have taken such a step, see Robin Bates's "Postscript: February 1990" to his "Reflections on the Kidd Era," *Studies in the Novel* 22 (Summer 1990): 136–38.

11. See Bates, "Reflections on the Kidd Era," 123–24. See also Kidd's much more extreme charge in his "An Inquiry into *Ulysses: The Corrected Text,*"

Papers of the Bibliographical Society of America 82 (December 1988): 514: "Somehow Gabler overlooked seven typesettings of *Ulysses* which came before his own, making his [edition] not the eleventh [as Gabler says in the *Critical and Synoptic Edition*] but the eighteenth."

12. Hans Walter Gabler, "A Response to: John Kidd, 'Errors of Execution in the 1984 *Ulysses*,'" *Studies in the Novel* 22 (Summer 1990): 252.

13. Hans Walter Gabler, "The Synchrony and Diachrony of Texts: Practice and Theory of the Critical Edition of James Joyce's *Ulysses*," *Text* 1 (1981 [published in 1984]): 310. Hereafter cited as "Synchrony and Diachrony."

14. Jerome J. McGann, "*Ulysses* as a Postmodern Text: The Gabler Edition," *Criticism* 27 (Summer 1985): 286, 287, and 290–91.

15. Gabler, "Synchrony and Diachrony," 309–10.

16. Wolfhard Steppe, "Reply to Paola Pugliatti's 'Who's Afraid of the 1984 *Ulysses*?,'" *James Joyce Quarterly* 27 (Fall 1989): 60.

17. See, once again, Steppe's "Reply," 55–57, where he argues that Pugliatti has misread the diacritical symbols. An added complication is that the symbols sometimes designate different documents in different episodes. See also Fritz Senn, "*Ulysses* between Corruption and Correction," in *Assessing the 1984* Ulysses, ed. C. George Sandulescu and Clive Hart (Gerrards Cross, Buckinghamshire: Colin Smythe, 1986), 188–206.

18. See, for example, *The Cornell Yeats* project for instances of editions that use different typefaces to represent different stages of composition (general editors Phillip L. Marcus, Stephen Parrish, Ann Saddlemyer, Jon Stallworthy).

19. See, for example, G. Thomas Tanselle, who concludes *A Rationale of Textual Criticism* (Philadelphia: University of Pennsylvania Press, 1989) with the claim that "our cultural heritage consists, in Yeats' phrase, of 'Monuments of unageing intellect'" (93). See also Michael Groden's inquiry into the monumental view of editing and its relation to New Criticism in "Contemporary Textual and Literary Theory," in this volume.

20. But see Clive Hart's corrective to Gabler's view, which clarifies the extent to which Gabler does not strictly adhere to what Joyce actually wrote. Hart would have an edition of *Ulysses* in which Joyce's errors and evidence of his forgetfulness are preserved, and he disagrees with Gabler's preference for the best formulations of a given phrase, and with Gabler's decision to correct obvious authorial errors. "Art Thou Real, My Ideal?" in Sandulescu and Hart, *Assessing the 1984* Ulysses, 58–65.

21. See Gabler, "Synchrony and Diachrony," 325. It is interesting to compare Gabler's insistence on writing as process with Derrida's "The end of the book and the beginning of writing," as well as to contrast the premium he puts on individual agency with that of Benjamin in "The Work of Art in the Age of Mechanical Reproduction."

22. Fritz Senn, "Inherent Delicacy: Eumaean Questions," *Studies in the Novel* 22 (Summer 1990): 184.

23. James Joyce, *Finnegans Wake* (New York: Penguin, 1939), 20.13. Hereafter cited as *FW*, followed by the page number and line numbers.

24. For a fuller account of the *Wake*'s emphasis on the conditions of its own production and printing, see John Paul Riquelme, *Teller and Tale in Joyce's Fiction: Oscillating Perspectives* (Baltimore: Johns Hopkins University Press, 1983), 14–19.

25. As A. E. Housman put it, "Textual criticism is . . . the science of discovering error in texts and the art of removing it." See his "The Application of Thought to Textual Criticism," *Proceedings of the Classical Association* 18 (1921): 67–84; reprinted in *Art and Error: Modern Textual Editing*, ed. Ronald Gottesman and Scott Bennett (Bloomington: Indiana University Press, 1970), 2. The best article on error and the Gabler edition to date is that of Patrick McGee, "The Error of Theory," in *Studies in the Novel* 22 (Summer 1990): 148–62. See in particular McGee's assertion that "For all of its errors, Gabler's edition represents a theoretical breakthrough even if it is editorially flawed. It may even be necessary to consider the errors as a byproduct of the theory. . . . Theory as a discourse is always in error, always moving away from certainties of the law. But the law itself is never stable and produces theory as the sediment of its own process. Any editorial practice taking place within our academic institutions can be read as theory. The language of the text is transformed by the editor into the discourse of theory" (157, 160).

26. Roland Barthes, "From Work to Text," in *The Rustle of Language*, trans. Richard Howard (Berkeley: University of California Press, 1986), 56–64.

27. See, for example, Margot Norris, "Narration under a Blindfold: Reading Joyce's 'Clay,'" *PLMA* 102 (1987): 206–15; and Jean-Michel Rabaté, "Silence in *Dubliners*," in *James Joyce: New Perspectives*, ed. Colin MacCabe (Sussex: Harvester Press, 1982), 45–72.

28. See the replies to Kidd's "The Scandal of *Ulysses*" by Jon N. Elzey and Beverly Fields in "'The Scandal of Ulysses': An Exchange," *New York Review of Books* 35 (18 August 1988): 64. On a more serious level, see Sandulescu and Hart, *Assessing the 1984* Ulysses; Philip Gaskell and Clive Hart, *Ulysses: A Review of Three Texts* (Gerrards Cross: Colin Smythe, 1989); and Rossman's special issue on editing *Ulysses, Studies in the Novel* 22, (Summer 1990).

Textual Criticism as Feminist Practice: Or, Who's Afraid of Virginia Woolf Part II

Brenda R. Silver

> RAFI *lies in bed in the half-lit room. He's asleep, having a nightmare. He cries out, then awakes. He lies there being stared at by Virginia Woolf, which becomes more horrible the more she looks at him. The noise from outside rises around him. It could be in his head or for real: he doesn't know. He sits up. On the edge of the bed he pulls cotton-wool out of his ears. He covers his face with his hands.*
>
> —*Sammy and Rosie Get Laid,* The Script

To begin with a question: what is Virginia Woolf doing in Hanif Kureishi's self-consciously postmodern depiction of 1980s London and why is she presiding over a race riot and the burning of the inner city? The poster of Woolf alluded to above hangs in the study of Rosie, social worker, feminist, sometime political activist; Woolf's writings, in their distinctive Hogarth Press covers, figure prominently in the center of her bookshelves. Rafi, Rosie's father-in-law, the Pakistani politician returned to the "Home Country" to escape death threats occasioned by the brutal persecution of his enemies, sees the flames from the riot superimposed on Woolf's image and experiences her gaze with horror. In a film where the text of T. S. Eliot's *Waste Land* covers the outside of a caravan parked on a waste ground reclaimed by a countercultural, multiracial community, the status of "high" modernism in the world of postmodern, postcolonial, metropolitan London is very much at stake, and "Virginia Woolf" seems to have become an icon representative of modernism itself. Yet has she? and if so, what do she and her gaze represent? Aloofness? a life and a writing style out of touch with the political realities of her own day let alone those of the present? Or is her presence more contemporary, and perhaps more sympathetic? Does it evoke her feminism, including her insistence on the interconnections of the public and private spheres, and her elevation by modern-day feminists such as Rosie (whose political commitments within the film, however, are highly ambiguous) into the position of "matron saint"?[1] Given the history of the British perception of Woolf as the elite, snobbish Queen of Bloomsbury and, oh yes, minor experimental writer, what does the prominence of her image in this distinctly political film suggest? Does she preside over this scene as modernist, as feminist, as pacifist, as highbrow, as sapphist, as suicide, as failed liberal anti-imperialist? And how do we begin to get beyond the surface of her enigmatic, silent, Mona Lisa–like stare?

The questions framing Kureishi's portrait of Woolf frame as well my concerns in this essay: the role that textual criticism, in particular the editing and reception of manuscript versions of Woolf's novels, have played in altering our image of the "author" and the way we understand her politics and art. More specifically, I want to make the claim that the centrality of Woolf to studies of contemporary culture such as *Sammy and Rosie* has a great deal to do with feminist critics in the 1970s and early 1980s who saw textual editing as a means to break through the surface of established texts and established views and bring to light "submerged" texts. (I am thinking here of Louise DeSalvo, Ellen Hawkes, Elizabeth Heine, Madeline Moore, Grace Radin, Lucio Ruotolo, and Susan Squier, among others.) This project can be compared to Woolf's discovery of her "tunnelling process" for *Mrs. Dalloway:* "[digging] out beautiful caves" behind the texts of her novels that "connect" and come "to daylight at the present moment."[2] The tunnels not only connected the earlier to the later versions of individual novels, but intersected with the multiple versions of the other novels and with the diaries, letters, memoirs, and essays that were concurrently coming into print. The results of this feminist project are the well-documented change in Woolf's status as both novelist and cultural critic and a broadening and deepening of the criticism about her.

But the story doesn't end there. Whether deliberately or not, in the act of shattering the surface of Woolf's novels, the editors shattered the idea of the stable text itself. Once we are aware of the manuscript versions and their alternate readings, it becomes impossible, except by a willed act of commitment to a particular interpretative stance, not to be conscious of their presence within the "final" text.[3] Once seen, once read, the words and the images found in the previous versions shadow and illuminate the impressions we receive from the familiar words on the well-thumbed page and create something new. And like all new works, the ones that emerged from the juxtaposition of the published and (previously) unpublished versions of Woolf's novels have created their own interpretative cruxes, including the vexed issue of self-censorship. For at the same time that feminist editors began to perceive and reveal the trenchant, frequently scathing, cultural criticism beneath the surface of the seemingly flawless, apolitical, aestheticized work of art, they began to debate where and how this criticism, including the expression of anger, was encoded, and whether it was deformed, transformed, or strengthened as the novel moved toward the public realm. And like the enigmatic, silent portrait of Woolf in Kureishi's film, the words that are both there and not there on Woolf's pages have proved resistant to any single "truth." Nevertheless, the choices made by Woolf's textual editors, like the choices made by "interpretative" critics, have a great deal to do with whether Woolf's readers, like Rafi, find her stare "horrible"—or empowering.

I

It has always seemed to me that one of the greatest ironies of the recent history of Woolf studies resides in the intersection of textual editing and feminist practice. This is an irony that Woolf herself would have relished. Think of the anger experienced by the narrator of *A Room of One's Own* when she is denied access to the Oxbridge library that housed the manuscripts of *Lycidas* and *Henry Esmond,* manuscripts that would have allowed her to study what alterations were made and whether they were "for the benefit of the style or of the sense."[4] Sexual politics and access to critical and creative tools were for Woolf clearly connected. Whether or not they were responding to this scenario, when critics in the late 1960s and early 1970s began to reclaim Woolf from the Leavisite orthodoxy that depicted her as a novelist of sensibility and reduced her to a footnote in the great tradition of ethical realism in the English novel, they found one of their strongest arguments in one of the most traditional forms of literary scholarship: textual editing, including the publication of manuscript versions of her novels.

Before I fill in the details of my argument, I want to make it clear that I am not concerned in this essay with the editorial questions surrounding the choice of copy-text for a critical edition of a novel and the place of the extant holographs, typescripts, galleys, and page proofs—the various versions—in this process. (The new editions of Woolf presently being prepared against the lifting of the copyright on her works in Britain will, however, have to confront these issues.[5]) Nor am I concerned with the publishing history of her novels, except for the circumstance that after her first two novels, Woolf published all of the English editions of her books and pamphlets with her own press, the Hogarth Press, which she and her husband Leonard Woolf owned and ran. While this factor eliminated the mediation of an editor who could ask for or make substantive changes—the only person who read her books before they went to press was Leonard, who gave an opinion but did not demand alterations—it did not eliminate the introduction of variants in the published texts, many of them consciously introduced by Woolf herself as she corrected two sets of identical page proofs, one for the Hogarth Press and one for her American publishers. In what might appear a distinctly poststructuralist manner if so many earlier writers had not also exhibited it, Woolf did not seem to care about "final authorial intention" or a stable text. She knowingly sent out different versions, different texts.[6]

I will come back to the significance of Woolf's publishing situation when I return to the question of self-censorship, but for the most part my focus here is on the reception rather than the production of Woolf's novels, and the role played in that reception by what Donald Reiman calls "versioning": the presentation of "enough different *primary* textual documents and states of major texts . . . so that readers, teachers, and critics can compare for themselves" the different versions and explore their "distinct ideologies, aesthetic perspectives, or rhetorical strategies."[7] The market that would allow such "versioning," he adds, "seems to arise whenever teachers and critics demonstrate enough intellectual curiosity to wish to analyze different versions of a major author's works—a desire usually produced by exposure to the primary evidence for one of them" (171). The conjunction of textual editing, "versioning," and feminist criticism that has occurred over the past twenty years has not only assured Woolf's status as "major author," but has contributed to the critical debates that redefined modernism as an ideological as well as aesthetic construct and located it as much in the critic/reader as in the text. To trace the circumstances and the language that surround and shape the "versioning" of Woolf's novels is to illustrate the centrality of the critical contexts and the historical moment that necessarily connect editing and interpretation. For the words editors use to describe their texts and their project simultaneously construct and deconstruct the structures and perspectives that critics call their own.

II

The first indications that Woolf's early drafts were not only available but worth critical study came in the late 1960s, initially in Wallace Hildick's pedagogical text *Word for Word: A Study of Authors' Alterations with Exercises,* which included extracts from the manuscripts of *Mrs. Dalloway,* and then in four essays by Charles Hoffman that described manuscript versions of several of Woolf's novels and discussed their differences from the published versions.[8] Both projects assume an audience curious about Woolf's alterations and both locate this curiosity in terms of her narrative experiments, her concern for the relationship of "art" and "reality," internality and externality, her use of imagery, and her presentation of "character": that is, in her formalist credentials. Hildick, for example, presents a series of versions of the opening of *Mrs. Dalloway,* which, he notes, some consider to be her best novel, as an illustration of Woolf's attempts to escape the "'ill-fitting vestments'" (Woolf's phrase) of conventional narrative methods and her "crystallization" of images and ideas (177, 187). But neither his comments nor the questions he asks about these passages direct the reader's attention to the relationship between Clarissa and Peter Walsh, who dominates the original opening, or to the significance of the images themselves.

Yet in his introduction to the volume as a whole, Hildick provides a rationale for looking beyond the formal values of a work when exploring the "intention" behind an author's alterations. His series of categories ranges from "tidying-up" and "roughening-up changes," through what he calls the "power-group" ("where the power to be increased is the power of penetration as well as of projection and persuasion" [14–15]), to major structural changes and, finally, the changes made for "ideological reasons." "Some," he notes, "would regard this as an extra-literary group, though if one declines to recognize any boundary between art and living, of which ideology is so extremely important a part, this description will not be applied" (21–22). Hildick's language not only grants this category of revision legitimacy by deconstructing the boundary between art and ideology (a surprising move in 1965), but also represents literature, as one strand of current textual criticism does, as an essentially social act performed within specific institutional contexts. Once this construct is in place, Hildick can identify its sources: changes made under a repressive political regime; changes made, usually several years after the publication of the work, to accommodate an author's change of views; changes made to reflect shifts in public taste, to avoid echoing a model, to defer to what the author "considers to be the taste of his public" or to the feelings of individuals who might recognize themselves (22–24). What is missing from this list is both the role of an external critic, such as an editor, and what will later come to dominate the attention of Woolf's textual critics and interpreters: the existence of a self-censorship that grows from an intertwining of personal and cultural factors and speaks to more than "public taste."

One other aspect of Hildick's representation of Woolf is worth noting: his assertion that while her manuscripts may give the "impression" of either disorder (by interspersing drafts of several different works) or an "indiscriminately impatient sketchiness" (located in the alterations themselves), they actually reveal "a keenly methodical mind at work behind the apparent disorder" and a writing method that is "ruthlessly logical" (177–78). Publishing in England at a time when the British curriculum was still dominated by the Leavisite canon, Hildick may well be reflecting a need to justify the inclusion of Woolf in the company of George Eliot, Lawrence, Pope, Butler, Hardy, Wordsworth, James, and Blake by emphasizing her seriousness, her discipline, as artist. This kind of assertion, which I read as part of the need felt by Woolf's early editors (and critics) to justify taking her seriously, emphasizes her artistic control as a way to defeat the prevailing view of her as "novelist of sensibility" and not as "artist." As late as 1979 Lucio Ruotolo, in the introduction to a collection of Woolf's previously unpublished works, described how "despite her renewed status on the curriculum, those who most influence the structure of humanities departments are disposed, with few exceptions, to find Woolf at best perplexing and at worst disruptively anti-intellectual. . . . The presumption . . . is that Woolf, like the women's studies programs surrounding her, invites students to indulge their feelings in unproductive ways, which is to say in ways that do not respect and perpetuate customary disciplines."[9]

The formalist representation of Woolf, and of critical practice, also governs John Graham's contribution to the 1972 collection *Editing Twen-*

tieth Century Texts, "Editing a Manuscript: Virginia Woolf's *The Waves,*" and the major project it describes: the transcription and presentation of the two holograph drafts of *The Waves.*[10] Graham was the first person to prepare Woolf's early drafts for publication, and his rationale—his need to defend what he portrays as a still rare editorial undertaking—illustrates clearly ideological debates within the editing and critical community: "The draft material for a text is . . . an historical document, like a letter or diary, and should take its place with these other documents in the library stacks." The reason it has not already, he speculates, reflects the "post-romantic feeling that the draft of a text is more sacredly private than are the sexual peccadilloes, financial disasters, or mystical experiences of the writer in question: the ashes left behind by the Promethean flame should be exposed to public gaze only on brief ritual occasions, preferably in glass cases in the lobby of the British Museum; and they may occasionally be examined by one of [the] priests, who can then allude cryptically in his footnotes to their presumed significance" ("Editing a Manuscript," 77–78). Graham's language here anticipates Jerome McGann's influential critique of "final authorial intention" on the grounds that it privileges a "Romantic conception of literary production" by emphasizing "the autonomy of the isolated author" and the unmediated text, thereby obscuring the fact that "the 'mode of existence of a literary work of art' . . . is fundamentally social."[11]

And yet it could be argued that Graham himself, while opening the way for the publication of the manuscript versions of Woolf's novels that followed his own, did not perceive the historicity or sociability of his own "document," including its critical assumptions. His strong prohibition in his anticipatory essay against editorial interpretation of the revisions—against presenting interpretation or speculation as fact ("Editing a Manuscript," 80, 91)—can be read as a manifestation of a discourse that believed there was such a thing as textual criticism or editorial practice divorced from critical and hence subjective perspectives. Even more striking, his presentation of Woolf's creative process in the light of a consistent vision and conception (a "fin in a waste of water"; "two realities in tension with each other"), and a "preoccupation with the total artistic effect" (*Holograph,* 22)—his contention that the preparatory notes and the revisions move toward a preconceived end and were "never altered by a fundamental shift in artistic intention" (*Holograph,* 28)—echoes not only G. Thomas Tanselle's arguments for "authorial intent" and the primacy of the integral, organic work of art that represents it, but Tanselle's belief that the editor will (objectively) recognize that "work of art" amidst all the possible versions.[12] Expectation and (re)presentation become one.

Another way to see the sociability of Graham's (and Tanselle's) assumptions is to say that his "interpretations" of Woolf's revisions reflect the critical ideology still dominant in North America at the time by pointing the reader toward the formal characteristics of the novel and the ways in which the revisions illustrate "the larger strategies followed by Virginia Woolf in her struggle to give a literary form to the original design" (*Holograph,* 40). *The Waves,* he argues in the introduction to the manuscripts, is a representative work of modernism, whose fictional experiments have been underrated and misunderstood (*Holograph,* 13–14). To support this contention, he focuses his introductory remarks on Woolf's experiments in form and perspective and reads all of Woolf's critical and personal writings during the novel's gestation through a strictly formalist lens. This perspective leads him, for example, to read "Women and Fiction," the precursor to *A Room of One's Own,* solely in terms of Woolf's predictions for a new poetic novel, to be written by "liberated" women, that "'will look beyond the personal and political relationships to the wider questions which the poet tries to solve—of our destiny and the meaning of life'" (*Holograph,* 24). What this reading elides is not only Woolf's insistence that fiction is never divorced from the material circumstances in which it is produced, but her prediction that women in the future would also write impersonal novels that would "become more critical of society."[13] While *The Waves* is clearly Woolf's most "poetic" novel, Graham's perspective and language effectively preclude "society" and social criticism from playing any role in the novel at all.

However unconscious Graham might have been of his critical assumptions, his contribution to the future of Woolf studies—and the role of "versioning" within it—was enormous. The availability of the two prepublication versions of the novel, each page transcribed exactly as it appears in the manuscript, provided the impetus and basis for future interpretations.[14] In fact, one of his major points is how few manuscript versions of works have been published and, as a result, how little we know about what these texts can teach us—not only about the "specific text in question, but [about] the foundation and superstructure of criticism itself." "If enough people seriously engage in this kind of discipline, it may lead slowly to the realignment of fundamental critical presuppositions, to the formulation of new questions, to the rephrasing of old questions, to a sharper appraisal of our old instruments of analysis and to the invention of new instruments more delicate and precise" ("Editing a Manuscript," 92). His prophecy, at least in the case of Woolf, has proved stunningly accurate in terms of the proliferation of editions and of critical approaches to them.

III

Graham's edition of the manuscripts of *The Waves* appeared in 1976; in 1977 two special issues on Woolf in very different journals—*Bulletin of the New York Public Library* and *Women's Studies*—signaled the growing intersection of feminist practice and textual criticism. Both of these issues were inspired by and included papers presented at conferences that set out to provide "Another Version of Virginia Woolf," a version that took the earlier versions of her works as the grounds for "exploring the often-neglected social and political aspects of Woolf's novels."[15] Suddenly the terrain of Woolf criticism began to shift, and textual criticism was at the center of the resulting fray. As feminist editors, versed in critical perspectives that challenged the isolation of formalist approaches to texts, made more and more of Woolf's texts available—including manuscript verions of those novels usually considered to be marginal to an oeuvre and a career defined solely in terms of aesthetic modernism—the critical discourse about all of Woolf's novels changed. It was not only, as Grace Radin argued in her 1981 study of the evolution of *The Years,* one of the central novels in this process, that critics turned to the drafts of these works to "learn more about Woolf's social theories"[16]—although this was crucial—but also that the presence of the early drafts of this and other works, which are often far more explicit in their social and political attitudes, led to a reappraisal of the whole of Woolf's published and unpublished writings, including a reappraisal of her artistry. By insisting on the significance of the recovered versions, and by altering the "texts" that critics used as the basis of their reading, feminist editors altered the nature of the critical enterprise.

The 1977 issue of the *Bulletin of the New York Public Library,* which could be said to have initiated this particular critical moment, took as its starting point a celebration of "the present strong interest in Woolf documents in our Berg Collection" and the imminent publication of the manuscript of *The Pargiters,* "the essay-novel portion of the manuscript that became *The Years.*"[17] Conceived as a historical critique of the status of women, including their sexuality, from 1880 to the 1930s, *The Pargiters* began by interleaving chapters of a fictional work with analytic essays but soon split apart, evolving not only into *The Years* but also into its polemic counterpart, *Three Guineas.* In the *Bulletin,* Mitchell Leaska, the editor of *The Pargiters,* and Radin, who charted its many transformations, provide a history and examples of the different versions of the work, which include the "Speech before the London/National Society for Women's Service" later called "Professions for Women"—the pre-text for the novel-essay—and the heavily corrected and excised galley proofs. Photographic reproductions of "two enormous chunks" deleted by Woolf from the galleys figure prominently at the center of the issue. The interpretative readings framing the texts move easily between the manuscript, galley, and published versions, as well as taking seriously Woolf's assertion that *The Years* and *Three Guineas* were "one book."[18]

Several areas of feminist and textual practice intersect in this important document. For one thing, it would be hard to overestimate the role that not only Woolf's manuscripts but the collections that housed them played in the feminist reappraisal of Woolf. To the extent that criticism, like works of fiction or poetry, is a social and not an individual act, the gathering of scholars at the Berg Collection and at the University of Sussex Library, the other major repository of Woolf's papers, became the crucible out of which a vital new critical enterprise emerged. The excitement and the collaboration generated by this gathering was palpable and public. Editors and critics, often the same, exchanged information and ideas, checked and double-checked each other's transcriptions, argued editorial formats and theories as well as interpretations, despaired, took heart, and continued to publish. The very existence of the first special issue of the *Bulletin* on Woolf, followed by a second one two years later devoted to the manuscript history and readings of *The Voyage Out* and announcing the publication of one of its manuscript versions, *Melymbrosia,* indicated an institutional commitment to the feminist impetus for change. Jane Marcus, in the "Front Matter" to the first *Bulletin,* called the essays "a collaborative reading of *The Years* and *Three Guineas,*" representative of "the cooperative ideal of contemporary Woolf scholars," and predicted that "this collective effort has rolled back the stone" before the tomb of *The Years* so that no one will call it a "'dead' novel again" (*Bulletin,* 139).

Marcus's prediction raises another important aspect of the revisionary feminist project: the choice of *The Years* as a work deserving serious critical and textual attention. Until this time, most critics of Woolf praised and studied her writings either in terms of psychology and "sensibility," or in the context of a modernism defined through formal experimentation, authorial perspective, symbolic systems, poetry, and a self-conscious attention to art itself. Within this latter context, they focused on *Mrs. Dalloway, To the Lighthouse,* and *The Waves* as the pinnacle of her achievement and viewed her writings in the 1930s, including *The Years* and *Between the Acts,* as a distinct falling off of her artistic powers. The early novels, *The Voyage Out* and *Night and Day,* were seen as interesting but false starts in a more realist manner, while *Jacob's Room* was read as a transitional text. The feminist essays *A Room of One's Own* and, even more so, *Three Guineas* had virtually disappeared. In this light it is not surprising that *The Waves,* situated as an underrated modernist masterpiece, should have been the first work whose manuscripts were considered worth publishing.

But with the publication of *The Pargiters* (1977) and, shortly afterwards, *Melymbrosia* (1982) and *Pointz Hall* (1983)—manuscript versions of *The Voyage Out* and *Between the Acts,* respectively—the perception of Woolf's artistry and the perception of "modernism," defined now as an ideological and gendered as well as aesthetic phenomenon, were indelibly altered. Works that were once considered marginal to Woolf's greatest achievements, and hence to modernism, disrupted the center and critics of Woolf could no longer ignore or dismiss either their presence or their importance.[19] The editors themselves were explicit not only about the ideological, revisionary nature of their project, but also about the role of textual editing within critical controversies. Lucio Ruotolo, for example, describes the special issue of *Twentieth Century Literature* on Woolf as being devoted entirely to previously "unpublished documents whose content further expands the ideological as well as the 'literary' context of her work."[20]

Radin, in her book on *The Years,* provides one rationale for the intersection of feminist and textual critique. In the past, she notes, "scant attention has been paid to [Woolf's] social theories, perhaps because they cluster around feminism, a point of view that has only recently been restored to serious consideration. For this reason *The Years* and its documents are at the heart of the current reappraisal of Woolf, since it is in these uncut documents that her social and political theories are developed most fully" ("*The Years,*" xxii–xxiii). For DeSalvo, the editor of *Melymbrosia,* who painstakingly reconstructed the multiple versions and at least two more or less completed drafts of Woolf's first novel, the convergence is more detailed. The emergence of an earlier, submerged draft, she argues, provides a document on the order of Joyce's *Stephen Hero* and Camus's *La mort heureuse:* "a document that can provide the basis for inquiry, not only into the genesis of Woolf's first novel but also into the creative processes of one of this century's most important writers." But the formal innovations are for DeSalvo, as for the other feminist editors, inseparable from the political contexts in which they occurred: "It is impossible," she adds,

> to read *Melymbrosia* and think of Virginia Woolf as an effete dreamer spinning out her private fantasies in the solitude of her study between bouts of madness. The narrative forces upon us the sense of her involvement with the most important issues of her day, of her awareness that every encounter between women and men occurs within the context of shifting and conflicting societal forces.[21]

But more than the image and understanding of Woolf and her artistry began to change during the period of intense editorial production in the late 1970s: the language used to talk about the manuscript versions and their relationship to the published text also began to shift, reflecting shifts in the idea of the "text" within the broader critical and theoretical environment, in particular the deconstruction of the concept of a stable, unitary text. While it was still common for the editors of Woolf's manuscript versions to talk about the "drafts" as "documents" that provided a "context" for reading the published novel, another discourse began to be heard. DeSalvo hints at this discourse when she calls *Melymbrosia* a "submerged" draft (xiii). Later in her introduction, borrowing terminology as well as theoretical ideas from Sandra Gilbert and Susan Gubar's *The Madwoman in the Attic,* she describes it as "palimpsestic" (xl): a work "whose surface designs conceal or obscure deeper, less accessible (and less socially acceptable) levels of meaning."[22] As a result, in DeSalvo's words, "there are two stories operating simultaneously," a surface story and a more radical "submerged story" that works to subvert and unsettle it, and both are present at once (*Melymbrosia,* xl). While DeSalvo's use of this terminology occurs in her interpretation of the specific text before her, extant draft B of *Melymbrosia,* it echoes backward to her discussion of the multiple texts that are submerged in and in fact constitute the work we now know as *The Voyage Out*. In this light, "the long history of hesitations and revisions in Woolf's composition of *Melymbrosia* and in its transformation into *The Voyage Out*" reveals not several distinct entities, but a vacillation between "mythical" and "realistic (and socially critical) dimensions" (xxxvi) within a single work. Read as one work, the "novel" contains both dimensions simultaneously, but each version foregrounds one or the other.

In this reading, the manuscript versions of a novel cease to be documents that provide background; instead, they produce a new figure, the composite work itself. In the process of effecting this transformation, however, DeSalvo suggests two different, and potentially contradictory, constructions of the relationship of the parts to the whole. One construction evokes Hans Zeller's concept of a "work" as "a diachronic succession of discrete semiotic systems": "If one imagines the textual history [of a work] in the shape of a 3-dimensional cylinder standing upright, then the different versions are horizontal planes perpendicular to the axis of the cylinder."[23] The emphasis both DeSalvo and Elizabeth Heine, whose independent excavations revealed a similarly multi-layered work, place on the discovery that several different distinct versions of the novel were indiscriminately interleaved in the extant manuscript materials supports this view of discrete if interconnected parts, as does DeSalvo's and Leaska's decision to use Woolf's working titles (*Melymbrosia, The Pargiters, Pointz Hall*) for the manuscript versions of the novels they edited. According to Zeller, even if everything else remains the same, a change in title indicates a different set of relationships among the elements in a text and hence a different semiotic system—and a different intention—than that signified by the same work with an alternate title (240–41). In this light, the editorial choice of *Melymbrosia* or *The Pargiters* as title signifies the editors' critical intention to trace the ways in which the versions, while interconnected and three-dimensional, illustrate Woolf's sequentially changing intentions.

But a second construction of the work, one evoked by a contradictory metaphorical system embedded in the image of the palimpsestic text, leads to a different critical project. While DeSalvo, like Zeller, appeals to an architectural metaphor for creation, borrowed from Woolf, in making her argument for Woolf's first novel as a palimpsestic text—"'the best novels are deposited, carefully, bit by bit; and in the end, perhaps they live in all their parts'"[24]—for the most part she and other commentators on the relationship between *Melymbrosia* and *The Voyage Out* echo Woolf's recurrent imagery of depths and merging (tunneling, or digging out caves) rather than hard, discrete objects in describing their perception of Woolf's texts. The goal is to blur the boundaries between planes of existence (or versions), not to distinguish or emphasize them. A typical example occurs in the repeated reference in the criticism to a passage in the earliest versions about the effect of *Religio Medici* on the heroine: "'the words lured her on, with a promise distinct though not definable, of wondrous caverns, and vast luminous vistas concealed below them, and in time they came to undermine her visible world with a labyrinth of dark channels, and to expand her heaven.'"[25]

Once the construct of the palimpsestic work is in place, critics can begin to read within its parameters without necessarily distinguishing between the different versions. What was once perceived as the single, integral work—the published novel—becomes multiple, intertextual. Radin illustrates the beginnings of this activity when she talks about "projecting" the episodes deleted from the galleys of *The Years* "back into the novel";[26] in her own discussion she goes back even farther to the holograph drafts. The effect is to suggest an archaeological project. Later critics, working more explicitly within a poststructuralist framework, have taken this approach even farther. Christine Froula, for example, in a study of Woolf's first novel as a precursor to her ongoing exploration of women's creative authority, agrees with DeSalvo's "view that much valuable material was submerged in the transformation of *Melymbrosia* into *The Voyage Out.* In my discussion, therefore, I treat the two versions as a single composite text, citing *The Voyage Out* when possible and *Melymbrosia* when necessary" to make her points.[27] Froula's textual choice reinforces her interpretative argument that the crucial metaphor within this "composite text" is that of the chrysalis, with its promise of an initiation, a transformation, for its artist-heroine that neither the society, nor the novel, can ultimately support.

One of the most explicit arguments for the critical implications—and potential—of the "composite, palimpsestic text" occurs in the recent work of Susan Stanford Friedman, which brings together psychoanalysis (in particular Freud's writings on dream-work, narrative as disguise, and the role of the "censor"), tenets of textual criticism (including "versioning"), and feminist perspectives. While not at the center of her inquiry, Woolf's multiversioned novels provide an exemplary instance of the "intertextual" reading she proposes. Presenting "women's writing as an insistent record—a trace, a web, a palimpsest, a rune, a disguise—of what has not or cannot be spoken directly because of the external and internalized censors of patriarchal social order,"[28] she turns to textual criticism, in particular the relationship among versions, to illustrate its possibilities for "deciphering the textual and political unconscious in clusters of texts by the same author":

> One kind of cluster is made up of what we conventionally consider the "final" text and its surviving "draft" or "drafts." Another kind is composed of serial texts on related subjects and characters. New Criticism would separate each text into a harmoniously constructed autonomous text. Most textual criticism would privilege the "final" text over the aesthetically inferior "drafts." And a Barthesian post-structuralist approach would ignore authorial and historical (con)texts to read these texts as part of an infinite series of signifying chains empty of meaning. A psycho-political hermeneutic, in contrast, would read these clusters intertextually, psychoanalytically, and politically—as sites of disguised repression and oppression produced by an author who reflects and re-presents a specific moment and process in history. . . . Read intertextually, "drafts" are potentially the "textual unconscious" of the "final" text. (144–45)

But Friedman is not arguing for privileging the "draft" versions any more than she is arguing for a teleological focus on final versions or ends. If "'drafts'" can represent more directly "narrative elements that are repressed and transformed as the author revises the text by the linguistic [and ideological] mechanisms of the dream-work," they can also be read as "'repetitions' in which the author is 'working through' conflicts in an effort . . . to move from 'repetition' to 'remembering.' Within this context, the earlier draft(s) might well be the most repressed, most subject to resistance and transference." What she wants is for critics to read "'both ways.' . . . Rather than searching for the 'authentic' version, this approach regards all versions as part of a larger composite, palimpsestic text whose parts or imperfectly erased layers interact according to a psycho-political dimension" (145, 146).

For Friedman, the dynamic of "reading both ways," which suggests "a new form of intertextual analysis for textual criticism" (146), can be applied to drafts and serial texts by men as well as women; her own extended project is to examine "the processes of self-censorship and the forms of disguised expression in the production of literary modernism."[29] Within this larger work, Woolf will play a major role, in particular for the ways in which the "'drafts'" of novels such as *The Voyage Out* and *The Years* reveal the workings of suppression and repression in the writings of modernist women. For Woolf, along with H.D., illustrates the process of condensing, displacing, or erasing an anger that is culturally forbidden from the "'final,'" public, published versions of their texts.

IV

Friedman's identification of Woolf's revisions with repression, suppression, and anger brings to the fore one of the most contested aspects of the intersection of textual criticism and feminist practice: self-censorship. From the moment Woolf's editors began to present and explore the manuscript versions and the documentary history of her novels as a primary source for understanding the depth and commitment of her cultural critique, they also began to debate the role of self-censorship in her revisions. Each novel poses its own set of questions about self-censorship, including those pertinent to the specific historical and personal contexts that surrounded its production. But one recurring issue is the fine line between self-editing and self-censorship, a distinction that is often difficult if not impossible to make, as Donald Pizer has suggested,[30] particularly when there is no external editor/censor: when, as in Woolf's case, the power of censorship seems to come from within. For as Woolf herself once commented, apropos of the Hogarth Press, she might well have been "the only woman in England free to write"—or publish—what she liked.[31] But that freedom was necessarily relative; and Woolf continually struggled with the question of what she could say out loud, and in what tone of voice, without alienating her readers. In this way, the specter of an external critic became one of the multitude of factors that inevitably play a role in the process of revision, including the writer's awareness of her audience.

Woolf's feminist editors and critics brought to her drafts a keen awareness of the social as well as aesthetic factors that make any published work, in Pizer's use of the term, a "palimpsest": a text that emerges out of and inscribes the tensions of the period in which it was written and revised ("Self-Censorship," 155). As a result the debates take as given not only Woolf's commitment to social analysis and critique but also the external and internal pressures inscribed in her expression of these views. This leads them to ask whether the early, private versions of the novels are more explicit and hence more powerful expressions of Woolf's social and political critique, including her anger, than the published versions, and if so, whether and why this critique was edited out as the novels moved into the public realm. Do the revisions constitute self-censorship and, if so, are they attributable to Woolf's belief that art and propaganda should not mix—that is, to aesthetic concerns—or to fear?

To pose the question in this way is to foreground the potentially binary distinction between self-censorship, with its connotation of either politics and ideology or unconscious psychic mechanisms, and self-editing, with its connotation of conscious artistry: an opposition that feminist criticism, often using Woolf as its example, has worked to deconstruct.[32] For fear, it seems to me, resides just as much in critics/readers as in writers. This raises the question, on the one hand, of how much the nervousness created by the term *self-censorship,* often located in nonfeminist responses, suggests a fear that Woolf the social critic, or Woolf the woman caught up in gender and its often unconscious inscriptions, might obscure Woolf the artist and hence the value of her art, while evoking, on the other hand, a fear, often located in feminist critics, that Woolf might have valued her art at the expense of her anger. To put this another way, why do critics often seem afraid of a Woolf whose own experiments in breaking down the boundaries between art and social commentary, internal and external, vividly exemplify the sociability of art's creation and reception?

An exploration of the broader questions of "art," politics, and value—and what constitutes an effective political art—lies outside the scope of this essay, but the issues raised by the debate about self-censorship within Woolf studies can help define its terms, particularly when the debate is situated within its historical moment. Although most of this debate has occurred in the realm we associate with interpretation, interpretation here cannot easily be separated from the documents that generate it and the discourses, or assumptions, that surround it. As Pizer notes, while self-censorship among artists has probably always existed, it became a major preoccupation in the editing and criticism of nineteenth- and twentieth-century fiction primarily because of "the availability of manuscript evidence demonstrating or suggesting that self-censorship occurred" ("Self-Censorship," 144–45). In Woolf's case, it was not until the mid-1960s and early 1970s that the vast amount of manuscript materials in the Berg Collection and, later, the University of Sussex, became available, materials that made it possible to know much more about her methods and her thoughts; it was also in the mid-1960s that women began to enter graduate schools in substantial numbers and to ask the questions that led to a feminist critique. The rise of the women's movement during this period, including consciousness raising, also played a crucial role. The timing here, the conjunction of historical factors (and I am providing only a cursory view), meant that almost from the beginning the assumptions brought to Woolf's manuscripts would reflect feminist perspectives and concerns. This conjunction also provides a historical gloss for Reiman's assumption that "versioning" implies an author and issues raised by the documentary history of her work—in this case those framed by a feminist analysis—important enough to warrant both extended critical discussion and a demand for more versions.

One of the major concerns framing and framed by the feminist contributions to "versioning" was anger. Whatever stance early feminist commentators took on the debate between self-editing and self-censorship, and whether they ultimately find the final work aesthetically better or worse, almost all of them agree that what was lost in the revisions was the explicitness of Woolf's cultural critique, including her expression of anger. It is not surprising that feminist editors in the 1970s, engaged in recuperating not only Woolf's submerged texts but their social and political implications, should have made anger a major site for assessing her self-censorship. As I have argued elsewhere, this moment in Woolf scholarship coincided with a reevaluation of anger as a political tool that was occurring simultaneously in a number of arenas, academic and activist alike.[33] What was being questioned was both the long history of political, critical, and psychological discourses that have condemned women's anger—along with that of other marginalized and subordinate groups—as destructive of "civilized" behavior and established authority, and the role these discourses have played in silencing personal and political expression. The effect was to deconstruct the supposedly universal rules governing critical discourse and reveal them as myths: rhetorical claims made "by the dominant about their legitimacy."[34]

Nor is it surprising that Woolf became a central figure for feminist critics struggling to find a voice to speak within the public realm, including the academy. Adrienne Rich both identified the struggle and located it in Woolf when she wrote how in rereading *A Room of One's Own* she recognized a tone common to herself and other women: "the tone of a woman almost in touch with her anger, who is determined not to appear angry, who is *willing* herself to be calm, detached, and even charming in a roomful of men where things have been said which are attacks on her very integrity."[35] The "willing" is crucial here, and it found support in Woolf's own statements about anger, including the comment in *A Room of One's Own* that in *Jane Eyre* "it is clear that anger was tampering with the integrity of Charlotte Brontë the novelist," interfering with the art and producing a book that is "deformed and twisted" (76, 72). This statement not only led feminist critics to look more closely at the anger in nineteenth-century women's novels—and helped support Gilbert and Gubar's contention that the submerged text in their novels, exemplified graphically in *Jane Eyre,* was often one of rage (*Madwoman,* 338)—but also encouraged them to look beyond Woolf's explicitly polemical tracts to her own novels for their political messages—and their "willfully" suppressed anger. And to the extent that Woolf's novels, like Brontë's, were perceived to be palimpsestic, it made sense to look to the submerged manuscript versions for their expression of anger and cultural criticism and to explore the revisions through the lens of possible self-censorship.

Within this context, *The Years* was the logical first choice for feminist "versioning" and analysis. For one thing, so many of the documents, ranging from drafts of the originary "Speech before the London / National Society for Women's Service, January 31, 1931" to galley and page proofs, were available, and Woolf so clearly deleted or altered passages with explicit sexual, feminist, or antiwar statements as late as the galley stage.[36] The holograph and typescript versions of the "Speech" proved especially fruitful, for in them Woolf not only illustrates how strongly she can express her opinions about "the masculine point of view" and war ("a stupid and violent and hateful and idiotic and trifling and ignoble and mean display"), but makes what are perhaps her clearest statements about the difficulty women writers have in describing their sexuality ("womens bodies for instance—their passions"), attributing it to the "prudery of men," the strength of literary and social conventions, and the danger inherent in defying those conventions ("I should need the courage of a hero") of becoming "hard and shrill and positive," of "[ceasing] to be writer."[37] In addition, the ample evidence of her early excitement and her subsequent struggle to finish the novel, provided by documents such as her letters and diaries, made it possible to argue that

Woolf's original intention was to write a novel that would trace "the sexual life of women" and contain "millions of ideas but no preaching—history, politics, feminism, art, literature—in short a summing up of all I know, feel, laugh at, despise, like, admire, hate and so on,"[38] and to use this as the basis for asking, Why the change? As Radin illustrates, one recurring note in the diary was her "horror of the Aldous [Huxley] novel," "something that I wont call propaganda" (*Diary* 4:281; in Radin, "*The Years,*" 61–62). Finally, the discovery that Woolf's name for her fictional family in the novel, the Pargiters, was rooted etymologically in the word "parget," defined in the *English Dialect Dictionary* edited by Joseph Wright (who appears by name in the novel-essay version) as "to plaster with cement or mortar," or "to whitewash," and that "pargeter" appears in the *Oxford English Dictionary* not only as "a plasterer; a whitewasher" but by figurative extension "one who glosses and smoothes over," aroused speculation about how much Woolf herself contributed to the process of cultural whitewashing she was illustrating in her text: how much, that is, did she "parget" in her revisions, including the change in the title of the novel from *The Pargiters* to *The Years*?[39]

The assumption was that she did "parget," not only in producing *The Years* but in other of her novels, and this assumption reflects another aspect of "versioning" implicit in feminist explorations of self-censorship: the debate among textual critics about "authorial intention" and whether one should read successive versions as if they are moving inexorably toward some better end (what Stephen Parrish calls the "Whig interpretation" of textual history).[40] Here, the two constructs of the composite "work"—Zeller's "diachronic succession of discrete semiotic systems" and the more intertextual palimpsest—come into play as well. Like Parrish, the advocates of both constructs appear to reject the belief, implicit in Graham's edition of *The Waves,* that there was a fixed intention, or even multiple intentions, that govern the outcome and establish the value of the final version. But their ways of reading the instability established by this rejection differ, as do their interpretations. To some extent, the timing of the versions is important here, as well as changes in critical and theoretical orientation; what emerges is a shift in the representation of the relationship of "original intention" to "final" work from a one-way street to a more complex network of impulses.

Based on the documentary material for *The Years,* both Leaska, who edited *The Pargiters,* and Radin, who traced the evolution of *The Years* as a whole, posit an original intention and a movement away from it.

Both agree that Woolf deleted and smoothed over—"pargeted"—materials that were more explicitly sexual and angry in the earlier versions, and both agree that in part the revisions are grounded in formal, aesthetic concerns. Where they differ is in their assessment of what was gained and lost, and this in turn suggests different perspectives on the relationship between Woolf's artistic demands and less easily indentifiable factors, including self-censorship. For Leaska, who asks "Is the author creating with one part of her mind and at the same time editing—perhaps censoring—with another part?" (*The Pargiters,* xxii), the pargeting did not necessarily constitute a loss, particularly in terms of its political explicitness ("some preaching does indeed cloud many of the novel's pages" [*The Pargiters,* xvii]). The framework for answering the question of self-censorship, provided in his "interpretative" essay rather than his introduction to the text, takes the reader into the recesses of Woolf's psyche; tracing the changes in the portrayal of Abel Pargiter, the Victorian patriarch, and his daughters' reactions to him, he attributes them to Woolf's awareness "that her unconscious mind was exhuming material of a seriously confessional kind" that "had in some way to be smoothed over and glossed if [it] were to be made acceptable"—although to whom is left unclear ("Virginia Woolf, the Pargeter," 180). But the results, in his view, are clearly beneficial: in the process of transforming the novel-essay into fiction only, "Woolf as novelist was also forced into becoming a pargeter—and ultimately one of great artistic fluency and moral courage" (*The Pargiters,* xix). Nevertheless, he defines his goal in his edition as providing "the reader with what might be looked upon as a slow-moving picture of Virginia Woolf—unobserved and uncensored—during those vibrant moments of creation" (*The Pargiters,* xxii).

In almost direct contrast, Radin, whose frameworks for assessing the revisions are more social and political than aesthetic and psychological, reads the revisions as a failure of courage and locates this failure in Woolf's "fear of becoming shrill and one-sided, of allowing her ideas to destroy her art" ("*The Years,*" xvii). Radin also directs readers to the earlier versions of the novel, which she describes as "a spontaneous outburst, an expression of anger, irritation, and disdain for the 'masculine point of view.' As was her wont," Radin continues, "when Woolf rewrote she softened her remarks and placed them in a broader context, believing that this would make them more palatable and persuasive" to her readers ("*The Years,*" 4). "By the time the novel was published," she concludes, Woolf "had softened, deleted, or made vague many of her strongest attacks on English society and its treatment of women and had eliminated most of the overt statements of her own beliefs," including her belief in women's need to acknowledge all of their impulses. "Sadly, the differences between her first draft and the novel and essay [*Three Guineas*] she published reveal that there had come a moment when her courage failed" (*"The Years,"* 35).

The identification and rhetoric of an original intention and a movement through sequential versions away from it also colors the early discussion of *The Voyage Out*. DeSalvo, for example, even as she represents *Melymbrosia* as a "submerged" draft of a palimpsestic work, shares with Radin the perception that Woolf concealed her anger by deleting the social and cultural criticism from the published version or making it more oblique; in terms of the novels' feminist and political content, both read the revisions as moving in one direction only and experience the changes as a loss. In *The Voyage Out,* the loss resides for the most part in the revisions that changed the heroine, Rachel, in Elizabeth Heine's formulation, from "an intelligent, outspoken, critical young feminist" to a "vague and innocently naive dreamer,"[41] and took the sting out of Rachel's aunt, Helen Ambrose's, ironic attitude toward men. Citing passages from a version that preceded even *Melymbrosia* and the response it evoked from Woolf's brother-in-law Clive Bell that her "prejudice against men makes [her] didactic 'not to say priggish,'" DeSalvo argues that Woolf began by writing "an angry novel" about the erosion of women's power and that she was "terrified by the force of her own prose, about the depth of the rage and anger which gave her prose its power—not an uncommon problem for women writers" (*Melymbrosia,* xxiii, xxxii–xxxiii). By the time Woolf completed *Melymbrosia* and began the draft of what became *The Voyage Out,* DeSalvo writes, "'Melymbrosia' indeed was becoming 'The Voyage Out'—a voyage away from the bluntness, candor, and the openness with which she had dealt with the reasons why women like Rachel and Helen are incapable of forming emotional attachments to men" ("Sorting," 284). The change in title for DeSalvo, as for Zeller, signifies a change in Woolf's perspective, or intention, and hence a change of the relations within the work as a whole.

Again self-censorship is implied, but not named, although DeSalvo does, tentatively, use the term in the companion book she published on the history of Woolf's first novel ("Her decision not to publish this version of 'Melymbrosia' seems to have been an act of self-censorship").[42] It "seems" as if Woolf's editors, at least in their role as editors, were wary of using the term, even if it appears in their more "interpretative" essays. Once the manuscript versions were known and available, however, and critics began to see a pattern in Woolf's revisions of her social critique, the discourse began to change. Alex Zwerdling, for example, who finds many feminist readings of Woolf ahistorical, unhesitatingly represents Woolf's historically situated choices—her "deliberate inhibition of anger" (*Virginia Woolf,* 245)—as "self-censorship" rather than "self-editing." Zwerdling's usage simultaneously undercuts and reinforces the disjunction between the political and aesthetic impulses in Woolf's revisions. On the one hand, he argues that Woolf's "decision to inhibit her anger . . . was not only literary; it was also political, and rooted in the tradition of nineteenth-century feminist writing" (247), a portrayal that makes Woolf an active agent rather than a passive victim of "fears." But he also feels that something was lost by this decision, and his description of this loss potentially reinscribes the aesthetic / political dichotomy: "Her self-censorship made her published work more refined and etiolated and helped to establish the image of her esthetic withdrawal. Fortunately," he continues, "what could not be published during her lifetime has been preserved" and published; "the manuscripts that have now found their way into print reveal that the words she kept from the public were often as striking as those familiar to an earlier generation of readers" (37).

In contrast to the unidirectional view of the revisions as self-censorship and loss that I have been outlining, Friedman's practice of reading "both ways" and her construction of a composite, palimpsestic text produce a dual discourse and a dual interpretation. Writing about the revisions that changed the representation of the heroine and distinguish *Melymbrosia* from *The Voyage Out,* Friedman agrees with DeSalvo's interpretation that self-censorship was at work and extends it to other women as well: "For a number of women writers in the modernist period, revisions of [their] texts reflected a sometimes conscious, sometimes unconscious negotiation between the desire to speak and the need to repress what was forbidden in their narratives of modernity. Often revisions, in making their texts more artfully modernist, also disguised the inscribed desire through mechanisms of condensation, displacement, and representation akin to the grammar of the dream-work described by Freud in *The Interpretation of Dreams.*" "However," she continues, "self-censorship does not fully explain the changes in Rachel. . . ."[43] Reading backward as well as forward, and using Freud's theories about repetition and recollection, she argues that in her later versions "Woolf was able to confront what she had repressed in the earlier drafts—namely, that part of herself which she considered 'dangerous' to her health." In other words, for Friedman, the revisions did not just censor Woolf's anger; they also allowed her to assess her own strength in comparison to that of her fictional heroine and illustrate the dangers of repression and censorship themselves. In this reading, Woolf not only becomes an agent in the act of revision, but actively confronts her fears rather than letting them control her.

Friedman's shift in emphasis, it could be argued, attests as much to contemporary feminist theory as it does to textual theory. Nevertheless, Friedman's insistence that the composite, palimpsestic work reveals continually shifting scenes of repression, censorship, and confrontation and not a linear progression both acknowledges McGann's influence and helps to validate his concept of the unstable text. Her concept of the "work" and how one approaches it is much closer, for example, to McGann's formulation of the "text" as unstable and multiple than it is to either Tanselle's integrated work of art or even Zeller's versions. Her reading of *Melymbrosia/The Voyage Out,* like Gabler's reading of Joyce's *Ulysses* in McGann's interpretation of it, "overhauls *the way we think about the text as a whole,*" and "forces us to think of [*The Voyage Out* or] *Ulysses* as something other than a given object of interpretation on the one hand (which is the traditional and New Critical view), or as an invention of interpretation on the other (which is the common poststructural view)." In this construction, "a number of different [*Voyage Outs*] begin to occupy the space of critical possibility."[44] In addition, Friedman's "interpretation," rooted as it is in a specific construction of a specific "text"—a composite, palimpsestic text—underlines McGann's contention that "the interpretative act 'constitutes meaning' . . . only in terms that are licensed by the received socio-history of the text. And that socio-history, for *texts,* is constituted at its most elementary level as a set of empirical documents whose meaning is intimately bound up with the socio-history of the documents" ("*Ulysses,*" 295). As a result, "textual meaning is not an 'idea' or an interpretive function—is not, that is to say, a textual supplement. Rather, textual meaning is always materially constituted *as* some particular text (in the documentary sense)" ("*Ulysses,*" 297).

Within this framework, the intersections of feminist practice and textual criticism outlined in this essay begin to reveal the inseparability of interpretations of Woolf's novels and the "author" from the socio-history of the manuscript versions and the way they alter both the "texts" we analyze and how we analyze them. In this light, the widely accepted view of Woolf today as a serious political and social commentator is inseparable from the publication of the manuscript versions by feminist critics for whom the existence of these "texts" necessarily destabilized the published versions of the novels and the versions of Woolf they had generated. To ignore the existence of the reconfigured texts that resulted is to limit what Woolf potentially "means" to her audience, to be afraid of Virginia Woolf and what her gaze can teach us. The palimpsestic text created by the presence of the manuscript versions and its critical reception, as in Pizer's construction, provides "a record of our civilization in the different ways that other men [and women] at other times have read it" ("Self-Censorship," 155–56).

Unfortunately, since the explosion of energy and editions that recorded the creative intersection of textual criticism and feminist practice, no new manuscript versions of Woolf's novels have appeared. The prepublication versions of many of her novels, as well as of her two polemical works, remain submerged.[45] Given the powerful rereadings of those novels that have been "versioned," this constitutes a powerful loss. The new editions of Woolf's novels that will appear in the next few years should alert readers to the presence of the manuscript versions, published or not, as well as necessarily altering, through their very presence, our perceptions of her work. The words on Woolf's manuscript pages, like the portrait of Woolf that hangs on the wall of my study, may not provide any definitive answers, but I do not view this situation with horror. Instead, Woolf's palimpsestic texts suggest to me, if not to Hanif Kureishi, the ways in which Virginia Woolf, the "writer" as well as the "author," speaks directly to a postmodern audience and continues to empower its cultural critique.

NOTES

My thanks to Mary Childers, Lynn A. Higgins, Lee Mitchell, and, especially, George Bornstein and S. P. Rosenbaum, who suggested bibliography and provided commentary on the different versions of this essay.

1. Alex Zwerdling, *Virginia Woolf and the Real World* (Berkeley: University of California Press, 1986), 33. Hereafter cited as *Virginia Woolf.*

2. *The Diary of Virginia Woolf,* ed. Anne Olivier Bell, vol. 2 (New York: Harcourt Brace Jovanovich, 1978), 272, 263.

3. See Jerome J. McGann on the "poetic presences" of the alternate versions of Auden's "September 1939" in any single version: "The Monks and the Giants: Textual and Bibliographical Studies and the Interpretation of Literary Works," *Textual Criticism and Literary Interpretation,* ed. McGann (Chicago: University of Chicago Press, 1985), 196. See also McGann's definition of "the 'work'" as "a series of specific 'texts,' a series of specific acts of production, and the entire process which both of these series constitute" in *A Critique of Modern Textual Criticism* (Chicago: University of Chicago Press, 1983), 52.

4. Virginia Woolf, *A Room of One's Own* (New York: Harcourt Brace Jovanovich, 1929), 7.

5. These include new editions planned by Hogarth Press, Penguin, Oxford University Press, and Basil Blackwell's Shakespeare Head Press.

6. The forthcoming editions of Woolf's novels will chronicle how extensive the differences are. Once the novels were in print, however, with the exception of *The Voyage Out,* Woolf did not revise them again. For a discussion of Woolf's revisions of her proofs and the results in one specific case, see Glenn P. Wright, "The Raverat Proofs of *Mrs. Dalloway,*" *Studies in Bibliography* 39 (1986): 241–61.

7. Donald Reiman, *Romantic Texts and Contexts* (Columbia, Mo.: University of Missouri Press, 1987), 169; hereafter cited in text.

8. Wallace Hildick, *Word for Word* (London: Faber and Faber, 1965); hereafter cited in text. Charles G. Hoffman, "From Short Story to Novel: The Manuscript Revisions of Virginia Woolf's *Mrs. Dalloway,*" *Modern Fiction Studies* 14 (Summer 1968): 171–86; "From Lunch to Dinner: Virginia Woolf's Apprenticeship," *Texas Studies in Literature and Language* 10 (Winter 1969): 609–27; "Fact and Fantasy in *Orlando*: Virginia Woolf's Manuscript Revisions," *Texas Studies in Literature and Language* 10 (Fall 1968): 435–44; "Virginia Woolf's Manuscript Revisions of *The Years,*" *PMLA* 84 (1969): 79–89. The publication of Woolf's *A Writer's Diary,* edited by Leonard Woolf, in 1953, followed by the publication of Leonard's diaries in the 1960s, had already alerted critics to the extended process of revision underlying Woolf's novels and to the existence of the manuscript versions. On the lack of interest in these manuscripts in England and Leonard's sale of them to American booksellers, see *Letters of Leonard Woolf,* ed. Frederic Spotts (San Diego: Harcourt Brace Jovanovich, 1989), 499–500.

9. Lucio Ruotolo, "Preface," *Twentieth Century Literature* 25 (1979): ii.

10. John Graham, "Editing a Manuscript: Virginia Woolf's *The Waves,*" in *Editing Twentieth Century Texts,* ed. Francess G. Halpenny (Toronto and Buffalo: University of Toronto Press, 1972), 77–92. Hereafter cited as "Editing a Manuscript." Graham's edition of *The Waves: The Two Holograph Drafts,* hereafter cited as *Holograph,* was published by University of Toronto Press (1976).

11. McGann, *A Critique of Modern Textual Criticism,* 8 and passim.

12. See, for example, G. Thomas Tanselle, "The Editorial Problem of Final Authorial Intention," *Studies in Bibliography* 29 (1976): 167–211. My argument is not intended to dismiss the role of aesthetic choices in Woolf's revisions or to deny her artistry, but to illustrate how critical assumptions at this time, as later, shape the presentation of her texts and the interpretations suggested by this presentation.

13. Virginia Woolf, "Women and Fiction," in *Collected Essays,* vol. 2 (New York: Harcourt, Brace and World, 1967), 147–48.

14. Graham's literal transcription of the manuscripts, with the strike-outs, substitutions, marginalia, and interlinear insertions presented just as they are on Woolf's page—a practice made possible in 1972 by the "flexibility and economy of a modern sophisticated typewriter and offset lithography" (Halpenny, *Editing Twentieth Century Texts,* 4)—is, when feasible, the preferable method, introducing the least editorial inference. The role of technology in editorial practice deserves more attention; Reiman, for example, notes the potential of the photofacsimile in making "versioning" a reality (*Romantic Texts and Contexts,* 172).

15. Madeline Moore, "Another Version of Virginia Woolf," *Women's Studies* 4 (1977): 149. Moore's title echoes that of the Virginia Woolf Seminar at the Modern Language Association Meetings in December 1974; the first Virginia Woolf Symposium was held at the University of California, Santa Cruz, November 1974.

16. Grace Radin, *Virginia Woolf's "The Years": The Evolution of a Novel* (Knoxville: University of Tennessee Press, 1981), xviii. Hereafter cited as *"The Years."*

17. "Front Matter," *Bulletin of the New York Public Library* 80 (Winter 1977): 137. Hereafter cited as *Bulletin.*

18. *The Diary of Virginia Woolf,* ed. Anne Olivier Bell, vol. 5 (San Diego: Harcourt Brace Jovanovich, 1984), 148.

19. The other manuscript version published during this period, Susan Dick's edition of the original holograph draft of *To the Lighthouse* (Toronto and Buffalo: University of Toronto Press, 1982), follows Graham's edition of *The Waves* both in its format (literal transcriptions) and its formalist, biographical approach to the revisions, including the assumption of an intentional movement toward an aesthetic end.

20. Ruotolo, "Preface," iii. The "documents" are "The Journal of Mistress Joan Martyn," edited by Susan M. Squier and Louise A. DeSalvo, a story about a woman social historian that includes the fictional diary of a young woman in the sixteenth century; "Friendships Gallery," edited by Ellen Hawkes, a "'spoof biography' of Woolf's friend and teacher Violet Dickinson" (iii); extracts from

the manuscript of *Orlando* deleted by Woolf in the published version and edited by Madeline Moore; and "Anon" and "The Reader," edited by Brenda R. Silver, reconstructions of the first two essays written for the history of English literature left unfinished when Woolf died.

21. *Melymbrosia: An Early Version of "The Voyage Out,"* ed. Louise A. DeSalvo (New York: New York Public Library, 1982), x, xxxvii. Hereafter cited as *Melymbrosia.*

22. Sandra M. Gilbert and Susan Gubar, *The Madwoman in the Attic: The Woman Writer and the Nineteenth-Century Literary Imagination* (New Haven: Yale University Press, 1979), 73. Hereafter cited as *Madwoman.*

23. Hans Zeller, "A New Approach to the Critical Constitution of Literary Texts," *Studies in Bibliography* 28 (1975): 244.

24. Woolf is quoted in Louise A. DeSalvo, "Sorting, Sequencing, and Dating the Drafts of Virginia Woolf's *The Voyage Out," Bulletin of the New York Public Library* 82 (Autumn 1979): 288. Hereafter cited as "Sorting."

25. See, e.g., Elizabeth Heine, "The Earlier *Voyage Out:* Virginia Woolf's First Novel," *Bulletin of the New York Public Library* 82 (Autumn 1979): 308.

26. Grace Radin, "'Two Enormous Chunks': Episodes Excluded during the Final Revisions of *The Years,*" *Bulletin of the New York Public Library* 80 (Winter 1977): 227. Hereafter cited as "'Two Enormous Chunks.'"

27. Christine Froula, "Out of the Chrysalis: Female Initiation and Female Authority in Virginia Woolf's *The Voyage Out,*" *Tulsa Studies in Women's Literature* 5 (1986): 89.

28. Susan Stanford Friedman, "The Return of the Repressed in Women's Narrative," *Journal of Narrative Technique* 19 (Winter 1989): 142.

29. Susan Stanford Friedman, *Return of the Repressed in Modernist Narratives.* Manuscript.

30. Donald Pizer, "Self-Censorship and Textual Editing," in *Textual Criticism and Literary Interpretation,* ed. McGann, 144–61. Hereafter cited as "Self-Censorship."

31. *The Diary of Virginia Woolf,* ed. Anne Olivier Bell, vol. 3 (New York: Harcourt Brace Jovanovich, 1980), 43. After she died the situation was different, and critics have questioned whether Leonard Woolf and Quentin Bell, her literary executors, have attempted to censor the more feminist, political aspects of her writing. See, e.g., Jane Marcus, "'No More Horses': Virginia Woolf on Art and Propaganda," *Women's Studies* 4 (1977): 265–89. But for the most part, the debates about censorship have focused on Woolf's revisions.

32. Other critics have also resisted the dichotomy. See, e.g., Pizer, "Self-Censorship"; and Zeller, "Critical Constitution of Literary Texts," 247: "if one has to reckon with purely literary and purely censorial motives for alteration, one must also reckon with a combination of the two." The status of the "self" in these debates needs further exploration.

33. See my essay "The Authority of Anger: The Case of *Three Guineas,*" *Signs: Journal of Women in Culture and Society* 16 (Winter 1991): 340–70.

34. The quotation comes from Peter Lyman, "The Politics of Anger: On Silence, Ressentiment, and Political Speech," *Socialist Review* 11, no. 3 (1981): 67.

35. Adrienne Rich, "When We Dead Awaken: Writing as Re-Vision," reprinted in Rich, *On Lies, Secrets, and Silence* (New York: Norton, 1979), 37.

36. See Radin, "'Two Enormous Chunks'" and "*The Years*"; see also Susan M. Squier, "A Track of Our Own: Typescript Drafts of *The Years,*" in *Virginia Woolf: A Feminist Slant,* ed. Jane Marcus (Lincoln: University of Nebraska Press, 1983), 198–211. Squier prints and discusses a typescript version of a debate among the Pargiter women about women's responsibility to patriarchal society and the possibility of a feminist society in the future—a debate considerably less combative, and less optimistic, in the published version.

37. These excerpts appear in Radin, "*The Years,*" 4, 6–7; and Virginia Woolf, *The Pargiters: The Novel-Essay Portion of "The Years,"* ed. Mitchell A. Leaska (New York: New York Public Library and Readex Books, 1977), xxxix. The latter work will be cited hereafter as *The Pargiters.* The full passage about war memoirs in the holograph reads, "If I were reviewing books now, I would say this [a participant's memoir of World War I] was a stupid and violent and hateful and idiotic and trifling and ignoble and mean display. I would say I am bored to death by war books. I detest the masculine point of view. I am bored by his heroics, virtue and honour." The holograph also reads, "literature which is always pulling down the blinds is not literature. All that we have ought to be expressed—mind and body—a process of incredible difficulty and danger" (Radin, "*The Years,*" 6).

38. *The Diary of Virginia Woolf,* ed. Anne Olivier Bell, vol. 4 (New York: Harcourt Brace Jovanovich, 1982), 6, 152. Hereafter cited as *Diary* 4.

39. Jane Marcus traced the connection; Mitchell Leaska quotes the definitions. See Marcus, "*The Years* as Greek Drama, Domestic Novel, and Götterdämmerung," and Mitchell A. Leaska, "Virginia Woolf, the Pargeter: A Reading of *The Years,*" both in *Bulletin of the New York Public Library* 80 (Winter 1977): 280 and 172–74. Hereafter Leaska's work is cited as "Virginia Woolf, the Pargeter." The novel also had a number of other possible titles between these two.

40. S. M. Parrish, "The Whig Interpretation of Literature," *Text* 4 (1988): 345, 349.

41. Heine, "The Earlier *Voyage Out,*" 294.

42. Louise A. DeSalvo, *Virginia Woolf's First Voyage: A Novel in the Making* (Totowa, N.J.: Rowman and Littlefield, 1980), 63.

43. Susan Stanford Friedman, "Virginia Woolf's Pedagogical Scenes of Reading: *The Voyage Out, The Common Reader,* and Her 'Common Readers,'" *Modern Fiction Studies,* forthcoming Spring 1992.

44. Jerome J. McGann, "*Ulysses* as a Postmodern Text: The Gabler Edition," *Criticism* 27 (Summer 1985): 291; hereafter cited as "*Ulysses*."

45. One exciting addition, however, is presently in progress: S. P. Rosenbaum's edition of the manuscript version of *A Room of One's Own*, which will be published by Blackwell's with Woolf's original title for the work, *Women & Fiction*.

Censorship and Self-Censorship in the Fiction of D. H. Lawrence

Eugene Goodheart

I begin with a confession. I have been one of the benighted who never took textual criticism seriously. The goal of achieving an impeccable text has a certain aesthetic appeal, but it never seemed to me that the small differences that preoccupied textual scholars seriously affected the matters of interpretation that concerned me. I do not therefore belong to the company of distinguished textual scholars among my companions in this volume. My testimony may have a particular interest, however. What happens when a literary critic who has already done some work on D. H. Lawrence reconsiders him in the light of issues raised by textual criticism? What has he learned from textual criticism that affects his understanding of Lawrence? The "authoritative" editions of Lawrence's work, recently published by Cambridge University Press, provide an opportunity for answering these questions.

I place *authoritative* in quotation marks because of the theoretical assaults that have been launched on the idea of an authoritative text with its implications of objectivity and autonomy. For some scholars and critics the first question may be not what kind of textual criticism should we require, but whether textual criticism is possible at all.

There is, of course, more than one kind of challenge to the autonomous text. The most radical challenge, which would make the textual enterprise an exercise in futility, denies the real existence of an objective text. This view has received its most influential expression in the work of Stanley Fish. Fish attacks the assumption "that there *is* a sense, that it is embedded or encoded in the text, and that it can be taken in at a single glance." Fish proposes to put "the readers' activities . . . at the center of attention, where they are regarded not as leading to meaning but as *having* meaning."[1] The issue here is not simply whether there is an authoritative text or not; it is whether the text exists at all apart from the readers' making of it through acts of interpretation. A reader-centered criticism attacks the root meaning of an *author*itative text. Such a view effectively invalidates the project of establishing authentic texts, since authenticity is in the eye of the beholder, and no particular perspective on the text is privileged.

One need not endorse the constitutive model of reader response to question the traditional assumption of textual criticism that a definitive text, based on a knowledge of the final intentions of the author, is possible. The claim for the objective text does not solve the problem of establishing an authoritative text. Thus in the interests of the enterprise itself Jerome McGann has advocated a revision of the assumptions of the editorial enterprise as they had been formulated by W. W. Greg and Fredson Bowers. According to McGann, the text is a historical phenomenon, a social construction, involving a collaboration of author and publisher. "Final authority for literary works rests neither with the author nor with his affiliated institution: it resides in the actual structure of the agreements which these two cooperating authorities reach in specific cases."[2] McGann's view is a version of the transactive model of reader response. It does not deny authorial intention and the structure realized by that intention, but it refuses to allow the author the final say, because the structure and what it contains (episodes, language, etc.) is shaped and reshaped by the way it is received and transmitted by the publisher to an audience, which in turn contributes to the making of the text. McGann's editorial model challenges not only the authority of "final intentions," but also the principle, in another traditional view of the editorial function, that the editor must seek the "best text" among the extant documents. Where the doctrine of final intentions gives authority to the author, the doctrine of the best text gives it to the editor's literary judgment. For McGann the text is not a determinate result, but a process, which the editor seeks to represent as accurately as possible. The McGann view is not uncontested, but it is the insurgent view, which has great appeal to those committed to historicist and sociological approaches. What happens when the text is regarded as a process: how does this view inform the particular judgments one might make in the concrete case?

What I propose to do is to examine various cruxes in the Cambridge Lawrence editions in order to test the claims of one or another editorial approach and, above all, to see what it is we learn about Lawrence's work in adjudicating these claims. I did not begin my study of the Cambridge edition with a commitment to a particular editorial theory and practice; I did begin with a strong sense of Lawrence's work, which helped me make judgments about the editorial decisions that were made. I tried, however, to keep my sense of Lawrence sufficiently in suspension so that it would be possible for the editorial process to enrich and even alter my sense of Lawrence. The works I will consider are *The White Peacock, The Rainbow, Women in Love, Aaron's Rod,* and *The Plumed Serpent,* with occasional references to *The Lost Girl* and *The Prussian Officer and Other Stories.* My omission of *Sons and Lovers* and *Lady Chatterley's Lover* is dictated by the simple fact that the Cambridge editions of those works were not available when I wrote this essay.

We might begin with a passage from Lawrence's first novel, *The White Peacock.* The first American edition, which preserves the manuscript version, gives the following: "God—we were a passionate couple and she would have me in her bedroom while she drew Greek statues of me—her Groton, her Hercules! I never saw her drawings." Believing that Lawrence's audience would find the passage objectionable, Heinemann, Lawrence's English publisher, asked Lawrence to change it for the English edition. Lawrence reluctantly agreed and produced the following: "Lord—we were an infatuate couple—and she would choose to view me in an aesthetic light. I was Greek statues for her, bless you: Groton, Hercules, I don't know what." "Passionate" and "bedroom" have been safely removed.[3]

The example of attempted censorship, whether externally imposed or reluctantly agreed to by the author, represents a formidable obstacle to a historicist approach to editing. The very idea of censorship brings the question of intention into the foreground, for censorship entails the counterforce of authorial desire or intentions. If there were no intention, then the alterations produced by an intentionless and consequently authorless text would not be described as censorship. The question of *final* intention may prove to be a diversion from the problem. We certainly don't need the notion of finality to recognize that Lawrence gave his publisher something he wanted printed and that the publisher compelled him to change the text in a manner that conformed to what the publisher wanted. Admittedly, there is a great variety of instances that are not so clear-cut. But the clear-cut counter-example illuminates the vulnerability, if not incorrectness, of the claims. The political and aesthetic implications of the historicist view in instances of the kind that I have just adduced are, I think, unacceptable to most readers of the text. Historicism is indifferent to the political idea of the freedom of the imagination to express itself against censorious established authority (whether the state or public opinion) and to the aesthetic idea that insists upon aesthetic discriminations among variants.

In providing the reader with the variant and in describing the process, Andrew Robertson, editor of *The White Peacock,* has done what McGann would require, but the description of the process does not itself dictate which variant should be selected. Indeed, the process, deplorable in this case, provokes the editors to resist it in the interests of considerations that are aesthetic and political. The editors chose the American edition as representing the preferred text for the aesthetic reason that it is, in their view, Lawrence's best style of vernacular expression, and for the political reason that it represents Lawrence's candor against the censorious culture in which he lived. The interactive process the editor describes is the process the author resisted. It is useful to know that process in order to understand the marks of censorship and self-censorship in the text. We want to know the extent to which Lawrence's writing may have been affected consciously and unconsciously by the always present threat of a censorious publisher and audience. Such knowledge speaks to the question of style as well as content. But a knowledge of the process of the production of a text and its reception does not by itself provide us with the text we may wish to read.

The Cambridge editions are based on an eclectic "theory" of editorial practice in which contending considerations are always at play. This, I think, is as it should be. In understanding and judging the editorial work of the Cambridge edition, I follow no particular theory or doctrine. My concern is with the persuasiveness with which the editors adjudicate among contending considerations. What interests me above all is the contribution editorial practice makes to the understanding and appreciation of Lawrence's work.

The editorial bias in the Cambridge edition is explicit and clear. The editors want to rescue the texts from "interference on the part of frightened publishers" as well as to free the texts from errors committed by editors, compositors, and printing-house conventions in order to give us the text that "Lawrence would have wished to see printed." This statement from the general editor's preface seems very much in the spirit of the doctrine of "final intentions," but it has in addition a political resonance implying advocacy of the freedom of imagination.

In order to accomplish their purpose, the editors had to decide which text of the several available was "the most *author*itative" (my emphasis). Sometimes it meant going "to a 'spoken' or a 'manuscript' rather than a 'printed' style. We have not wanted to strip off one house-styling in order to impose another." The editors speak of editorial intervention as necessary to recover from bowdlerization, carelessness (author's, printers', typists') what Lawrence wanted to see printed. "Paradoxical as it may seem, the outcome of this rescension will be texts which differ, often radically and certainly frequently from those seen by the author himself."[4]

Each volume provides the reader with a general introduction and an introduction to the particular work, which includes its publication history, its reception at the time of publication, a discussion of base text and variants, and separate sections at the end devoted to explanatory notes and textual apparatus. In some instances, appendixes are provided (e.g., the diary of Helen Corke, a model for the character of the heroine in *The Trespasser*). What is missing, what any historicist would find lacking, is a history of the reception of the novel to the present. (Editions do not customarily give us the history of reception up to the present moment, but the logic of historicism, which asserts the perpetually changing life of the text history, would seem to require it.)

The Cambridge edition of Lawrence's second novel, *The Trespasser,* aims to represent, insofar as it is possible, Lawrence's final intentions. The determination of final intentions has an element of uncertainty; it is also complicated or confused by aesthetic considerations. The base text is the final manuscript rather than the earlier partial manuscript ("The Saga of Siegmund"). The final manuscript reflects Lawrence's intention to make "war against adjectives." "The process of condensation in MSI [the early manuscript] and MSII [the final manuscript] strongly suggest that the final, more concise form was his own."[5] The editor Elizabeth Mansfield also notes that "collation of the uncorrected proofs and text of the first edition reveals that this process continued: 121 adjectives were removed, and many adjectival phrases were eliminated as well." Since the corrected proofs are not extant, the editor cannot be sure that all the changes were made by Lawrence, so the base text is the final manuscript and not the first edition. "Any judgment about variant readings introduced between the final [manuscript] and the first edition must take into account the direction in which Lawrence was moving during composition and revisions previous to proof stage" (36). "Final intention" then is a deduction from a perceived sense of direction and the choice of final intention is enforced by an aesthetic bias that prefers concise form. What would Mansfield have said if Lawrence had showed a proclivity for adding adjectives and adjectival phrases? Would she have decided on the basis of final intention or of aesthetic judgment? She never raises the question.

Mansfield does not have a problem, because, as I have remarked, aesthetic judgment and the doctrine of final intentions do not conflict. Indeed, her own language seamlessly combines literary judgment with final intentions. In comparing passages from the early and final manuscripts, she finds the language of MSII (the final manuscript) "more familiar to readers of his later works. . . . Lawrence's sense of artistic integrity overcame his vulnerability to criticism; he wrote what he now believed had to be said, using the words that conveyed it most effectively." Here is the passage and the editor's comment upon it:

> He covered her with his coats, and crushed her into his breast. He had borne for many months a dull, empty feeling on his chest; this had sometimes concentrated into a deep, almost unbearable pain, which he knew would never be healed till he pressed the bosom of Sieglinde into his. Now he strained her savagely to his breast, and she lay there hurt and stifled, but very willing [that] death should come that way, if it came at all. Siegmund remained perfectly still, his muscles set hard, holding Sieglinde. It was just a burning bush, [flaming] passionate relief and joy flaming through their tissues.
>
> Revising this passage in MSII, Lawrence began to use language more familiar to readers of his later works: 'his blood flushed up, and up again, with fire, till all Siegmund was hot blood, and his breast was one great ache', and 'at that moment, he was tense, vivid body of flesh without a mind; his blood, alive and conscious, running towards her' (35).

The editorial judgment here is by no means self-evident and it is unargued. Both passages have a strong adjectival bias. Concise form was hardly the hallmark of Lawrence's characteristic prose, even in his best and most mature work. The editor makes two vulnerable claims:

(1) that Lawrence's intention was to achieve a more concise form and (2) that concise form is artistically superior to a more expansive form.

The insertion of unpersuasive aesthetic judgment in a textual argument for choosing one variant rather than another simply confuses our understanding of Lawrence's achievement. It is not enough to say that literary or aesthetic judgment must play a part in textual criticism: that judgment must be as informed and sophisticated as any strictly textual argument. Unfortunately, the combination of talents is rare. Moreover, the exercise of both talents might create more problems than it solves, for if one is committed to the principle of "final intentions," one might not necessarily wind up with the best text, that is, the aesthetically superior text.

Not all the editors are inclined toward making aesthetic judgments, and the failure to do so may weaken editorial authority by default. Mara Kalvins, the editor of *Aaron's Rod,* notes

> a puzzling anomaly in the Secker [i.e., American] first edition where an alteration has been made, presumably by someone in the publisher's office, to one of the censored passages. The English first edition at this point reads: "a long, live thread of electric fire"; a variant reads: "a long, live thread excruciating, but also an intensely gratifying sensation". . . . the Harry Ransom Humanities Research Center contains seven copies of the English first edition, four have the former reading, three the latter.

Since subsequent reprints preserve "a long, live thread of electric fire," Kalvins speculates that "Secker chose to adopt . . . the original reading . . . rather than the more explicit revision, given his anxiety about sexual connotations." The editor doesn't quite explain her choice of "the more explicit revision."[6] Is it a matter of final intentions or of explicitness that is supposed to represent the true Lawrence?

Here is the passage from chapter 19:

> . . . And this night, in his extreme, he felt his passion drawn from him as if a long, live nerve were drawn out from his body, a long living nerve finely extracted from him, from the very roots of his soul. *It was an excruciating, but also an extremely gratifying sensation.* As his passion broke from him to her, he felt the long live hot fire-thread drawn downwards through him, terribly down his legs and through

> his heels, leaving his heels feeling bruised, and himself feeling vacant. . . . (272; my emphasis)

The question is: what difference does it make? Is the sentence more explicit than the rest? Hardly, it seems to me. I would argue that it is the weakest sentence in the passage, lacking as it does the metaphoric vividness of the other sentences. It is a sentence that tells about rather than shows the experience. It represents Lawrence at his worst: his overexplicit need to persuade the reader, perhaps from an insecurity that his imagination had not done its job. (The sentence is certainly not consistent with an aesthetic of concise form, which the editor of *The Trespasser* valued.) I am of course on contestable ground in making an aesthetic judgment. I am grateful to the editor for providing me with the evidence of variants, but I find no effort on her part to enter the terrain of reasoned literary judgment, which makes her edition less gratifying than it might be.

One value of learning about the variants for me is that it crystallizes a sense I have of Lawrence's style. Lawrence's erotic imagination is at once graphic and indirect; its power lies not in its physical explicitness (what occurs between bodies often remains obscure), but in its capacity for metaphoric displacements, which convey the experience of passion. "Electric fire," "roots of his soul," "discharge of lightening": eroticism in Lawrence becomes a mystical animism, in which cosmic energies inform the sexual act. The focus is on those energies, not on the "mechanical" physicality of the act.

What role does censorship or self-censorship play in the making of the erotic style of Lawrence's prose? Would Lawrence have been more physically graphic, if his society were less censorious in sexual matters? It is a very difficult question to answer. I suspect that Lawrence himself had internalized much of that puritan morality: that his powerful erotic imagination instinctively sought the metaphoric religious displacements and that paradoxically it intensified his erotic imagination, as repression often does. As Lawrence once explained to his editor Edward Garnett apropos of *The Rainbow,* he was primarily "a passionately religious man, and my novels must be written from the depth of my religious experience."[7] Censorship may have been Lawrence's enemy, but in a sense it was a necessary and empowering enemy. By taking seriously the prohibition, Lawrence allowed sexuality to become a transgressive force in his work, in contrast, for example, to the imaginative sexual vacuity of many contemporary writers in which the absence of prohibitions results in a lack of tension, an evaporation of the passional side of erotic writing.

Lawrence's relationship with his publishers and his audience was equivocal. He wanted to be both true to his daimon and successful, and the two desires were not always compatible. For instance, writing *The Rainbow*, he clearly wanted the authority to decide what was to be printed, but for *The Lost Girl*, composed at the same time, he was willing to follow the lead of his publisher. As the editor John Worthen remarks, Lawrence's willingness to make the extensive revisions that the publisher requested is "evidence of the extent to which he viewed *The Lost Girl* as a commercial enterprise."[8] How does this knowledge affect our view of Lawrence's intentions? How important is the integrity of *The Lost Girl* in light of Lawrence's willingness to do the publisher's bidding? Does the view that the book is a commercial enterprise belong to his intention? Lawrence did not always insist upon final authority, indeed on occasion he was only too willing, for whatever reason, to delegate it to others. For instance, Lawrence told Douglas Clayton, his typist of 1913–14, "Please alter anything that seems to you wrong."[9] Of his typist for *The Rainbow*, Viola Meynell, Lawrence requested that she "keep an eye open for 'repetitions and the things I can cross out' and also parts 'the publisher will decidedly object to'"(xxxviii). Final intentions would seem to be impossible to determine in such situations. Indeed, in a case where Lawrence shows an indifference to the result, final intentions would seem to be irrelevant. Knowing the process of interaction with his publisher or typist may enable us to judge what the criteria for a critical edition should be. Where Lawrence didn't seem to care, the proper course might be for the editor to consult his own literary judgment about what seems to him or her consistent with the character of the work.

Final intentions, the interactive processes of author, publisher, and audience, and aesthetic judgment all need to be considered in the making of editorial decisions and in the critical understanding of the text. A problem arises when one of the editorial doctrines is exclusively and systematically applied. This is not the case with the Cambridge editions. What is the case is that in a number of instances the various considerations do not seem to be properly sorted out and thought through. Sometimes a final intention is viewed as decisive without sufficient argument. On other occasions literary judgment goes unargued. An acknowledgment of process cannot decide matters by itself.

Consider the following instance from *The Plumed Serpent*. Lawrence is shown to have deleted a third of a dialogue in which there is a heated exchange between Kate and Don Ramon. The editor, L. D. Clark, remarks, "This revision leads more naturally to the ending of the passage, in which Ramon goes quietly away." Clark goes on to cite other revised passages, which he declares to be "clearly authoritative" on the grounds that "the author's later intention obviously supersedes the former." "Obviously" because the later intention is aesthetically superior? But this is not obvious at all. Or is it because the later intention is the final intention? Note, however, what the later intention means: "At the time of writing MS he had a concept of the novel as a whole which he no longer enjoyed during later revision, when he concentrated only on a few passages."[10] The later revision then, more likely or not, might distort the shape of the novel and yet it is supposed to be authoritative. Why? We do not get beyond tautology. "The author's later intention obviously supersedes the former."

The deleted passages are given to us in the section entitled "Textual Apparatus" and they give us at great length the mythic doctrine of the Queztalcoatl cult as expounded by Don Ramon. It is the message that Don Ramon wants Kate as his evangelist to take to Europe. As it turns out, Kate decides to remain, though she appears at the end uncertain about her future in Mexico. The concluding chapter in the Cambridge edition is sparer, more dramatic, less laden with doctrine than the typescript version. The editor goes along with Lawrence's deletion of Ramon's symbolic message and his decision seems a reasonable one, but apart from invoking Lawrence's later intention the decision is not really argued on literary grounds. The argument for the later intention is clearly insufficient on Clark's own testimony. Nowhere in the introduction are we given an account of "a concept of the novel as whole" that Lawrence had in writing his manuscript. I doubt that such an account could ever be given, because it probably never existed.

The ideal textual edition would be one in which the editor could determine final intentions (if they were determinable), grasp the interactive social process of artistic production, and make cogent literary interpretations and judgments when necessary.

In *The Rainbow* Mark Kinkead-Weekes displays an admirable combination of critical and editorial powers. But his theory about the nature of *The Rainbow* is problematic. "What seems most important is to remain true to the nature of *The Rainbow*, as the work of a continuously revising and recreating author; whose theory of creativity (which he began to formulate in his 'Hardy') was essentially theory of process, of continuous and organic change, and whose individual works kept evolving out of themselves, continually refusing to be 'finished'"(xiii). Kinkead-Weekes follows Lawrence's own belief in organic and continuous change without end. There are difficulties in such a view. Organic form implies the possibility of fulfillment or realization, but Lawrentian organicism is mystifyingly endless. I don't see how Lawrence or Kinkead-Weekes can have it both ways. Moreover, the organic implies an inviolable process ("evolving out of itself"). Any attempt to revise by typist, publisher, even the author himself compromises the process. The actual histories of the making of Lawrence's fiction do not illustrate organic form. Even Lawrence's defense of it in the case of *The Rainbow* is unconvincing.

> I have cut out, as I said I would, all the *phrases* objected to. The passages and paragraphs marked I cannot alter. There is nothing offensive in them, beyond the very substance they contain, and that is no more offensive than that of all the rest of the novel. The libraries won't object to the book any less, or approve it any more, if these passages are cut out. And I can't cut them out, because they are living parts of an organic whole. (xliii–xliv)

Why aren't the phrases that he agreed to delete part of "the organic whole"? The organicist metaphor for the imagination already in Aristotle and powerfully formulated in Romantic theory, dies hard. I think the solution is to abandon the organic metaphor as a vehicle for critical understanding, while appreciating it as an event in Lawrence's self-understanding. One may do so without also abandoning intentionality. In any event, Kinkead-Weekes's sense of Lawrence's achievement is much closer to its spirit than Clark's, for whom Lawrence's intention is a closed concept that becomes the standard for judging subsequent revisions.

The view of *The Rainbow* that emerges from Kinkead-Weekes's account is of continuous revision in the direction of overcoming the one-sided single perspective in order to achieve "a better balance" between opposing attitudes. Lawrence "reconceived [the cathedral scene in which Will's soul leaps from stone to stone to the apex of the spire] to achieve a better balance between Anna and Will, and to insure that their partial failure to achieve the marriage of opposites is attributed as firmly to her as to him" (xiii–xiv). By showing Anna in a spirit of mockery and resentment toward the little faces on the church facade, Lawrence qualified the portrait of an expansive, freedom-loving woman, thereby redistributing responsibility for the failure of their marriage. The textual evidence, as Kinkead-Weekes makes clear, supports a view of Lawrence as an artist with a powerful lyric gift, who sought to overcome the one-sidedness of the lyric perspective in order to achieve dramatic justice.

But the process of revision does not always have this confident narrative shape. Revisions of erotic language (made by Lawrence) do not necessarily reflect censorship or self-censorship, but rather uncertainty or two minds about the erotic situation. Kinkead-Weekes offers the following interesting example. Lawrence altered "There would be pretty places in her body, that he wanted to discover . . . to know and enjoy . . . to have his fill of them" to "Her childishness whetted him keenly. She would be helpless between his hands". Kinkead-Weekes notes that "the 'eroticism' is hardly diminished, only . . . changed in emphasis. In the earlier passage the change points to a different kind of sexuality than thoughts of places in the body; the kind that depends on a sense of power and makes some men 'whetted' by rather childish girls"(lxvii–lxviii).

Here we have an instance that would seem to belie the theory of organic form. Organic form moves continuously in a single direction. Lawrence seems to have leaped discontinuously from one formulation to another as if he were of two minds about the scene. To look for intentions does not mean that the task is an easy one or that the problem is always soluble. One might discover conflicting intentions in which no intention has priority, that is, finality. The only resort, it seems to me, would be the literary judgment of the editor. The effect of tracking the textual revisions is to discover how volatile Lawrence's erotic imagination is. Lawrence's development during the "middle period" of his career (from *Aaron's Rod* to *The Plumed Serpent*) has been described as a passage from the love mode to the power mode: the textual changes show love and power intimately connected in a manner that makes the division of Lawrence's work into periods oversimple.

Kinkead-Weekes is particularly illuminating in his attempt to distinguish among the censorious effects of the publisher, advice that Lawrence may have solicited from his typists, who were knowledgeable as writers and readers, and his own uncertainties about choices he had to make, particularly in matters of sex and religion. Kinkead-Weekes admits that it is often difficult to distinguish motives for revision. His solution is to rely on the first English edition, if arguments on both sides of an issue "are equally poised." The arguments are based on aesthetic considerations, a knowledge of Lawrence's character, and speculation about his intentions. Thus a change in the generation of Ursula's future man from "the loins of God" in the manuscript to "from the Being of God" in typescript to "out of Eternity" in the variant that Kinkead-Weekes chooses is justified by what he takes to be "Lawrence's own [religious] sensitivity," not simply fear of offending the reader (lxv). For the same reason, Kinkead-Weekes speculates Lawrence may have eliminated references to King David, whom Anna Brangwen had "always loved," and to the "unseen Lover whose name was unutterable," as she dances naked, substituting "the unseen Creator . . . to Whom she belonged," because he might have "wanted Anna's impulse to spring, not from a youthful 'crush' or an erotic memory of David dancing naked [before the Ark], but from her own inner urgency to reach out to the Unknown and the Unseen Creator—precisely the emphasis he had underlined at several points" (lxvi).

None of Lawrence's other fictions compares with *Women in Love* as an example of Lawrence's revisionary disposition. David Farmer, Lindeth Vasey, and John Worthen provide a vivid and detailed account of the many versions of the novel from its inception as *The Sisters* (a version that included what was to become *The Rainbow*) through *The Wedding Ring* and the five versions of *Women in Love*. The story they tell is one of intertwined considerations: publisher's fears, threats of libel action by aggrieved models for characters (e.g., Ottoline Morrell's indignation at the portrait of Hermione Roddice), uncertainty in Lawrence himself about the success of his imaginative adventure (he solicited opinions from his publisher friend Edward Garnett), and the interventions of his wife Frieda. Indeed, Frieda's transcriptions, apparently erroneous, are at times accepted by Lawrence in later redactions and accepted by the editors. Frieda at those moments becomes Lawrence's collaborator, but the editors are also concerned to resist Frieda's "collaborative" efforts.

The text that the editors offer is intended to

> strip off layers of error and mistranscription which affected both first editions [English and American] produced in the author's lifetime, and which have been enshrined in all subsequent printings. It also restores passages which were censored or changed in [the first English edition] through threat of legal action. For the first time, Lawrence's

> 'terrible and horrible and wonderful novel' appears in a text in which his own expectations may be said to have been realised.[11]

This act of recovery is a sort of counterpart to the extraordinary accretive process by which the novel grew. The editors promise a supplementary volume "to be entitled *The Sisters* [which] will be issued at a later date . . . [it] will provide both the text of the novel as it stood at the end of November 1916 (when it might conceivably have been accepted by a publisher), and the variant and deleted readings of MS, TSIa and TSIb" (lvi–lvii).

The Cambridge edition of *Women in Love* has occasioned a fierce exchange between Charles Ross, who reviewed it for *Essays in Criticism,* and John Worthen and Lindeth Vasey, the editors. Anyone interested in the details may read the exchange in the issues of *Essays* for October 1988 (342–51), April 1989 (176–84), and January 1990 (95–97). I think Worthen and Vasey have much the better of the exchange.

Worthen and Vasey are interested in Lawrence's "final intentions" to the extent they can be determined and they argue that the first English edition provides the best base text, though they emend the text wherever they feel necessary from other sources. Occasionally, Ross quarrels with the editors on the grounds of Lawrence's intention. But his essential difference from them is in his view that "emendation can[not] be done piecemeal, without considering the holistic meaning of a draft or sequence of revisions."[12] Ross wishes to see Frieda as a collaborator whose emendations are to be taken seriously. What holism entails in the light of the revisionary process the novel underwent (a process acknowledged by Ross and the editors) Ross doesn't say. Is holism (a word in organicist discourse) a concept of the whole that existed at the moment of composition or is it the reflection of a process in time that comes to a teleological fulfillment? Neither alternative can serve as a model for practice: how could the editor determine what the whole was in the mind of the author at a particular moment or over a period of time? May we assume without argument at this late date that a work is an organic whole (especially the work of an untidy, explosive genius like Lawrence)? Worthen and Vasey are, I think, right in saying that Ross himself becomes the arbiter of what the best version of the novel is. The reader (in this case Ross) is given authority over the author. One example reveals how arbitrary and unreliable a readerly exercise of authority might be. "Where Lawrence wrote 'she did not know why she hated him, she had no reason for hating him,' Frieda improved the second clause to 'her hate was quite abstract'" (347). It is not obvious at all that the change is an improvement—it seems much flatter than the original. Moreover, the meaning is changed, the original version implying that she could not figure out why she hated (perhaps there was an undiscovered reason for it), the changed version in effect settling the matter.

What view of Lawrence emerges from a consideration of the textual scholarship? Does it change our understanding of his achievement in a significant way? Any intelligent reader of Lawrence, of course, knows that he was an embattled writer, that his is a transgressive imagination, constantly challenging cultural taboos. The scholarship shows the toll that it took, the compromises that Lawrence had to make for his work to see the light of day. But it also shows his uncertainties and equivocations. Lawrence's dogmatic manner conceals the uncertainties: the effect of looking at variants is to make us see the ambivalences, the alternatives that Lawrence had to confront in making choices. The uncertainties, one may speculate, may reflect not a fear of censorship, but a sense of undiscovered and unknown terrain, what lies beyond the prohibitions that Lawrence has chosen to transgress. It should not surprise us if Lawrence, in writing his revolutionary novel *The Rainbow,* declares at a moment in the creative process that he doesn't know his own intention. "I am doing a novel which I have never grasped. Damn its eyes, there I am at page 145, and I've no notion what it's about. I hate it. F[rieda] says it is good. But it's like a novel in a foreign language I don't know very well—" (xxi).

Lawrence's famous injunction "never trust the artist, trust the tale, because the artist is a liar" could of course be applied to Lawrence's own work. His uncertainty about *The Rainbow* during the process of composition would seem to subvert the doctrine of authorial intention. I don't think it so much undermines the idea of intention as it compels us to qualify it. For a writer not to know what he is about as he writes is not to deny that he is about something and that the creative process is the effort to discover his intention without interference from publishers and censorious readers.

Lawrence himself was given to appropriative readings of other writers, as in his studies of the classic American writers and Thomas Hardy. His claim to have discovered what they were really up to as against what they thought they were doing need not be accepted, however brilliant

Lawrence's readings and misreadings are. In rewriting the novels of others (in effect turning them into Lawrencean fictions), Lawrence may be exercising an artist's privilege, but his appropriations must not be confused or identified with what the subjects of the appropriation were about.

If the making of a book is a collaborative process, authorial intention relinquishes much of its authority to publisher and audience. In a sense, authorial intention is always already determined by a sense of its audience. It may also be determined by a desire to resist its audience, to tell it a story it may not even wish to hear. We diminish the audacious authority of Lawrence's work, its subversive message, if we prematurely absorb it into an author-publisher-audience collaborative. It has long been fashionable to scoff at a respectful view of authorial intention as a pious fetishizing of the text, a needless submission of the reader to authorial tyranny. But publishers and readers may constitute their own tyranny (Lawrence's career provides ample evidence).

Intention is a sign of *authority,* and our democratic society dislikes authority. The book that has had ultimate authority until recently in our culture has been the Bible and the intention never to be questioned, whether it could be determined or not, was God's intention. Much of the political resentment against authority and intentionality in contemporary literary discourse derives, I think, from a misguided belief about where and what the sources of contemporary literary authoritarianism are. The modern writer is not God, though he or she may on occasion, as in the case of Joyce, put on divine airs or, as in the case of Shelley, pretend to legislative powers. At best, the writer is a critic of the prevailing power. And the prevailing power in "free modern societies" is not a government whatever the form, but public opinion: the publisher and the audience toward whom the book is directed. If this is so, the truly liberating critical act is to discover and preserve the intentions of the writer against the appropriating, bowdlerizing efforts of communities of readers to domesticate the intentions to the mere needs and desires of the readers.

I am of course speaking of modern texts rather than ancient ones, where the effect of censorship may have little relevance to our own political situation. It may indeed be a mark of our freedom as imaginative readers that we not be overwhelmed by the feeling of piety toward every word an ancient author might have intended, if we could possibly know what he or she intended. But even in the case of ancient authors our indifference to the question of intention may allow for another kind of tyranny: the unexamined and uncontested role of prevailing contemporary assumptions. The past may enable us to see the present as the present does not permit. An ancient text that we don't simply appropriate to our immediate concerns may give us a sense of life alternative to our present senses.

Historicism is inimical to the individual will, or rather it transforms intention into an instrument of forces always greater than itself. And it does so with a certain pleasure, for "history" (or the historicist's version of history) is a sort of God. One need not be a historicist to value historical perspectives. The interaction between history and self, between context and text, however, is possible only if the integrity of each term is preserved; in historicism the integrities are dissolved and absorbed into "process," an appealing word with sinister potential.

The debate in textual criticism between the historicists and the final intentionalists can be read, I think, as an allegory of the politics of the literary profession. One reading, the one that would come to mind to most of the conforming citizens of the contemporary academic community, is to see the debate as a struggle between progressives and reactionaries, between those who wish to advance our historical understanding of literature and those who remain stuck in an old-fashioned, quasi-religious piety in the presence of the text. In contrast, the debate, as I see it, is a struggle between those who in effect diminish and those who wish to preserve the political and aesthetic powers of literature. A text without boundaries, seamlessly extending itself to every audience's appropriation of it, ceases to have anything critically aggressive to say to its audience. The work of Lawrence, Solzhenitsyn, Kundera, Havel (to name writers of our momentous present) would lose its necessary force. Between the tyranny of Lawrence's genius and the tyranny of the publisher's timidity or the reader's herdlike scandalized response, I have no trouble choosing. Whatever the process, I would think that the scholar, the critic, the reader would be interested first in what the author wished to say.

NOTES

1. Stanley Fish, *Is There a Text in This Class?* (Cambridge, Mass.: Harvard University Press, 1980), 158.

2. Jerome J. McGann, *A Critique of Modern Textual Criticism* (Chicago: University of Chicago Press, 1983), 54.

3. D. H. Lawrence, *The White Peacock,* ed. Andrew Robertson (Cambridge: Cambridge University Press, 1983), xxxiv–xxxv; see 150 nn. 22–24.

4. See General Editor's Preface in all volumes, viii.

5. D. H. Lawrence, *The Trespasser,* ed. Elizabeth Mansfield (Cambridge: Cambridge University Press, 1981), 33.

6. D. H. Lawrence, *Aaron's Rod,* ed. Mara Kalvin (Cambridge: Cambridge University Press, 1988), xxxviii.

7. D. H. Lawrence, *The Rainbow,* ed. Mark Kinkead-Weekes (Cambridge: Cambridge University Press, 1989), xxxii.

8. D. H. Lawrence, *The Lost Girl,* ed. John Worthen (Cambridge: Cambridge University Press, 1981) xxxix.

9. D. H. Lawrence, *The Prussian Office and Other Stories,* ed. John Worthen (Cambridge: Cambridge University Press, 1983), xxxvi.

10. D. H. Lawrence, *The Plumed Serpent,* ed. L. D. Clark (Cambridge: Cambridge University Press, 1987), xl.

11. D. H. Lawrence, *Women in Love,* ed. David Farmer, Lindeth Vasey, and John Worthen (Cambridge: Cambridge University Press, 1987), lxi.

12. Charles Ross, "The Cambridge Lawrence," *Essays in Criticism* 38 (October 1988): 345.

Where the Comma Goes: Editing William Faulkner

Noel Polk

Scholarly editing is the ultimate act of criticism, because it involves a wider range of issues—from macrocosmic ones like the author's or text's meaning to more mundane and practical microcosmic ones like *where does the comma go?*—than interpretation alone does. Dealing with all these issues responsibly requires extensive knowledge of publishing history and of publishing techniques and procedures, of standard usage in the author's period, of the author's preferences at any period of his or her career, of the author's relationship to commercial editors, to financial considerations, and to the political and cultural times, and of the author's practices in composing, revising, and proofreading. The editor must be sensitive to an author's most subtle nuances of style, punctuation, and spelling, as well as to larger issues in the work, but also constantly aware of the complex interaction between his or her own aesthetic sense and the author's (or text's), because in order to determine where the comma goes the editor must constantly differentiate between authorial *error* and authorial *intention*. Finally, the editorial act is central to the critical enterprise because editorial decisions impinge directly upon questions of canon and literary history.

This is not just an apologia for editors, but rather to suggest the variety of complex issues involved in editing any text. And if these issues impinge on the editing of works up through the nineteenth century, during which time grammar and punctuation usage was at least evolving toward some theoretical point of "correctness" against which the quality of any work could be measured, they are much more central to the editing of the works of the high moderns, who merely demanded that readers rethink the entire semiotic system by which they had read the precedent literary generations.

Thus the immediate problem in editing a modernist text is that the editor can no longer usefully call on W. W. Greg's distinctions between "substantives" and "accidentals" (those variations that affect meaning directly and those that do not; in practice the distinction has come to be that between words and punctuation)[1] because Greg assumed a stability in language that it was precisely the purpose of many modernists to challenge. How useful would Greg be to the editor of e. e. cummings, for example, who must decide whether an unpaired close-parenthesis, or a comma or a colon in the middle of a word, is correctly placed or whether its placement is a compositorial, editorial, or even authorial error? The gap between substantives and accidentals, then, never a very large one, virtually disappears in modernist texts, especially in radically modernist ones like *Ulysses* and *The Sound and the Fury* and *As I Lay Dying,* wherein every jot and tittle is at least potentially substantive.

Cummings is, of course, the most extreme example of an author at odds with the conventions of written language, at play with the relationship between the signifier and the signified; he indeed uses that relationship as the absolute meat and meaning of some of his poems. Of fiction writers, William Faulkner was clearly the most radical experimenter with the visual representation of language, more radical, in some ways, than Joyce; a great deal of Faulkner's fiction is intimately concerned with the inadequacy of words, written and spoken, and some of his most memorable passages articulate this inadequacy, as in Addie Bundren's poignant complaint that "words are no good; that words dont ever fit even what they are trying to say at."[2] Doomed by his craft to deal with inadequate words, Faulkner perforce resorted to an inventive array of other visual devices—italics, double and single quotation marks, flush left paragraph margins; dialogue separated by dashes; uncapitalized and unpunctuated and ungrammatical passages in characters' speeches and thoughts; extremely long compound-complex sentences (which, however, always parse); spaces, gaps in the text; and line drawings of a coffin and of an eyeball as part of the text—to try to communicate what words by themselves could not. Even though there are large issues in editing Faulkner's texts, nearly all of the most perplexing editorial problems center around the regularity, or irregularity, of Faulkner's manipulation of these textual devices, the extent to which either regularity or irregularity is part of the texture of his intention; the problems of that "intention" anyway; the extent to which any editor can hope to differentiate those things that should be emended from those that should be left alone; the ways in which any editor's aesthetic sensibilities—his or her sense of what literary art *is*—affect editorial decisions. Applied to all authors, solutions to these problems force us to consider the effect such decisions eventually have on literary history and on the canon.

In this essay I'd like to lay out some of the problems I have faced in editing the texts of William Faulkner, but I must note at the beginning that I make no claim that the texts I have edited[3] can be considered "definitive"—whatever that means—by any of the general standards accepted over the years by followers of W. W. Greg and Fredson Bowers and promoted by the Modern Language Association's Center for Editions of American Authors (CEAA) and its successor, the Committee on Scholarly Editions (CSE). Although I have been the grateful beneficiary of lots of help and advice from colleagues and friends in Faulkner studies, these new texts are essentially a one-man show, for which I happily take credit where due and, less happily, blame. I've made extensive use of the available holographs and galleys, letters and other evidence, but my procedure for the "New, Corrected Texts," as they are called, has been essentially to trust Faulkner and his typescripts, documents he himself prepared and, where possible, to restore his typescript readings in preference to editorial and, occasionally, even authorial revision. A "definitive" edition of Faulkner will have to await a more extensive project that will more thoroughly examine all the available evidence; the new texts are intended to restore Faulkner's typescripts, to *de-edit* them,[4] as it were, in order to get into print texts as close to Faulkner's typescripts as possible.

But accepting the typescripts as expressing Faulkner's intentions begs several questions about how well they actually contain them. The typescripts are very clear, generally, but they are marred by a number of typos, revisions, irregularities in patterns of narration and punctuation, and perhaps by outright misreadings of his own handwriting.[5] Some of the differences between the published texts and these typescripts prove that Faulkner or somebody did some revising or polishing or changing on now lost galley or page proofs—the only places where such changes could have occurred. Likewise, there are some problems caused by Faulkner's acquiescence to editorial emendation and the extent to which he, in James West's phrase, delegated his intentions[6] to editors who were expected to divine those intentions through the typescript, through correspondence or conversation, and then to execute them in places where Faulkner failed to.

Except for the well-known instances of *Sanctuary* and *Requiem for a Nun,* Faulkner but rarely initiated revisions in galleys; such revisions as he did make there normally were to correct typos; to respond to editorial queries with a correction, a minor revision, or a *leave as is;* or, occasionally, to repair damage that editorial intervention had caused. The evidence suggests Faulkner did not normally get terribly exercised at editorial intervention; he did, of course, object to Ben Wasson's editing of *The Sound and the Fury,* and he insisted that his typescript readings as regards italics be restored;[7] and with *Pylon* he repaired one problem by adding a bridge between two scenes.[8] In no instance did he insist that editors leave his apostrophe- and period-less contractions and abbreviations alone, and I don't recall a case in which he restored edited material to short stories as he collected them.[9] It is true that he objected to the Random House editors' wholesale revision of *Absalom, Absalom!*, and to their bowdlerization and retitling of *If I Forget Thee, Jerusalem;*[10] but it is also true that he never made any effort, even in the 1950s, as a powerful Nobel laureate, to have those alterations corrected in new editions. How close, then, is it possible to get to Faulkner's intentions, in large or small matters, even as they express themselves on typescripts he prepared, when he himself did not often protest editorial intervention?

To a large extent, of course, *all* authorial intentions are delegated intentions—to the extent, that is, to which any author must entrust the work to other hands to bring it to publication, and nearly all do; even writers who publish or revise themselves are in effect delegating their intentions to another self, a self different even if only older than when she or he originally submitted it. I now think, for example, that Faulkner eviscerated a really fine novel when he revised *Sanctuary* in galleys; Hershel Parker and Brian Higgins have argued that Fitzgerald was well on his way to doing the same thing when he revised *Tender is the Night*[11] after its publication. Parker continues to argue[12] that authorial revision is not necessarily improvement, and I believe we have to admit the corollary, that not all editorial changes are necessarily bad ones. If we insist upon the primacy of what authors actually put on paper, at the expense of their intentions, we may as well publish all literary works in typescript and manuscript facsimiles; if we accept the author's agreement with or acquiescence to editors' or collaborators' alterations, we have little choice but to stick with the text's first published edition; in either case we, as editors, have unintentionally theorized ourselves out of work. Taken to one extreme, answers to questions about authorial intention aid and abet those who want to see texts as cultural documents, products not of an author alone but of a time and a place, which should therefore be studied only as they were originally *published,* not as they were written. Taken to the other extreme, answers that insist upon the absolute primacy of what the author wrote, instead of on what he or she intended, may in some cases actually diminish the perceived aesthetic or artistic value of a work, a consequence that could have profound effects on the canon.

Thus the editorial enterprise raises several crucial questions about complex relationships among author, editor, art, and salable artifacts. If such editorial interventions have produced "better" novels than the author could have written alone, could we? should we? knowingly downgrade the work back to the author's "intentions" if an editor's emendations were somehow demonstrably superior to what the author had written, superior even to what the author had *intended,* whether the author had delegated that intention or not? The question is not just one of error; indeed, the larger questions address themselves directly, perhaps even antagonistically, to aesthetic considerations: simply, what makes one work or one author "better" than another? What are the standards—aesthetic or commercial or political—that make such judgments possible, or necessary? Most of the debate about James West's new edition of Dreiser's *Sister Carrie* and of Henry Binder's edition of Crane's *The Red Badge of Courage,*[13] both of which audaciously claimed to restore what the author wrote, has centered less on the finer points of editorial theory than on whether the new texts are "better" than the ones we have grown comfortable with.[14] Try as we must to keep them at bay, aesthetic considerations, always highly subjective and personal, can never be very far from the editor's decisions. More than one friend has argued with me that Faulkner's editors at Random House did him a big favor in editing *Absalom, Absalom!* so heavily: among other things they rewrote significant portions of that novel by deleting many passages, by drastically altering the punctuation, and by "clarifying" many of Faulkner's deliberately ambiguous pronoun references. Questioned whether I was going to restore one particular passage, I was able to respond with an enthusiastic *Yes,* partly because I do not think it my job to improve Faulkner or to impose my editorial powers on his aesthetic prerogatives, although obviously an editor cannot always escape doing so. But since my own aesthetic sensibilities have largely been shaped by Faulkner himself, I am forced to confess to a profound, perhaps even blind, confidence in Faulkner's sense of himself as an artist (he told a friend that he thought *Absalom* was "the best novel yet written by an American"[15]) and in his attention to the details of his text. I readily grant that such special arguments for Faulkner allow me to slip off the theoretical hook as regards other authors. For me in editing Faulkner there is hardly ever a conflict between aesthetics and intention, or between intention and accomplishment; and so when possible, as I say, I trust him, allow him to stand, dingdongs of doom and all, and I doubt that there are enough dings in the new editions of *Absalom, Absalom!* and *The Sound and the Fury* to cause a general lowering of our estimates of these works. With other authors whose self-confidence, not to say achievement, was not so great as Faulkner's, the gulf between intention and accomplishment might be wide indeed, and how I might edit them is another question altogether.

Discussions of complex aesthetic issues can be enhanced by access to as many different "versions," as many different stages of composition of any work, as are available, so that we can contemplate the novel as a *process* rather than as a completed *object*. I have, for example, argued that we ought not think of a single *Sanctuary,* that we should think of the two versions[16] as "forming a single literary text that is far more significant that either of the versions taken singly."[17] But the critic's understandable desire to have many versions of a text is precisely the problem for the editor, who must deal in particulars—particular texts, particular commas and semicolons, particular paragraphs. This is partly why the CEAA and CSE have expended so much energy on apparatuses for their editions: the historical collations and the tables of variants and emendations seek to provide access to as many different reconstructions of the in-process text as possible. Not many editors will have the luxury that I fortunately have had of editing and publishing multiple versions of the same novel;[18] most editors will have to choose what to do, line by line, comma by comma, and readers will be stuck with these choices for some time to come, especially if Norton, in its canonical (marketplace) wisdom, decides to transubstantiate our meager bread into the actual living body of its literature anthologies.

Generally speaking, for the Faulkner texts up through *Go Down, Moses* in 1942, there are relatively few problems figuring out who, Faulkner or editor, did what to which texts, and it is nearly always possible to speculate intelligently about what Faulkner wanted—and what he wanted is usually contained pretty plainly in the typescripts, despite my previous disclaimers. Nor does his seeming acquiescence to editorial collaboration make it necessary to accept those editorial alterations. Editing the novels of Faulkner's late career, however, is complicated considerably by Faulkner's desire to enforce some consistency between the last two novels of the Snopes Trilogy, *The Town* (1957) and *The Mansion* (1959), and the first, *The Hamlet* (1940), and by his failing memory and apparent refusal to reread the earlier works. In *The Hamlet,* for example, Mink Snopes's ambush victim is Jack Houston; in the typescript of *The Mansion* (1959) Faulkner called him Zack. Albert Erskine, Faulkner's last editor at Random House, with Faulkner's full approval, changed Zack to Jack throughout; and, again with Faulkner's apparent approval, altered other minor ingredients of the narrative to give the entire trilogy more consistency. Clearly, at one level at least, it was Faulkner's intention that the submitted typescript be revised toward conformity with the other novels of the trilogy. Should a modern editor, discovering other discrepancies, then feel free to impose total consistency?

Editing his later novels is problematic indeed. Upon completing *A Fable* (1954), *The Town, The Mansion,* and *The Reivers* (1962), Faulkner's practice was to send a complete or nearly complete typescript to Random House, then follow it to New York after Saxe Commins and then Erskine had had a chance to go over it. Commins, then Erskine, and Faulkner would sit in the editor's office at Random House, the text between them, Faulkner sometimes fully engaged in the work, sometimes not. They would go over it together, working through editorial questions, Faulkner initiating some changes and directing Erskine to make them, Erskine asking questions or making suggestions, and Faulkner would either revise the text himself or get Erskine to do so. In short, there seems to have been not only delegated (negotiated, at any rate) intention, but absolute collaboration on certain details of the text of the late novels—for Faulkner an efficient merging of composition with editing—and, since Faulkner and editor frequently used the same grease pencil to mark the text, it is sometimes impossible to tell who made a particular mark, much less who originated it. How *is* an editor to figure out "intention" in all this? Not to accept the edited typescript is to deny Faulkner certain kinds of consistencies and regularities he seems to have wanted, and it is an act of scholarly supererogation to try to second-guess either Faulkner or the editor who worked directly with him on the typescript; on the other hand, to emend toward any form of regularization is to valorize regularity, control, and *neatness* as an aesthetic standard, and to work against the manifest and deliberate untidiness, even tastelessness, of such writers as Faulkner and Thomas Wolfe.[19] But to accept *every* emendation on one of these typescripts is to accept a lot of readings that were made by the editor acting alone and that are in my judgment demonstrably wrong or inferior to what Faulkner typed, no matter who altered it. Yet to accept some emendations, selectively, is to impose my own aesthetic judgments upon the author's, which all editors—and critics too—ought to be loath to do, even though, I repeat, the editor finally has nothing else to fall back on; to think otherwise is simply to be hamstrung by editorial theory.

But here we are back at the question of how to determine the difference between authorial error and authorial intention: can one always tell the difference between a misspelling or misuse and a neologism or coinage? Faulkner had an exceptionally large vocabulary, but there were some words he misused—he didn't always get the difference between "arrogate" and "abrogate" right, for example—and several he misspelled, or used archaic forms of: for example, "knowlege," "penetentiary," "rythm," "irreconciliable," and "indefatiguable" are listed in the *Oxford English Dictionary* as historic—and therefore presumably legitimate[20]—forms of these words, which Faulkner may have encountered in the *OED* itself or in his vast reading. Did he really prefer "rythm"? As Faulkner's editor in such instances, I am forced to walk the very, very fine line between protecting him from error and allowing him his archaisms and idiosyncracies.

My not entirely satisfactory approach to solving such problems is to look at the context in which such words appear, and to treat those words whose unconventional spellings seem to affect the sentence's rhythms somewhat differently from those that are simply spelled phonetically. Thus "indefa*tig*uable" and "irrecon*cili*able" do affect the prose's rhythms, and may well be the way Faulkner heard those words; in contrast, "rythm" and "knowlege" do not affect pronunciation or rhythm and, further, as unmodern spellings, seem to call attention to themselves in ways I do not believe Faulkner intended; they thus can detract from other, more important things going on in the text. Obviously, Faulkner sometimes intended to call very specific attention to certain words, and on those occasions it is crucial to allow him his own usages and idiosyncracies. But, again, what's the difference between an allowable idiosyncracy and an error?

I can suggest how these considerations work to affect the editing of particular texts by paying some attention to two of Faulkner's most highly regarded novels, *The Sound and the Fury* (1929) and *Absalom, Absalom!* (1936), two quintessentially modernist texts. Faulkner submitted the typescript of *The Sound and the Fury* to Cape and Smith in the late fall of 1928; the publisher turned it over for editing to Ben Wasson, who decided that the text's many intricate time shifts could be more efficiently indicated with extra line spacing than with Faulkner's own system of alternating italic and roman passages. When Faulkner saw the galleys, he was sufficiently moved to write Wasson the well-known letter in which he declared, "I know you mean well, Bud, but so do I. Put it back." He went on, in that letter, to say that he was going to add a few more italic passages, and directed Wasson to oversee both the restoration of the original italic passages and the installation of the new ones.[21] How else Wasson or any other editor at Cape and Smith tampered with the text of *The Sound and the Fury,* much less what changes Faulkner made on the ribbon typescript or galleys, we do not know, since neither document is known to exist. What we do have are: (1) a holograph manuscript, which differs from the carbon typescript so extensively as to be of little use as a representation of final intentions; (2) a carbon typescript, the major document for any new edition, on which Faulkner inked several experimental changes from the typed text; (3) a sample gathering of the first few pages, which preserve the text as Wasson edited it; and (4) about forty pages of a preliminary version of the Quentin section—a ribbon typescript copyedited at Cape and Smith and sent back to Faulkner—which, unfortunately, don't tell us what we need to know to edit the rest of the novel.

In editing *The Sound and the Fury* I made every effort to follow Greg whenever it was reasonable to do so. Given the extant documents, it would normally be proper to choose the carbon typescript as copy-text, and to adopt its accidentals unless there was good reason not to. But to accept all of the carbon typescript's accidentals would mean throwing out many changes Faulkner himself made, or instructed somebody else to make. For example, he seems to have typed portions of the Benjy section at least three times, using three different systems of punctuation. He finally evolved a system that called for a period at the end of all quotations, whether a comma, question mark, or exclamation mark should normally have been there; this method of punctuation brilliantly conveys Benjy's limited perception of emotion or tone. But Faulkner came to this method only after considerable experimentation. The holograph manuscript is not heavily underlined for italicization and is punctuated normally. The first typed version of the Benjy section is also punctuated normally: commas, question marks, and exclamation points come inside the quotation marks. He tried again, however, and when he retyped, he removed all end punctuation from direct quotations. The fact that no more than one method of punctuation appears on any single page, however, makes it clear that the carbon typescript is really a composite of at least three different whole or partial typings of the Benjy section. We do not know whether the ribbon typescript setting copy was also a composite or a completely new typing. If it matched the carbon typescript, we have to assume that Faulkner himself made the punctuation changes in ink before submitting it or instructed Wasson or some other editor to make the changes.

I can discover no pattern in the carbon typescript's punctuation of the Benjy section that would justify retaining the three different methods in the new edition—that is, there are no punctuation distinctions between black and white speech, for example, or between past and present time. Clearly, then, we have to accept the regularized punctuation of the published book's Benjy section as more nearly representing Faulkner's intention than the carbon typescript does; but doing so raises questions about the Quentin section. Faulkner read galleys at least for italics in the Benjy section, but there is no evidence that he ever saw proof of the other three sections. For example, in the Quentin section, he typed two important passages—Quentin's recollection of his fireplace conversation with Caddy's fiancé, Sidney Herbert Head, and his painful memory of his encounters with Dalton Ames and with Caddy in the well-known suicide/incest scene—with no paragraph indentations: all paragraphs in these passages begin flush with the left margin. This device calls visual attention to these passages, which erupt out of similar stimuli to Quentin's consciousness, and which Faulkner seems to have wanted readers to see as thematically related to each other; they were printed, however, with normalized paragraph indentation. Did Faulkner ink these paragraphing changes on his ribbon typescript? Did he instruct Cape and Smith to make these changes? Did Wasson or another editor take it upon himself to change this, too, while altering the Benjy section? Faulkner in fact revised the typescript of the Quentin section some time after it was copyedited. Did he see galleys for the Quentin section? If so, did he accept the altered typescript "intentions" as a fait accompli when he saw galleys? We have no evidence that he saw galleys for any but the Benjy section. For the "New, Corrected Edition" of *The Sound and the Fury*[22] I restored the flush left readings of the carbon typescript, not with a great deal of confidence that Faulkner did not make or order the changes himself, but only with the evidence that the flush left paragraphs indicate a pattern in the section's visual apparatus that is demonstrably part of Faulkner's intention at the time he submitted the typescript to the publisher. The carbon typescript of the Benjy section does not *contain* Faulkner's intention but does seem to point toward it clearly enough to make it possible to reconstruct it. The carbon typescript of the Quentin section contains one intention demonstrably Faulkner's; there is no evidence to indicate whose intention the published text might represent.

Absalom, Absalom! poses very few problems in its accidentals, largely because preserved among Faulkner's papers are the copyedited typescript setting copy at the University of Virginia, and a set of corrected galleys at the University of Texas, which record the editorial process that made the 1936 published text so different from the typescript that Faulkner submitted. A rough estimate suggests that there are nearly fifteen hundred variants, accidental and substantive, between the typescript and the published book. Three editorial hands delete and add punctuation; replace purposefully ambiguous pronominal references with their proper name referents (Faulkner caught one change in galleys and irritably chastised the editor for getting the antecedent wrong!); shorten Faulkner's lengthy sentences and lengthen his short ones; make regular sentences out of passages Faulkner enclosed in parentheses; shift and, worse, even delete entire passages, sometimes as much as ten lines at a time. The 1936 Random House *Absalom,* then, is the most heavily and worst edited of any of Faulkner's novels. The new text will make it necessary to reconsider the novel's stylistic complexities; whether we shall be more or less pleased with those complexities, I am not prepared to say.

In most cases, there was no question for me but to restore Faulkner's typescript readings. Only one major problem in editing *Absalom* required some care not to impose meaning where there was none or, by the same token, to deny it if it were there. This problem concerned whether the appended chronology and the genealogy were merely appendixes, or whether they bore other relationships to the narrative proper. As published in the 1936 first edition, the chronology contains several discrepancies from the novel proper: for example, Ellen, according to the chronology, was born in 1818, but the tombstone in the novel gives her birth as 1817; in the chronology Charles Bon was born in 1829, but the evidence of the novel suggests 1831. There is an early manuscript and an early typescript version of the chronology; nothing remains of the genealogy but the published version, and neither chronology nor genealogy is connected to the extant manuscript, typescript, or galley proofs of the novel. Given Faulkner's many experiments with novelistic structure, it is certainly possible that discrepancies between the chronology and the narrative proper are deliberate, that these appendixes are part of the modernist technique of *Absalom* and in fact are as much a part of the novel proper as the concluding newspaper account of the incident on board the *HMS Bellipotent* is a part of *Billy Budd*. This is a bellipotent argument against correcting the chronology to agree with the "facts" of the novel; indeed, in a novel full of (and even built around) interpretative voices, each positing a set of "facts" designed to make its own case about Thomas Sutpen, in a novel full of disquieting ambiguities about the nature of historical truth, one might well see those appendixes as yet another voice, more or less external to the novel proper.

Yet I was persuaded to make the chronology's "facts" agree with the "facts" of the novel, when it was possible to do so; the evidence persuaded me to treat these appendixes as aids to the reader of a very complex novel. Two pieces of information decided the issue for me. First is the outright error in the chronology which lists the fall of 1910 as the date on which Quentin and Rosa Coldfield go out to the Sutpen house and find Henry there: this is an absolute, glaring error that cannot even remotely be considered a "commentary" on the novel. Second, perhaps more telling, is that according to the novel proper, Judith Sutpen and Charles E. St. Valery Bon die, in 1884, of yellow fever; according to the 1936 published chronology, they die of smallpox. The manuscript version of the chronology says simply that they "died." The holograph manuscript of the novel has them dying of smallpox, as does the published chronology. Page 258 of the typescript setting copy, however, shows that Faulkner, following the manuscript, originally typed "smallpox" and at least the next word, then went back, typed *x*'s over "smallpox," and typed in "yellow fever" above. He did *not,* however, go back and change the manuscript or the chronology to agree with his revised thinking.

This bit of evidence suggests, though of course does not prove, that Faulkner got confused about relationships among events in this very complex novel, and manufactured the chronology for himself—perhaps after he came back to it from his brief interlude of work on *Pylon*—to help him keep straight all the dates and relationships, then discarded it, for his own purposes, as he wrote past a particular date. Perhaps someone at Random House suggested that it be appended to the book, and Faulkner allowed this to happen, without correcting or updating it—and apparently none of the original editors, for all their wholesale revision, had read it or the novel closely enough to be aware of the discrepancies. The evidence thus suggested that the appendixes were not modernist adjuncts to the novel, but merely aids to the reader, and so I treated them as appendicular material, separate documents with separate if related purposes; I corrected their dates, where possible, to conform with the "facts" of the novel, and so confirmed them in what the evidence testified about their original "intention."

The editorial enterprise, then, is uncertain at best, and editors who claim to have produced a "definitive" text may well spend eternity in a special circle of hell proofreading *Finnegans Wake,* and they would deserve no less. No fewer than a dozen proofreadings by at least four different pairs of eyes left me with at least one glaring typo in *The Sound and the Fury:* "treees",[23] which had persistently hidden itself from us in *all* stages of proof. So much for "definitive," much less for "final intentions," which can, probably must, change from day to day for any writer engaged with his or her material. The whole notion of a final intention is at bottom an intensely romantic one that assumes that at some point, any point, in the composition process, a writer is in full and complete control of *every* aspect of the work, from comma placement to large and profound themes; I doubt seriously that this *ever* happens, except as an illusion, even though I cling to the old-fashioned notion that authors are essentially smarter than we are, or at least better-informed about the work they are writing, and that what we perceive as problematic in any text may simply be our own blindness.

To conclude, I'd like to detour slightly from Faulkner to report an instructive exchange with Eudora Welty regarding the text of her first collection of stories, *A Curtain of Green.* For years the most available text of this important collection was that of the Modern Library's *Selected Stories* (1954), a plate reprint of the 1947 Harcourt Brace second edition.

But its textual antecedents are quite problematic. The first edition (Doubleday Doran, 1941) was set from Welty's typescript, which shows numerous and, to my eye, injurious editorial interventions in matters of style and punctuation. When Harcourt asked her for printer's copy, she sent them, curiously, a copy of the 1943 first British edition, which had been set from the Doubleday text after its editing toward British usage and house-styling. The Harcourt Brace text was, then, with numerous changes from the original (among which were four completely dropped lines, including a whole paragraph of dialogue), even further distant from those typescript intentions, and the popular Modern Library text perpetuated those differences. Nearly thirty years later Welty apparently used the Modern Library text, dropped paragraphs and all, to revise from when preparing the *Collected Stories* of 1980.

In 1984, Michel Gresset, translating *A Curtain of Green* for the first time into French, wrote asking for help on some Southern idioms and for advice on what to title the translation (*A Curtain of Green,* he said, did not translate meaningfully into French; he proposed *L'Homme Pétrifié*). I noted that his queries were keyed to the Modern Library text and wrote back proposing that he use the Doubleday first edition for his translation. Gresset counterproposed that, in view of Welty's revisions for the *Collected Stories,* we ask her.

I wrote her, proudly enclosing a copy of my learned essay on the text of *A Curtain of Green;*[24] she wrote back as follows:

> Thank you for your interesting letter. I appreciate your being of good assistance to M. Gresset, of the University of Paris. In regard to your questions, I think *Petrified Man and Other Stories* is a good title and perfectly acceptable as a substitute one for *A Curtain of Green* (which was the editors' choice in the first place only because nobody had anything special against it, out of all the titles in the collection). About the translation text and my own preference, it is of course that text I most recently provided, for *The Collected Stories.* As you saw, I had made changes, and my reason was in every instance toward clarity, I believed—clarity was my object. I don't see much use in retaining something cloudy or confusing just because it was earlier, though I am not of the scholarly persuasion and I expect you demur. Anyway, while of course I respect you and am grateful to you as the bibliographer, I feel as I do from the author's wish to get the meaning

across, which is probably undying, don't you imagine? Thank you for your aid.[25]

I have no doubt that James, Irving, Whitman, and other late revisers of their works would have responded similarly. There are, or should be, lessons for us all in such completely understandable authorial attitudes, even if some of them are painful and even if none is particularly helpful to an editor. The lessons are multiple, and contradictory, and for critics involve such considerations as the meaning of "clarity" in Welty's letter. Creators do not stand still in time, and neither do their works. Neither, in painful fact, do critics. But editors and texts *must.* Editors are by definition charged to produce *a text,* to make pedestrian decisions about where the comma goes and to make sure it gets where it's supposed to be. The *ideal* of scholarly editing is to make all possible forms of a text available to the reader, since that is the only way to bridge the gap, the abyss, between and among any set of authorial "intentions" and outside influences on any given work of art; but that is only an ideal, and most editors will have to choose one version or text to produce; most will have only one comma to wrestle with, and that comma may well be the still point of a turning critical world.

The sheer impossibility of the task, then, makes the editorial enterprise an awesome, sobering responsibility. At the same time, and paradoxically, of course, that very impossibility relieves us of some measure of that responsibility, and perhaps ought to give us enough distance from comma placement to consider some of the larger implications of editorial responsibility: that is, if the texts we edit are as close as some of us will ever come to justifying the ways of God to *man,* it cannot be lost on anybody that the greater part of our editorial energy is being expended by white men working to establish—or, rather, to *re*-establish, *re*-canonize—the already canonized texts of other, already established white men and who are therefore in effect mostly justifying the ways of white men to each other. This is an understandable result of the forces that have shaped the canon, and it may be that the editorial enterprise is the most effective way to address the problems at the heart of the canon itself: serious discussion of the arduous and particular process of making large and small editorial choices (where a comma goes, where an author goes) and, especially, of the cultural and aesthetic training that influences those choices, will, I think, eventually, inevitably, give a voice to the legitimate claims that female and black and other minority readers have on the canon. We need obviously to take our editorial responsibilities seriously, and to get all those commas where they ought to be, but we ought at the same time always keep in mind that our texts—even those of Faulkner, Joyce, Shakespeare—are *not* the Graven Tablets nor the Pentateuch, no matter who is justifying what to whom, no matter what tradition is being reified in the editorial process. Perhaps in fact we should all do well to remember that the Father/author of the Ten Commandments delegated a good deal of his intention to a male editor who, with a good deal of editorial supererogation, proceeded to destroy the original hand-printed plates and then reconstruct the text from memory—no doubt making the author's meaning clear with some accidentals of his own.

NOTES

1. W. W. Greg, "The Rationale of Copy-Text," *Studies in Bibliography* 3 (1950–51): 19–36.

2. William Faulkner, *As I Lay Dying* (1930; rpt. New York: Library of America, 1985), 115.

3. These are Faulkner's *Sanctuary: The Original Text* (New York: Random House, 1981); *The Sound and the Fury* (New York: Random House, 1984); *Absalom, Absalom!* (New York: Random House, 1986); and *As I Lay Dying, Sanctuary, Light in August,* and *Pylon* (collected in William Faulkner, *Novels 1930–1935* [New York: Library of America, 1985]); all but the first of which were published by Vintage Paperbacks in 1987. *Absalom, Absalom!, The Unvanquished, If I Forget Thee, Jerusalem* [*The Wild Palms*], and *The Hamlet* (collected in William Faulkner, *Novels 1936–1940* [New York: Library of America, 1990]) are scheduled for publication by Vintage in 1990 or 1991.

4. James B. Meriwether's excellent term, noted in his classes and in numerous conversations with him about editorial problems in Faulkner.

5. Faulkner once told a group at the University of Virginia that he wrote so fast "that somebody said my handwriting looks like a caterpillar that crawled through a ink well and out on to a piece of paper. If I leave it until tomorrow I can't read it myself, so it's got to be put down quick and then typed quick." Quoted in Frederick L. Gwynn and Joseph Blotner, eds., *Faulkner in the University* (Charlottesville: University Press of Virginia, 1959), 194.

6. James L. W. West III, "Editorial Theory and the Act of Submission," *Papers of the Bibliographical Society of America* 83 (June 1989): 169–85.

7. Noel Polk, *An Editorial Handbook to William Faulkner's "The Sound and the Fury"* (New York: Garland, 1985), 3–6.

8. *William Faulkner Manuscripts,* vol. 12, *Pylon,* ed. Noel Polk (New York: Garland, 1987).

9. As with the stories collected in *The Unvanquished,* he probably sent to book editors tearsheets of inconsistently *Post-* and *Scribner's-* and *Collier's*-edited stories pasted to his typing paper, without bothering to correct their bowdlerizations, their repunctuation or reparagraphing of his prose, or their normalization of his dialect.

10. See *William Faulkner Manuscripts,* vol. 13, *Absalom, Absalom!,* ed. Noel Polk; vol. 14, *The Wild Palms,* ed. Thomas L. McHaney (New York: Garland, 1987).

11. Hershel Parker and Brian Higgins, "Sober Second Thoughts: Fitzgerald's 'Final Version' of *Tender is the Night,*" *Proof* 4 (1975): 129–52.

12. Hershel Parker, *Flawed Texts and Verbal Icons: Literary Authority in American Fiction* (Evanston, Ill.: Northwestern University Press, 1984).

13. James L. W. West, III, ed., *Sister Carrie,* by Theodore Dreiser (Philadelphia: University of Pennsylvania Press, 1981); Henry Binder, ed., *The Red Badge of Courage,* by Stephen Crane (New York: Norton, 1976). See also Parker, *Flawed Texts,* 147–80 and *passim.*

14. On the latter, see Parker, *Flawed Texts,* 147–80.

15. Joseph Blotner, *Faulkner, A Biography* (New York: Random House, 1984), 364.

16. *Sanctuary: The Original Text* reproduces the typescript text of that novel's original version, the text Faulkner submitted to Cape and Smith, then revised when he saw it in galleys. The Library of America text (New York, 1985), published as a Vintage paperback (New York, 1987) as *Sanctuary: The Corrected Text,* is a text of his revisions, published originally in 1931.

17. Noel Polk, "The Space Between *Sanctuary,*" in *Intertextuality in Faulkner,* ed. Michel Gresset and Noel Polk (Jackson: University Press of Mississippi, 1985), 16–35.

18. I have been able to edit *The Sound and the Fury,* to make corrections for the Vintage paperback, and will be able to make other corrections as necessary. I have overseen publication of that novel's manuscript and carbon typescript in facsimile—four different versions of a single novel. I have edited the two different versions of *Sanctuary* and have overseen facsimile reproductions of Faulkner's typescript, a third version, and of his holograph manuscript, from which can be reconstructed, I suspect, a large number of other "versions" of the original text of *Sanctuary. William Faulkner Manuscripts,* Garland's 44-volume facsimile edition of the most important of the extant Faulkner manuscripts at the Alderman Library of the University of Virginia and at the New York Public Library, in fact make available for reconstruction *all* versions of Faulkner's texts;

Garland and other publishers are also publishing facsimiles of other authors' manuscripts and typescripts.

19. Faulkner wrote to Warren Beck in 1941: "I discovered then that I had rather read Shakespeare, bad puns, bad history, taste and all, than Pater, and that I had a damn sight rather fail at trying to write Shakespeare than to write all of Pater over again so he couldn't have told it himself if you fired it point blank at him through an amplifier." *Selected Letters of William Faulkner,* ed. Joseph Blotner (New York: Random House, 1977), 142. See also Hershel Parker, "Regularizing Accidentals: The Latest Form of Infidelity," *Proof* 1 (1973): 1–20.

20. It is fairly common for editors to rely on the *OED* as a final authority for many of their editorial decisions. This may be a mistake: since the *OED* is based on printed, not manuscript, sources, a bow to its authority in usage may in fact merely perpetuate house-styling or printing conventions rather than actual *usage.*

21. Polk, *Editorial Handbook,* 5–8.

22. See especially 107–11, 149–64; in the Vintage edition, 123–27, 171–87.

23. See the Random House edition, 6.

24. Noel Polk, "The Text of the Modern Library *A Curtain of Green,*" *Eudora Welty Newsletter* 3, no. 1-A (Winter 1979): 6–9.

25. Eudora Welty to author, 26 November 1984. I am grateful to Miss Welty for allowing me to use this letter.

Contemporary Textual and Literary Theory

Michael Groden

What is the nature of the literary work (text, object)? What is an author, and what authority does the author have over the work? What are the work's relationships to its social contexts? to its modes of composition, production, and distribution? to its readers? How do these relationships affect a reader's or critic's views of the work?

Literary critics and theorists have been asking questions like these for years, and so have textual theorists. Yet, as many people from both groups have noted, there has been relatively little contact between the two and not much recognition of common interests. Literary theorists and critics have tended to see editing and bibliography as activities that are preliminary to criticism[1] and the textual theorists and critics themselves as concerned only with empirical evidence, often with minute details (commas, watermarks). Textual critics, on the other hand, have accused their literary counterparts of being insufficiently interested in the editions of texts upon which they base their readings or theories and naive in their unquestioned assumptions that the texts they are using are reliable.

Textual critics have not been reticent in charging literary critics with limited vision. In 1959, for example, Fredson Bowers remarked that "we should be seriously disturbed by the lack of contact between literary critics and textual critics" and claimed, memorably, that "many a literary critic has investigated the past ownership and mechanical condition of his second-hand automobile, or the pedigree and training of his dog, more thoroughly than he has looked into the qualifications of the text on which his critical theories rest." His recommended prescription was that "every practising critic, for the humility of his soul, ought to study the transmission of some appropriate text."[2] Over the last thirty years the talk has been less about "humility" and "soul," but the complaint remains the same; for instance, G. Thomas Tanselle has recently noted that "critical sophistication in extracting the meaning from words on a page can—and frequently does—coexist with the most uncritical attitude toward the document itself and the trustworthiness of its text."[3]

Textual critics have also repeatedly emphasized that literary critics give up or risk a lot by ignoring textual activities. Bowers notes that "the common ignorance of textual conditions and of editing standards . . . puts the critic quite at the mercy of the editor" (4), a statement put in a different key by Jerome McGann: "The literary criticism of English and American works has ceded to textual and bibliographical specialists almost total authority to pronounce upon matters relating to their fields" (*Beauty,* 76). Tanselle says that "readers cannot be expected, every time they pick up a book, to examine all the written and printed documents relevant to the transmission of the work represented by the text in that book. But they ought to have sufficient understanding of the nature of verbal works to know that a failure to do so involves risk, and they can then judge whether, given the occasion, the risk is worth taking" (*Rationale,* 47). Finally, Peter Shillingsburg notes that "editors *are* critics, too; an edition reflects the editor's critical biases. . . . Edition-users have a very high stake in knowing what principles were used to produce the edition they are relying upon."[4]

On the other side, textual critics have been criticized (more from within than from without, since literary critics have tended to ignore textual criticism) for paying insufficient attention to developments in literary criticism and theory. Shillingsburg notes that "new trends in literary criticism have not noticeably influenced textual editing" (11). Gary Taylor has recently remarked that, when Bowers made the statements already quoted from *Textual and Literary Criticism* in 1959, he still thought of the New Criticism as dangerously new.[5] Even as late as 1985 Bowers was saying that "the great principle of the search for authorial integrity, which is to say for authenticity, remains forever constant,"[6] as if such terms as *author* and *integrity* were transparent and unproblematical. D. C. Greetham, noting that "for the most part, the literary theorists have continued their work as if there had been no advances in textual-critical theory in the last few decades," goes on to say that "the *editing* of texts has sometimes continued without a full or articulated investigation of the theoretical *choices* involved in each separate editorial task."[7]

The gaps may be starting to close. Greetham has recently suggested parallels between various current textual theories and the work of such literary theorists and philosophers as Husserl, Gadamer, Jauss, Shklovsky, Barthes, and Derrida, and he has compared three broad approaches to editing to the literary theories of Stanley Fish, E. D. Hirsch, and the French Structuralists; Hans Zeller evokes the Prague Structuralists, and Louis Hay builds on work by Barthes and Kristeva; Hans Walter Gabler conceives of textual variants in terms of structuralist binary oppositions and talks of authorial intention as "not a metaphysical notion to be fulfilled but a textual force to be studied"; Gerald M. MacLean proposes editing not an author but a discourse.[8] Gabler's edition of *Ulysses,* Jerome McGann claims, "raises all the central questions that have brought such a fruitful crisis to literary work in the postmodern period," while Christine Froula argues that an edition of Pound's *Cantos,* by necessarily confronting issues of error, might foreground debates over matters of authority, power, and ideals of perfection that are prominent in current literary theory.[9]

This essay looks at some central issues in textual criticism and theory, emphasizing matters that also concern literary theory. The following section traces the growth of the dominant theoretical and practical position in Anglo-American textual studies today, the approach associated most readily with W. W. Greg, Fredson Bowers, and G. Thomas Tanselle. I will then consider recent refinements of this approach and various alternatives to the position in terms of two broad issues: author/authorial intention and work/text. By looking at different responses to these two vexed issues, I hope to suggest ways in which textual and literary theorists can challenge each other and ways in which the gaps between the two groups might be further narrowed.

I

Modern Anglo-American textual theory begins with W. W. Greg's "The Rationale of Copy-Text," delivered as a lecture in 1949 and published in 1950–51. Greg was responding to earlier theories of editing Renaissance works, principally R. B. McKerrow's, that argued that an editor should select the "best text" among those available and follow it in all its readings except for those that are demonstrably erroneous. Against this, Greg proposed a copy-text of divided authority. Since our knowledge of conventions of the English language in the Renaissance is limited (and different printers followed different conventions), Greg suggested that a document closest in time to the author's own text, usually the first edition, should be chosen as copy-text and followed in its accidentals (spelling, punctuation, etc.). For substantives (words), the editor should consult all authoritative texts and, where necessary, emend the copy-text. The resulting text is eclectic because, in Bowers's later formulation, the editor "synthesize[s] the authority of the revised substantives with the authority of the original accidentals."[10] The eclectic edited text will necessarily differ from all the authoritative texts of the work that the editor used to produce it, indeed from any previous text. For Greg, a copy-text is chosen "only on grounds of expediency," not for critical reasons, and he designed his rationale to free the editor from "the tyranny of the copy-text" by protecting his or her freedom to emend the substantives while at the same time providing a text that he or she could fall back on when all choices were equal (indifferent variants) and for accidentals, which Greg distinguishes from substantives on "practical" and not on "philosophic" grounds.[11]

Greg designed his rationale to deal with Renaissance drama; for those works, authorial manuscripts have not usually survived and "philological ignorance" and "linguistic circumstances" prevent a critic from being certain about the accidentals (377). In the 1950s and 1960s Fredson Bowers explained, adapted, and applied Greg's thinking in a series of papers and in editions of such later authors as Dryden, Fielding, Hawthorne, Crane, and William James. In so doing, he argued for and sought to demonstrate the validity of the rationale for diverse post-Renaissance works. In the late 1960s and 1970s Greg's rationale became the principle for editions prepared under the auspices of the Modern Language Association's Center for Editions of American Authors (later the Center for Scholarly Editions),[12] where it became highly influential and controversial in both theory and practice. By this time Greg's model of divided authority had been recast in some important ways: if the copy-text, chosen to preserve the author's system of accidentals, is usually the document closest to the author, then the author's manuscript, if it survived, would probably best suit the purpose, whereas the editor should consider all later authoritative versions in order to reproduce the "final authorial intentions" for the substantives. (Greg did not talk about final authorial intentions, but the concept is a major aspect of Bowers's interpretation and application of Greg.)[13]

From the start there were two major areas of controversy: the applicability of extending Greg's concept of copy-text to works from the nineteenth and twentieth centuries and the justification for selecting the document closest to the author as copy-text while looking for the author's final intentions in the substantives. (A third area of controversy was the editions' formats and the nature of their apparatuses.)[14] Defenders of the Greg-Bowers approach repeatedly emphasized both its flexibility (it doesn't mandate the choice of first edition or manuscript as copy-text) and its pragmatic advantages (in Tanselle's words, "What Greg's method provides editors is a procedure to follow when they would otherwise be undecided: when in doubt, he was saying, stick to the copy-text").[15] While defending the approach, they also modified, refined, and extended it. For instance, in 1978 Bowers "revisited" Greg's "Rationale of Copy-Text" article from the perspective of editors of modern texts, who are likely to feel a "conviction that the accidentals are an inseparable whole with the substantives in transmitting the author's total meaning." For these editors, "the choice of copy-text transcends the grounds of expediency and must be recognized as having a critical significance beyond that which Greg conceived." Bowers concludes that, with modifications and variations, Greg's rationale is sound for literature of all periods.[16]

In recent years G. Thomas Tanselle has become the most prominent, consistent, and authoritative defender of the Greg-Bowers approach to editing. He has written three omnibus accounts of textual criticism that discuss and respond to various issues and debates (in 1975, 1981, and 1986; collected in *Since Greg*), as well as other articles on specific topics (the problem of final intentions, relations between editing classical and modern texts). Tanselle appeals to logic, coherence, and consistency in his arguments, and, while holding to the basics of what is by now the dominant theoretical and practical position in Anglo-American editing, he has sought to reduce its contentious aspects and to accommodate legitimate critiques of its limitations. He no longer speaks much about copy-text in terms of substantives and accidentals (he agrees with others that the terms should be dropped both because of their confusing connotations and, following Bowers, because a critical distinction between a text's words and its spelling or punctuation is often not relevant);[17] copy-text has now become essentially a document of "presumptive authority" for indifferent variants (*Since Greg,* 106). He has continually emphasized the openness and flexibility of the position. He sees debates about specific issues in textual criticism as part of a much loftier general enterprise: at the end of the last essay in *Textual Criticism since Greg* he says that "scholarly editing appears . . . as one of the most demanding and rewarding forms of the critical study of history" (154), and he argues at the close of *A Rationale of Textual Criticism* that "our cultural heritage consists, in Yeats's phrase, of 'Monuments of unageing intellect.' . . . [Textual criticism] puts us on the trail of one class of our monuments and helps us to see the process by which humanity attempts, sometimes successfully, to step outside itself" (93).

II

For Anglo-American textual critics the most contentious issue in the past twenty-five years has probably been "final authorial intentions." All three words are problematical. First, what are "intentions," and how are they manifested? We may accept the New Critical "intentional fallacy" and refuse to look to the author for matters of value or meaning, but does this rule out the author's intention to put a specific word or mark on a page?[18] Can or should intentions be extended to expectations about what other people will do to the text, whether the author requests or desires collaboration (he or she asks a publisher to correct spelling errors and to regularize grammar and punctuation) or, more or less reluctantly, accepts it (the publisher will impose a house style on the manuscript)?[19] Second, what does "final" mean? Are final intentions simply the last ones, or can they be the fullest or most developed, whether or not they are chronologically last?[20] Most complicated is "author." Is the author always engaged in the "creative process" or only up to a point, after that point becoming more a reviser or editor?[21] Are we concerned with an isolated human being who conceives and writes a work, or the social being who, willingly or reluctantly, collaborates with others (manuscript editor, copyeditor, printers, proofreaders) to achieve a public text? Can an author, or any of these individuals, be seen as an autonomous, unified subject isolated from other forces (social, economic, historical, psychological)?[22] Obviously, answers to these questions will affect definitions of the other terms. If the originating person can be considered the author only during a creative phase, then "final" intentions will be limited to that phase. Other answers affect the goal at its core: if the human being who wrote the text is not conceived as isolated, integral, and unified, then "final authorial intentions" can become highly problematic and even meaningless. Attempts to define these three words involve several of the most basic questions that not only textual critics but all theorists who work with literature have to ask.

Greg's rationale, and Bowers's development and refinement of the theory and methodology, took place during the heyday of the New Criticism in the 1950s, even if it came to dominate editing theory and practice only in the 1960s and 1970s. In some ways Greg-Bowers editing and New Criticism are diametrically opposed, since New Criticism, following Eliot, eliminated the author as a source of interpretation and set up the poem as a self-contained "verbal icon." In their well known argument against the "intentional fallacy," W. K. Wimsatt and Monroe C. Beardsley concluded that "critical inquiries are not settled by consulting the oracle" (*Verbal Icon,* 18). Greg-Bowers editing, of course, requires "consulting" the author to settle textual inquiries; as a result, the literary theorist from the 1960s most commonly and readily associated with this approach to editing has been E. D. Hirsch, whose *Validity in Interpretation* is an explicitly anti–New Critical argument for rescinding the critical banishment of the author: "To verify a text is simply to establish that the author probably meant what we construe his text to mean. The interpreter's primary task is to reproduce in himself the author's 'logic,' his attitudes, his cultural givens, in short, his world. Even though the process of verification is highly complex and difficult, the ultimate verificative principle is very simple—the imaginative reconstruction of the speaking subject."[23]

Beyond these real differences, however, there are perhaps more important parallels and similarities. The New Critical poem, despite the emphasis on construction in terms like Wimsatt's "verbal icon" or Cleanth Brooks's use of Keats's "well wrought urn," was an organic entity: "The elements of a poem are related to each other, not as blossoms juxtaposed in a bouquet, but as the blossoms are related to the other parts of a growing plant. . . . The relation between part and part is organic"; "If we should compare a poem to the make-up of some physical object it ought not to be to a wall but to something organic like a plant."[24] As D. C. Greetham has recently noted, the organicism of this poem and "the New-Critical reliance on cohesion arising from a reconciliation of the multiple ironies in a poetic utterance unavoidably rested upon the unacknowledged concept of an intentionalising consciousness"; the "single, static artifact" was inextricably linked to "the concept of the single, informing consciousness as a unifying and unitary vehicle" ("Matrix," 14–15n.4).[25] Similarly, in Greg-Bowers textual theory, the practice of conflating readings from different documents produces an edited text that is different from any previously existing text, and it has become controversial because it draws eclectically from different texts, but the theory is held together by a concept of an organic work and a unified originating consciousness. Tanselle has distinguished different versions of a work in terms of a "conception of an organic whole" ("Final Authorial Intention," 340, 353), and his recent "rationale of textual criticism" hinges on a distinction between work and text that ultimately locates the work in the author's mind (*Since Greg,* 109; *Rationale,* 80, 90).

A few further parallels between New Criticism and Greg-Bowers editing are worth noting. A cornerstone of New Critical thinking and practice has been the severance of the author from the work once it is released into the world, as in such statements as Eliot's "We can only say that a poem, in some sense, has its own life; that its parts form something quite different from a body of neatly ordered biographical data; that the feeling, or emotion, or vision, resulting from the poem is something different from the feeling or emotion or vision in the mind of the poet" and "A poem may appear to mean very different things to different readers, and all of these meanings may be different from what the author thought he meant. . . . The reader's interpretation may differ from the author's and be equally valid—it may even be better."[26] Tanselle sounds quite similar to Eliot when he claims that a

> scholarly editor sets as his goal the reconstruction of the text intended by the author. . . . The text he produces can, like any other text, be the subject of critical speculation by those who have no interest in the author's intention; but it can also serve the needs of those critics who are concerned with the work as the product of a particular mind. That an interpretation by one of the former turns out to seem more satisfying to many readers than an interpretation by one of the latter has no bearing on the importance or desirability of the task which the scholarly editor has set himself. ("Final Authorial Intention," 324)

Thus, both for Eliot and the New Critics in his wake and for Tanselle, the processes and premises of creation (or recreation) and of criticism are kept firmly distinct. For Tanselle, critics have an obligation (usually ignored) to learn how an edition was produced, but, like the author, the editor cannot and should not be concerned with assumptions that subsequent critics might hold.

Tanselle no longer describes the goal of a scholarly editor in as limited and categorical a way as he did in this statement from 1976, but this parallel between the New Critical author and the Greg-Bowers editor in relation to subsequent criticism suggests, I think, one important reason why textual and literary critics have had so little interest in each other's activities. Textual and literary critics have moved away from (or toward) the literary object from opposite directions but have stopped short of meeting. Rather, they have established a line (the object of their study itself) that neither is interested in crossing; each group has in effect declared the other side off limits. To the extent that textual critics are trying to establish a text of a work, their efforts stop at the point of that establishment. They make no claims to influence the readings or interpretations that subsequent critics might make. Literary critics, on the other hand, have tended to banish the author from any evaluative or interpretative authority over the work and have extended that banishment to any questions about how the text was produced (or, more typically, to take for granted that questions about the author and the text's production relate exclusively to questions of meaning and interpretation). It is for this reason that Jerome McGann can make this sardonic assessment of the relationship between the two groups:

> The academy has ceded a privilege to textual scholars and bibliographers which allows them to live and move and have their being at the periphery of literary studies as such. It is a privilege that has been agreed to by all parties: the scholars have thereby gained a considerable freedom and autonomy to pursue their (often highly technical and specialized) work, and the critics have been released from the oligation to develop certain skills which are not easily or quickly acquired. As a result, the angels of hermeneutics have long feared to tread in the fields of textual/bibliographical studies, which are widely regarded, in fact, as a world well lost. Reciprocally, the bibliographers, editors, and textual critics have largely agreed to assume the bad eminence they have achieved, whence they may hurl defiance at the heavens of the interpreters. (*Beauty,* 70)

Elsewhere, McGann argues there should be a "tension and struggle between these opposing interests, rather than an agreement to let each go its own way" (*Beauty,* 94). However, if textual and literary critics continue to espouse positions that perpetuate the line between textual production and reception, each group will probably remain uninterested in the other's activities.

Lately, there have been moves from different directions to weaken or dissolve the line. Tanselle's recent thinking, most notably his *Rationale of Textual Criticism,* involves an attempt to discuss the nature of literature and of critical and scholarly activities in a way that unites literary and textual criticism. This thinking hinges on an insistence on the critical nature of scholarly editing and on a distinction between a literary "work" and a "text."

Tanselle and others emphasize the critical nature of editing because of the common accusation that Greg's rationale, as extended by Bowers, provides an editor with an overly objective, even mechanical, way of resolving textual disputes. Defenders of the Greg-Bowers approach and other textual theorists have spent a great deal of energy dispelling these charges, from such projects as attempting to eliminate the word *definitive* from the textual vocabulary ("Since every verbal work must be reconstructed, no text of any such work is ever definitive" [Tanselle, *Rationale,* 74]; "edited texts will not be definitive, any more than any other product of literary criticism is definitive. The word *definitive* should be banished from editorial discussion" [Shillingsburg, *Scholarly Editing,* 93]) to frequent insistence that editing involves subjectivity, judgment, and criticism: "One sometimes hears complaints about the subjective element in editing, and there is a long tradition . . . of searching for a procedure that eliminates human judgments. No such system has been found, of course, nor will it be. . . . We should instead embrace the inevitable and concentrate on defining the role of judgment" (*Rationale,* 82). Hardly any editor or textual theorist would disagree with these statements, although they still tend to come as surprises to the larger literary community, as some readers' shock regarding the subjective nature of aspects of Gabler's contested edition of *Ulysses* would seem to indicate.

The second change in emphasis involves the articulation of a general theory of literature. Whereas in 1976, as quoted above, Tanselle defined the goal of scholarly editing unequivocally as "the reconstruction of the text intended by the author," he has more recently attempted to place arguments for editing according to author's intentions into a full-scale theory of literature and a "rationale of textual criticism." Central to this attempt is a distinction between "work" and "text." Textual critics must always ask certain basic questions: how are various extant documents related to each other? are they all texts of the same work? if so, how do we know? Likewise, if documents contain errors (and editing a previously published text is necessary only if they do), then against what standard of accuracy is error measured? The goal of editing according to author's final intentions provides a standard and a grounding, but if intentions are not automatically the goal, then a more inclusive standard is needed. For Tanselle, "a work, at each point in its life, is an ineluctable entity, which one can admire or deplore but cannot alter without becoming a collaborator with its creator (or creators)" (*Rationale,* 13–14). We can't know a work directly; it "lies behind" a text and "can be transmitted only indirectly" (18). We can know only literary texts, which are imperfect and accessible to us through documents. Since texts for Tanselle are only approximations of the "ineluctable entity," they are indeterminate, and none of them, including a critically edited text, can be definitive. According to this argument, textual criticism is an effort to get nearer to an always elusive goal, since we can never reach the work itself; "we can never know, from surviving physical artifacts, what constitutes the texts of . . . works" whose media are those of the sequential arts (literature, music, film, etc.; 30). Textual criticism is seen as both a doomed and a heroic enterprise: it is doomed because "the world of documents is a world of imperfection" (65) and (if works are identified with Yeats's "Monuments of unageing intellect") "those monuments come to us housed in containers that . . . are . . . constantly changing. Verbal works, being immaterial, cannot be damaged as a painting or a sculpture can; but we shall never know with certainty what their undamaged forms consist of" (93). At the same time, textual criticism can "help us to find a way through chaos" (74); it "helps us to see the process by which humanity attempts, sometimes successfully, to step outside itself" (93). Finally, its debates and cycles of thought "have served . . . to satisfy the persistent human craving for absolute truth" (97).

Tanselle presents his "rationale" as a set of observations on "the essential nature of the medium of literature" (16) from which textual criticism and theory can proceed; it claims to permit almost any theory of textual criticism without requiring any particular one. But the rationale may be less inclusive than Tanselle implies. A distinction between work and text is obviously crucial for any editing theory or practice, since an editor has to determine whether the differences in some details in two or more literary texts are variants or errors in versions of one work or differences that make the texts representatives of different works. Perhaps to counter the linking of Greg-Bowers editing with authorial intentions, Tanselle rests his discussion of the "essential nature of literature" not on authors but on works and texts. However, if any text is an imperfect approximation of an "ineluctable entity" that is the work, where can this work be located? Tanselle places the work in the author's mind: the result of editing is "a historical reconstruction, even though it may not correspond with any text that ever existed in tangible form, because the goal is what once existed in the author's mind" (90). The author thus reappears in the conception of the work; any attempt to manifest the work in print, in speech, or even presumably in a word-for-word formulation in the author's mind, is already an imperfect text. The author is an isolated, stable entity, and Tanselle's work seems to have no existence without this author, in whose mind alone it exists. If approaching this work is the goal, even an unattainable one, a theory of editing according to authorial intention would inevitably bring us closer than a different kind of theory.

Tanselle aims for theories that are logical, coherent, and consistent (*Since Greg,* ix, 154; *Rationale,* 74, 75, 83), but in defining "work" as he does and in positing the author's mind as the location of the work, he makes an odd leap out of logic that has links with New Criticism. Terry Eagleton, in a critique of New Criticism, notes that "the New Critical poem, like the Romantic symbol, was . . . imbued with an absolute mystical authority which brooked no rational argument. . . . New Criticism was at root a full-blooded irrationalism."[27] (McGann makes a parallel argument for "the fundamental Idealism" of New Criticism and various subsequent formalisms [*Beauty,* 117n.8].) The New Critical claims for the organic nature of a poem are not logical ones, even though logical critical procedures follow from the claims. Likewise, Tanselle's specific concepts of work and author's mind do not follow inevitably from the observation that no particular text *is* the work; they have to be posited, and believed in, before logical arguments can be constructed from them. As such, they too can be seen as irrationalist moves that maintain the author as central in the way that, as Greetham suggests, the author is central for the anti-intentionalist New Critics.[28] Greg-Bowers textual theories have certainly been logical, coherent, and self-consistent; probably few textual theorists would disagree with McGann's assessment that the Greg-Bowers theory of editing according to final authorial intention is "the most powerful and coherent that we currently possess" (*Critique,* 35). However, the coherence rests on a set of beliefs in a certain kind of human agent who is the author and in a certain relationship between knowable, imperfect human constructs and an imagined less imperfect state, a set of beliefs that McGann treats as ideological (37ff.).[29] Thus, on the one side is an argument for the "essential nature of literature" and on the other a claim that those arguments are rooted in unacknowledged ideology.

III

Several other models of the work/text distinction have been proposed, and they can be usefully observed as alternatives to Tanselle's. For example, Peter Shillingsburg has attempted to map out specific theories of editing within a framework of multiple possibilities. In *Scholarly Editing in the Computer Age* he sketches four main orientations toward literary forms: historical, which emphasizes the accurate presentation of documents as they existed historically or might ideally have existed; aesthetic, which relies finally on the editor's taste; authorial, which emphasizes authorial versions of a text over nonauthorial ones; and sociological, which emphasizes the social nature of text production and does not grant complete authority to the author alone (19–29). He argues that "these editorial positions are all internally coherent and viable, but no single text will satisfy the needs of all four" (29). Moving through a series of contentious issues that are central to textual theory (and many of them, in different ways, to literary theory)—authority, forms, intention, ontology, expectation, completion, ideal texts—Shillingsburg posits a relationship between work and text that parallels Tanselle's but is fundamentally different. For him, a text is "the actual order of words and punctuation as contained in any one physical form" (49), but a work, which has "no substantial existence," is still not "a platonic ideal which the author strove to represent in some final or best version" (46). Against Tanselle's idea that the work "lies behind" all texts and that the editor strives to approach the work as a parallel to a search for "absolute truth," Shillingsburg cites Morse Peckham's claim that a work is an editorial or theoretical "construct," a "'postulated work'" (46, citing Peckham, "Reflections," 127). Shillingsburg argues that "there is a pleasing simplicity in the notion that texts grow or develop or are shaped toward a final form," but the notion is misleading, since a work is the product of "shifting, developing, and sometimes contradictory intentions" (47). Shillingsburg's distinction is still primarily authorial and intentional (although he distinguishes between what he calls "intention to mean" and "intention to do" and argues that only the latter—to have a certain word appear in a particular place—is recoverable by the editor [36–37]), but it is less insistent on a particular relationship between work and text as a criterion for coherence and logicality.

Other arguments that run counter to Tanselle's move away from Shillingsburg's authorial orientation. The best-known recent alternative has been what Shillingsburg calls the sociological orientation, and the most prominent representative of this position is Jerome J. McGann. In attempting to expose what he calls the "ideology of final intentions" (*Critique,* 37), McGann argues that the concept of "the autonomy of the isolated author" (8) is a holdover from Romantic conceptions of the isolated creative genius that is flawed in general and inapplicable in many specific instances (8, 42, 103). Instead of the isolated creator, McGann argues that "literary works are fundamentally social rather than personal or psychological products" (43–44) and that they "are not produced without arrangements of some sort" (48). As one practical result, McGann argues for an approach to editing that treats the process of publication (contributions from the manuscript editor, correction of spelling and grammar, house styling, etc.) as potentially part of the text to be critically established; the first edition, because it reflects arrangements and compromises that McGann considers inevitable, will "normally" be preferred as a copy-text over a manuscript or other prepublication document (113).

McGann's project goes much farther than suggesting an argument for a different copy-text, however. Like the contributors to the present collection of essays, McGann wants to reinstate textual studies as a central part of literary studies, not as a preliminary tool but as something all literary critics should know and, he argues, practice. Unlike my emphasis in this essay, editing is for McGann only one aspect of the broader and wider-ranging enterprise of textual scholarship and criticism.[30] This enterprise assumes a continuum between textual production, reproduction, and reception (*Beauty,* 78, 82–84), and for McGann it is "a special method which students of literature must and should use when they examine, interpret, and reproduce the works we inherit from the past" (77). The method consists of three stages that McGann calls "the originary textual moment," "secondary moments of textual production and reproduction (individual and related sequences)," and "the immediate moment of textual criticism" (82–83), and it involves

> first, an elucidation of the textual history of the work, and second, an explication of the reception history. Neither of these operations can be performed independently of the other because the two historical processes are dialectically related. (This is why no textual criticism, however specialized, can be produced without at least an implicit reference to certain more broadly established social phenomena which impinge on a work's various textual constitutions.) None the less, in textual criticism the attention will focus, necessarily, on a work's shifting verbal forms on the one hand, and on its changing bibliographical states on the other. (84)

Since McGann wants to ground all aspects of production, reception, and scholarship and criticism in their specific historical contexts, it is not surprising that, even though he too insists on a distinction between work and text, his "work" is far from Tanselle's "ineluctable entity." A work is a "related series of concretely determinable semiotic events that embody and represent processes of social and historical experience" (10); the work is "a series of specific 'texts,' a series of specific acts of production, and the entire process which both of these series constitute" (*Critique,* 52) rather than "an *Ur*-poem or meta-work whose existence is the Idea that can be abstracted out of all concrete and written texts which have ever existed or which ever will exist" (*Beauty,* 117).

McGann has been criticized for being inconsistent and for oversimplifying the positions he is opposing (Tanselle, *Since Greg,* 127–35; Shillingsburg, *Scholarly Editing,* 32), and he has not yet demonstrated what an edition that follows from his principles would look like. (He has analyzed such prose works and poems as Poe's "Von Kempelen and His Discovery" and Tennyson's "The Charge of the Light Brigade" as examples of the critical method that he is proposing [*Beauty,* 102ff., 173ff.].) The part of his proposed reformulation of textual criticism that has received the most attention is the argument in *A Critique of Modern Textual Criticism* for a reorganization of the way editors and critics view the participants in the process of textual production, a movement away from author alone to author in collaboration with publishers. This is how Tanselle (*Rationale,* 83–85) and Shillingsburg (*Scholarly Editing,*

24–25, 27) view McGann's alternative to editing according to final authorial intention. But elsewhere McGann seems to be arguing for an alternative conception of these participants themselves and of the literary product: "Every work of art is the product of an interaction between the artist, on the one hand, and a variety of social determinants on the other" (*Beauty,* 119), "Poems are artistic works produced, and maintained, under specific socialized conditions" (120), "A work of poetry is not a thing or an object, nor should criticism conceive it as such; it is the result of an interactive network of productive people and forces" (343). McGann sees a work as a nexus of people and forces, but he doesn't make an argument for the relationship between the forces and the people themselves. Poems are not things or objects, but the people remain as entities. As a result, McGann's arguments do not sustain as thoroughgoing a challenge to the premises of prevailing editorial theories as they might.

As we move from Tanselle to Shillingsburg to McGann, we can see shifts in the concepts of author, work, and text, and also in suggested relationships between textual and literary theory. Tanselle and Shillingsburg are both very insistent on the need for literary critics and theorists to be aware of textual theory and practice; for both of them, critics need to know the premises and theories under which the editors worked to produce the editions they are using (Tanselle, *Rationale,* 47; Shillingsburg, *Scholarly Editing,* 94). These arguments, I would suggest, maintain the line I have been positing between textual and literary theory; their main point (a convincing and important one) is that critics need to be aware of what is happening on the other side. McGann's position attempts to dissolve the line, making textual production and reception part of a continuum that is central to the activity of literary criticism. We can proceed one step further by looking at the ways some theorists have conceived authorship as an additional challenge to prevailing textual theories; even though these concepts have not yet resulted in fully developed textual theories, they would, if they are accepted at all, have to be accommodated within a theory of textual criticism.

At the opening of *Scholarly Editing in the Computer Age* Shillingsburg briefly mentions "trends in literary criticism" that "have directed attention away from authority and authenticity which concern historical critics, focusing it instead on forms and structures deriving from the culture as a whole and from language itself rather than from the individual author" (11). This formulation seems to polarize positions that do not need to be kept completely separate (although it is certainly true that many literary theorists have tried to make literature a product of language and not of authors). Perhaps the most useful challenge that so-called literary theory can offer to editing theory would be to suggest alternative views of human agency that would have consequences both for literary criticism and theory and for textual theory and practice. Theories that argue against the assumption that humans are unified, integral entitites have been prevalent in contemporary literary theory, and I want to close this section by glancing at two such suggestions.

Not surprisingly, much literary theory seems irrelevant to textual theory because, when it mentions the author at all, it does so only in terms of interpretation and valuation. One exception is Michel Foucault, who discusses authorship in "What Is an Author?" and "The Discourse on Language." For the most part in both essays, Foucault is talking about the author in relation to meaning, interpretation, and value, "the author as the unifying principle in a particular group of writings or statements, lying at the origins of their significance, as the seat of their coherence."[31] But for Foucault the author is not independent; he or she is always bounded by and locked into discourse. In "What Is an Author?" Foucault replaces the concept of the integral author with that of the discursive "author-function": "it is a matter of depriving the subject (or its substitute) of its role as originator, and of analyzing the subject as a variable and complex function of discourse."[32] The unifying principle that is the author-function works by establishing limits: "the author is the principle of thrift in the proliferation of meaning. . . . He is a certain functional principle by which, in our culture, one limits, excludes, and chooses."[33] Foucault also makes an analogy between "commentary," which "limited the hazards of discourse through the action of an *identity* taking the form of *repetition* and *sameness*," and "the author principle," which "limits this same chance element through the action of an *identity* whose form is that of *individuality* and the *I*" ("Discourse," 222). For textual theorists it is important that Foucault also considers the writer as the human originator of the text's words, even though he insists that this human agent cannot be separated from the discursive author-function: "Of course, it would be ridiculous to deny the existence of individuals who write, and invent. But I think that, for some time, at least, the individual who sits down to write a text, at the edge of which lurks a possible *oeuvre*, resumes the functions of the author" ("Discourse," 222). In other words, the writer is always permeated by the author-function, discourse always intrudes on individual autonomy. If the author is located at the juncture of individuality and discourse, a textual theory would have to account both for intentions and the force of the discourse.

Psychoanalysis, Marxism, and feminism offer three theoretical positions from which human agency and autonomy are strenuously questioned. An example from a Marxist orientation that is relevant here is Janet Wolff's *The Social Production of Art.* Discussing the production of both visual art and literature, Wolff attacks both what she sees as "an overemphasis on the individual artist as unique creator of a work" and "a simplified account of the [writing] subject as a coherent, rational entity" that "impos[es] an artificial unity on the individual as subject."[34] Arguing that all art is situated art, she claims that "humanist criticisms of the sociology of literature and art are often actually attempts to rescue a notion of 'creativity' which allows to art a special transcendence of all contingencies, particularly social and ideological contingencies" (69); works of art themselves are "not closed, self-contained and transcendent entities, but are the product of specific historical practices on the part of identifiable social groups in given conditions" (49). In contrast to Tanselle's use of Yeats's "monuments" to describe works, Wolff refers to Jeffrey Mehlman's claim that "the text must be regarded less as a monument than as a battlefield."[35]

Wolff's analysis is useful in the context of theory because, unlike most studies not directly concerned with textual criticism, she is careful neither to reduce the writing subject to social and ideological contingencies nor to dismiss the human author from consideration: "showing the ideological nature of art does not eliminate authors/artists as analytical categories (or as real people)" (70). Her author, however, is a conceptually diminished one: referring to Roland Barthes's pronouncement of the "death of the author,"[36] she writes that "the author as fixed, uniform and unconstituted creative source has indeed died. . . . But the author, now understood as constituted in language, ideology, and social relations, retains a central relevance" (136). Wolff ultimately locates the author in the work of art by citing Pierre Bourdieu's description of "the creative project as a meeting point and an adjustment between determinism and a determination."[37] Developing a textual or editing theory from a concept of the author such as the one Wolff offers would be a much more elaborate project than can be offered here, but it would have to differ in crucial ways from any theory based on authorial intention or even one based on social relations if the people involved are conceived as unified entities.

If engagements between textual and literary theory are to be fully fruitful, they will have to involve conceptualizations of the author and work as drastically different as are Tanselle's and Shillingsburg's, on the one hand, and Wolff's and those of psychoanalytic and feminist theorists on the other.[38] Textual theorists, often branded as hopelessly conservative and recalcitrant, have been confronting these different conceptions for some time now, as the biennial conferences of the Society for Textual Scholarship and its journal *Text* readily show. Two examples of preliminary attempts to apply concepts of authorship and textual production similar to McGann's and Wolff's can be briefly mentioned; both are indications of the kinds of projects that at least some textual scholars and theorists will be pursuing in the future. One is Gerald M. MacLean's project of editing a discourse rather than an author. MacLean's project of editing poems on the Restoration of Charles II rejects "the integral author" ("Editing a Discourse," 319) as the unifying principle in both theory and practice. Theoretically, MacLean criticizes "the typical false consciousness in that commitment to the unified authorial self who produces a text, viewed as a reified object the history of which is necessarily "'corruption'" (334). Practically, his basis for choosing a copy-text is not the author but the historical event: "the governing principle from which I shall work is to choose as copy-text that state of the text closest to the events it describes" (322). MacLean's concluding arguments attempt to provide an alternative to the situation described by Foucault, in which the author-function serves to limit and exclude: "Editing a discourse involves principles of multiplicity different from those employed in editing an author. Against the centrality of the creative author we may oppose the discursive heterogeneity of the mode of production" (340).

A second example is Katie King's consideration of "a feminist apparatus of literary production."[39] For King (who follows McGann's call for a continuous field of textual-critical study) textual studies open up "the political histories of the technologies of print culture" (91) in ways that "challenge a modernist preoccupation with interpretation as the center of literary practice" (92). Arguing that "scholars who privilege interpretation . . . will have different 'world views' about the center of literary studies than editors, and they may see not just different elements in the apparatus of literary production, but perhaps also fewer elements" (93), King uses Mark Schulman's challenge to "the centrality of originary moments of artistic creation," a challenge that "foreground[s] large social formations rather than individual authors or acts of creation."[40] This allows her to "examin[e] a set of systems of literary production in feminist terms," which she does via "the stories we tell about the shifting, problematic, and always multiple boundaries between those only seeming stabilities, 'the oral' and 'the written'" (95). For King, bibliography or textual studies provide a "window" through which to glimpse "technology and commerce, . . . historical specificity and commodity formation," areas that are usually neglected in interpretative studies but that make a project involving "feminism and writing technologies" (91) (with specific attention to Audre Lorde) possible.

IV

I have tried so far to suggest some ways in which literary theory can help to broaden the scope of such central terms for textual theorists as author, work, and text. On the other side, literary theorists can benefit from textual theory in ways that go beyond recognizing the principles upon which specific editions are based.

One way is for literary theorists to follow the developments of various theories as they are adapted into textual theory and practice. Hans Walter Gabler partially bases his edition of *Ulysses* on an adaptation of the structuralist idea that the elements of a system are not entities but exist only in relation to one another. When Gabler discusses variants (which are always central for a textual critic because of the potential for a variant to be an error in need of correction), he suggests that variants are more likely to be interesting as alternatives or as revisions than as corruptions, and thus he reverses the usual order of the formulation. Variants "command attention no longer by the degrees of textual deviation . . . from an assumed ideality of the work." Instead, they are "alternatives of expression and meaning within the total structure of the text, as revealed in the choices made manifest by the variation which is an integral element of that structure. The variation forms patterns of opposition" ("Synchrony," 309–10). For Gabler "the work may be said to comprise all its authorial textual states. . . . Its total text presents itself as a diachronous structure correlating the discrete synchronous structures discernible, of which that conferred by publication is only one, and not necessarily a privileged one" (309). Gabler is adapting Hans Zeller's notion of "versions," an explicitly structuralist, relational concept ("New Approach," 240, 258) in which ideas of the work as movements toward a goal (teleological) or as an organism (morphological) are replaced by a concept of a series of discrete versions that are not more or less contaminated approximations to some ideal (242–43, 256–57).[41]

Jerome McGann finds in Gabler's edition of *Ulysses* a demonstration that a text is neither "a given object of interpretation" nor "an invention of interpretation" but rather that "all texts are unstable to the extent that they are all processive and (in Gabler's terms) 'continuous'. At the same time, all are fixed within certain real, determinable limits" (*Social Values,* 181–82). "Gabler's work reminds us that fictive works do not exist in 'definitive' forms (or editions); by the same token, it also reminds us that the indeterminacy of texts is a determinate and determinable matter" (184). These determinate limits seem to place sharp bounds on any concept of the "work" that prevent it from becoming an "ineluctable entity," bounds that Gabler also sees. For Gabler authorial intention, leading to a work, "is not a metaphysical notion to be fulfilled but a textual force to be studied" ("Text as Process," 112). As a result, the synoptic text in his edition of *Ulysses* is not designed to be "mimetic," where the typography shows the text moving "by successive revision towards intermediary or final stable textual states," but rather to be "analytic," where the reader can "move as freely along the type-line in print as forwards and backwards along the axis of diachrony of the work's total text" ("Synchrony," 320). Considerations like these cause McGann to state that Gabler's *Ulysses* "raises all the central questions that have brought such a fruitful crisis to literary work in the postmodern period" (*Social Values,* 174).

The last theoretical piece that I want to consider is an attempt by a textual critic to analyze a book of literary theory. In "Textual Criticism and Deconstruction" Tanselle, noting "an increasing tendency for literary critics to refer to literary works as 'texts'," discusses the five essays by Harold Bloom, Paul de Man, Jacques Derrida, Geoffrey Hartman, and J. Hillis Miller in *Deconstruction and Criticism* by "look[ing] at the use of the word 'text' in the five essays . . . and consider[ing] the implications of that usage for the arguments they make."[42] In each case, although in different ways, Tanselle finds that the critic has blurred the distinction between *work* and *text* so that, most often, the two words come to mean the same thing. As a result, each critic is talking sometimes about the specific manifestation of the poem he is discussing, sometimes about the poem apart from its particular manifestation, but the terms *work* and *text* fail to carry any distinctions. Following this line, Tanselle is able to point out places where the five critics' terminology and thinking become sloppy, especially in examples of the word *text* shading into what he means by *work* (2, 4, 23, 24). He attempts to show how the distinction blurs the points the critics are making, and in the case of Derrida's "Living On: Border Lines," he uses the work/text distinction to try to show Derrida's essay deconstructing itself (16–17).

Tanselle is able to point out serious inconsistencies in the critics' thinking when he notes that "if we are interested in language as the driving force, and not the individuals who have used it (or been used by it), we have no reason to notice 'authors'" (28); why, then, are the critics concerned with the poets Shelley or Wordsworth at all? Likewise, in his preface Geoffrey Hartman "identifies a central concern of the volume to be the 'priority of language to meaning'; but he does not acknowledge the failure of the volume to consider an equally fundamental matter—the logic of accepting any sequence of words as it comes to us. Such acceptance implies a reverence for artifacts; otherwise the words or their arrangement could be freely altered" (2). Had the critics been aware of textual theories, they would have known about other attempts to struggle with problems they are dealing with: "Editors, like everyone else interested in the past, try to establish a framework of facts not subject to interpretation (though they have exercised judgment in arriving at it) and then supplement it with interpretation. The boundary line between fact and interpretation is forever indistinct" (12). In the case of Derrida, Tanselle regrets that he halts his consideration of indeterminacy at the level of meaning alone: "What is more remarkable still is that a piece so full of word-play, so full of twists and turns and bypaths in its exploration of the nature of works, could fail to find its way to a confrontation with the ultimate indeterminacy of the texts (not just the meanings) of verbal works" (17; also 5 and *Rationale,* 24).

There are problems with Tanselle's analysis. For example, it is useful to point out that the Yale critics' failure to consider the distinctions between work and the text has led them to incoherencies, confusions, flaws, and weaknesses—although it is maybe not so useful as to require the number of reminders that Tanselle offers in the essay—but when he assumes that the relationship between work and text must be his own distinction, then his critique becomes as limited as he accuses the five essays of being. His observations, however, provide useful checks on a group of critics' claims for free play and indeterminacy that can come from someone who, starting from a very different set of concerns and premises, is nevertheless concerned with the same terms.[43] Just as literary theorists can, from their side, suggest possibly fruitful ways of opening up the concepts of author, work, and text, so textual critics can show how literary critics and theorists may too quickly and easily have glossed over problematic implications of the terms and concepts they are using and perhaps taking for granted.

V

It has been the central premise of this essay that any connection between textual and literary theorists would be preferable to the current lack of contact. Now that textual critics acknowledge that the products of their efforts are as much a matter of criticism as of objective scholarship, literary critics should begin to recognize their obligation to analyze and assess those products with the same scrutiny and skepticism that they grant to rival interpretations and theories. Tanselle argues that "textual critics must try to understand the works they are editing (however one defines 'understand') in order to make choices among variant readings and decisions about emendations; they inevitably engage in literary criticism. So-called literary critics, for their part, should recognize—though they rarely do—that they must evaluate the makeup of particular texts in the process of analyzing literary works"; "If textual criticism is . . . truly 'criticism,' literary criticism cannot simply accept its conclusions but must examine them as part of the process of reading" ("Deconstruction," 1, 9). Literary critics might discover, as Katie King has suggested, that critics who are concerned only with interpretation and not with textual matters "may see not just different elements in the apparatus of literary production, but perhaps also fewer elements" ("Feminist Apparatus," 93). Whether a broadening of interest on the part of textual and literary theorists produces a mutual recognition of "parallel conceptual or methodological issues at stake," as Greetham suggests ("Matrix," 5), or a "tension and struggle between these opposing interests, rather than an agreement to let each go its own way," as McGann argues (*Beauty,* 94), textual and literary theorists and critics would be much better off with more interest in and understanding of each other's theories and activities.

NOTES

1. For instance, René Wellek and Austin Warren, *Theory of Literature* (1949), 3d ed. (New York: Harcourt, 1962), 57; discussed in Jerome J. McGann, *The Beauty of Inflections: Literary Investigations in Historical Method and Theory* (Oxford: Clarendon, 1988), 69. McGann's work cited hereafter as *Beauty.*

2. Fredson Bowers, *Textual and Literary Criticism* (Cambridge: Cambridge University Press, 1966), 4, 5, 4. Originally the Sandars Lectures in Bibliography, 1957–58. I regret the persistent use of "he" as a generic pronoun in textual criticism.

3. G. Thomas Tanselle, *A Rationale of Textual Criticism* (Philadelphia: University of Pennsylvania Press, 1989), 16. Hereafter cited as *Rationale.*

4. Peter L. Shillingsburg, *Scholarly Editing in the Computer Age: Theory and Practice* (Athens, Ga.: University of Georgia Press, 1986), 94; hereafter cited as *Scholarly Editing.* Italics in the original. Unless indicated otherwise, all italics in quotations are in the originals.

5. Gary Taylor, "The Rhetoric of Textual Criticism," *Text* 4 (1988): 48.

6. Fredson Bowers, "Unfinished Business: Presidential Address, The Society for Textual Scholarship, April 26, 1985," *Text* 4 (1988): 11. See also Peter L. Shillingsburg, "An Inquiry Into the Social Status of Texts and Modes of Textual Criticism," *Studies in Bibliography* 42 (1989): 79n.42.

7. D. C. Greetham, "Textual and Literary Theory: Redrawing the Matrix," *Studies in Bibliography* 42 (1989): 2. Hereafter cited as "Matrix."

8. Greetham, "Matrix," 6–13, and "A Suspicion of Texts," *Thesis* 2 (Fall 1987): 23–24; Hans Zeller, "A New Approach to the Critical Constitution of Literary Texts," *Studies in Bibliography* 28 (1975): 258; Louis Hay, "Does 'Text' Exist?," *Studies in Bibliography* 41 (1988): 66–68; Hans Walter Gabler, "The Synchrony and Diachrony of Texts: Practice and Theory of the Critical Edition of James Joyce's *Ulysses,*" *Text* 1 (1981 [published 1984]): 310, and "The Text as Process and the Problem of Intentionality," *Text* 3 (1987): 112; Gerald M. MacLean, "What Is a Restoration Poem? Editing a Discourse, Not an Author," *Text* 3 (1987): 340 and throughout. Zeller's essay cited hereafter as "New Approach"; Gabler's essays as "Synchrony" and "Text as Process"; and MacLean's as "Editing a Discourse."

9. Jerome J. McGann, *Social Values and Poetic Acts: The Historical Judgment of Literary Work* (Cambridge, Mass.: Harvard University Press, 1988), 174; hereafter cited as *Social Values.* Christine Froula, *To Write Paradise: Style and Error in Pound's "Cantos"* (New Haven: Yale University Press, 1984). For Pound, see also McGann, *Social Values,* 192–94, and Gabler, "Text as Process," 113–15.

10. Fredson Bowers, "Textual Criticism," in *The Aims and Methods of Scholarship in Modern Languages and Literatures,* ed. James Thorpe (1963), 2d ed. (New York: Modern Language Association of America, 1970), 48.

11. W. W. Greg, "The Rationale of Copy-Text" (1950–51), in his *Collected Papers*, ed. J. C. Maxwell (Oxford: Clarendon, 1966), 377, 382, 376n.2.

12. Center for Editions of American Authors, *Statement of Editorial Principles and Procedures: A Working Manual for Editing Nineteenth-Century American Texts* (1967), rev. ed. (New York: Modern Language Association of America, 1972); "The Center for Scholarly Editions: An Introductory Statement," *PMLA* 92 (1977): 583–97.

13. In "The Editorial Problem of Final Authorial Intention," G. Thomas Tanselle quotes the phrase "author's final intentions" from Bowers's 1964 essay, "Some Principles for Scholarly Editions of Nineteenth-Century American Authors" (Tanselle [1976], in his *Selected Studies in Bibliography* [Charlottesville: University Press of Virginia, 1979], 310; Bowers, *Studies in Bibliography* 17 [1964]: 227). Hereafter cited as "Final Authorial Intention." Tanselle argues that an appeal to intentions (or "wishes") is implied in Greg's rationale (310), whereas Jerome McGann claims that such an appeal is not in Greg at all but is instead Bowers's "special variation" on Greg's rationale (*A Critique of Modern Textual Criticism* [Chicago: University of Chicago Press, 1983]: 27–28, 38; hereafter cited as *Critique*).

14. See, for example, Tom Davis, "The CEAA and Modern Textual Editing," *Library*, 5th ser., 32 (1977): 61–74; Paul Baender, "The Meaning of Copy-Text," *Studies in Bibliography* 22 (1969): 311–18; Donald Pizer, "On the Editing of Modern American Texts," *Bulletin of the New York Public Library* 75 (1971): 147–53; Edmund Wilson, "The Fruits of the MLA," *New York Review of Books*, 26 September 1968, 7–10, and 10 October 1968, 6–14. For accounts of the controversies and defenses of the editions, see G. Thomas Tanselle, "Greg's Theory of Copy-Text and the Editing of American Literature: 1950–74" (1975) and "Recent Editorial Discussion and the Central Questions of Editing: 1974–79" (1981), both reprinted in his *Textual Criticism since Greg: A Chronicle, 1950–1985* (Charlottesville: University Press of Virginia, 1987). Hereafter cited as *Since Greg*.

15. G. Thomas Tanselle, "Textual Scholarship," in *Introduction to Scholarship in Modern Languages and Literatures*, ed. Joseph Gibaldi (New York: Modern Language Association of America, 1981), 40.

16. Fredson Bowers, "Greg's 'Rationale of Copy-Text' Revisited," *Studies in Bibliography* 31 (1978): 125, 128–29, 147.

17. Tanselle, *Since Greg*, 82. See also Morse Peckham, "Reflections on the Foundations of Modern Textual Editing," *Proof* 1 (1971): 123–26; and Davis, "CEAA and Modern Textual Editing," 66–69. Peckham cited hereafter as "Reflections."

18. W. K. Wimsatt and Monroe C. Beardsley, "The Intentional Fallacy" (1946), in Wimsatt's *The Verbal Icon: Studies in the Meaning of Poetry* (Lexington: University of Kentucky Press, 1954), 3–18; hereafter cited as *Verbal*

Icon. Tanselle, "Final Authorial Intention," 321–22, and *Rationale,* 77; Shillingsburg, *Scholarly Editing,* 37–39.

19. For example, Tanselle, "Final Authorial Intention," 328–33, *Since Greg,* 104–6, and *Rationale,* 76–79; McGann, *Critique,* 75, 78, and elsewhere; Shillingsburg, *Scholarly Editing,* chap. 5; James Thorpe, *Principles of Textual Criticism* (San Marino, Calif.: Huntington Library, 1972), 37–49, 165–66; Philip Gaskell, *From Writer to Reader: Studies in Editorial Method* (Oxford: Clarendon, 1978), 3–4. Other questions regarding intention are posed by William Proctor Williams and Craig S. Abbot in *An Introduction to Bibliographical and Textual Studies* (1985), 2d ed. (New York: Modern Language Association of America, 1989), 57–58.

20. Tanselle, "Final Authorial Intention," 352–53, and *Introduction to Scholarship,* 42; Shillingsburg, *Scholarly Editing,* 89; Steven Mailloux, *Interpretive Conventions: The Reader in the Study of American Fiction* (Ithaca, N.Y.: Cornell University Press, 1982), 110–13; Hans Walter Gabler, Afterword to James Joyce, *Ulysses: A Critical and Synoptic Edition,* 3 vols. (New York: Garland, 1984), 3:1901, also 1882, 1895, 1903; McGann, *Social Values,* 179–80.

21. Hershel Parker, *Flawed Texts and Verbal Icons: Literary Authority in American Fiction* (Evanston, Ill.: Northwestern University Press, 1984), chap. 2 and elsewhere.

22. Donald E. Pease, "Author," in *Critical Terms for Literary Study,* ed. Frank Lentricchia and Thomas McLaughlin (Chicago: University of Chicago Press, 1990): 105–17; Peckham, "Reflections," 136–55, esp. 143–44; McGann, *Critique,* 8 and elsewhere. See also Paul Eggert, "Textual Product or Textual Process: Procedures and Assumptions of Critical Editing," in *Editing in Australia,* ed. Paul Eggert. Occasional Paper no. 17 (Canberra, Australia: English Department, University College, Australian Defence Force Academy, 1990), 19–40. (This paper will also appear in the *University of Texas Library Chronicle.*)

23. E. D. Hirsch, Jr., *Validity in Interpretation* (New Haven: Yale University Press, 1967), 242.

24. Cleanth Brooks, "Irony as a Principle of Structure" (1951), in *The Critical Tradition: Classic Texts and Contemporary Trends,* ed. David H. Richter (New York: Bedford/St. Martin's, 1989), 799, 804; Cleanth Brooks, Jr., and Robert Penn Warren, *Understanding Poetry: An Anthology for College Students* (New York: Holt, 1938), 19. Brooks discusses the "well wrought urn" image in Cleanth Brooks, *The Well Wrought Urn: Studies in the Structure of Poetry* (New York: Harcourt, 1947).

25. Tracing a twentieth-century history of editing Shakespeare, Paul Werstine has recently argued that "it is only our desire for New-Critical unity that may have caused us to ignore [various accounts] and to fix the origins of the early printed versions upon single agents" ("Narratives about Printed Shakespeare Texts: 'Foul Papers' and 'Bad' Quartos," *Shakespeare Quarterly* 41 [1990]: 86).

26. T. S. Eliot, *The Sacred Wood: Essays on Poetry and Criticism* (London: Methuen, 1920), x; and "The Music of Poetry" (1942), in *Selected Prose,* ed. Frank Kermode (London: Faber, 1975), 111.

27. Terry Eagleton, *Literary Theory: An Introduction* (Oxford: Blackwell, 1983), 49.

28. In his discussion of editing Shakespeare, Paul Werstine considers "the category of 'foul papers'" as "the product not of reason but of desire—our desire to possess in the 'good' quartos Shakespeare's plays in the form in which he, as an individual agent, both began and finished them" ("Narratives," 75). He goes on to argue that it "becomes possible to represent twentieth-century textual criticism as having been produced by the desire for a certain kind of narrative, one which calls into being certain individuals—solitary author or lone actor—for the purpose of holding them solely responsible for the production of the most diverse phenomena" (82).

29. Tanselle's concepts of work and author's mind seem to me the latest manifestations of a persistent theological tendency in Greg-Bowers editing. Almost every major aspect of the theory and practice, from Greg's terms *substantives* and *accidentals* to the author whose final intentions are followed, has been at some time called theological, incarnational, hagiological, metaphysical, etc. See, for example, Peckham, "Reflections," 125–26, 137; Davis, "CEAA and Modern Textual Editing," 64n.19, 66; McGann, *Beauty,* 118; Shillingsburg, *Scholarly Editing,* 11, 32. The work and mind that Tanselle posits as the groundings for stability in an otherwise chaotic observable world are like arguments for God as a source of order and stability in the world. To someone who already believes in such a God, the resulting scheme will be coherent, convincing, and even self-evident (Tanselle talks about "fashion[ing] a whole out of what seem the fragmented facts" [*Rationale,* 74]); to a nonbeliever, the scheme may be coherent and self-consistent, but it will probably also seem meaningless and beside the point (and a "whole" may be out of the question).

30. McGann, *Beauty,* 73, 75, 76–77, 78. The essay to which these page numbers refer ("The Monks and the Giants: Textual and Bibliographical Studies and the Interpretation of Literary Works") originally appeared in *Textual Criticism and Literary Interpretation,* ed. Jerome J. McGann (Chicago: University of Chicago Press, 1985). This collection contains several other essays that demonstrate ways in which textual studies are relevant and even essential for literary studies; see in particular the articles by Lee Patterson and Derek Pearsall.

31. Michel Foucault, "The Discourse on Language" (1971), in *The Archaeology of Knowledge and the Discourse on Language,* trans. A. M. Sheridan Smith (New York: Pantheon, 1972), 221; hereafter cited as "Discourse."

32. Michel Foucault, "What Is an Author?" (1969), trans. Josué V. Harari, in *Textual Strategies: Perspectives in Post-Structuralist Criticism,* ed. Harari (Ithaca, N.Y.: Cornell University Press, 1979), 148, 158.

33. Foucault, "What Is an Author?," 159. This passage does not appear in the earlier version of the essay included in Foucault, *Language, Counter-Memory, Practice,* ed. Donald F. Bouchard (Ithaca, N.Y.: Cornell University Press, 1977).

34. Janet Wolff, *The Social Production of Art* (1981; rpt. New York: New York University Press, 1984), 137, 138.

35. Wolff, *Social Production,* 120, citing Jeffrey Mehlman, *Revolution and Repetition: Marx/Hugo/Balzac* (Berkeley: University of California Press, 1977), 107.

36. Roland Barthes, "The Death of the Author" (1968), in *Image-Music-Text,* ed. and trans. Stephen Heath (New York: Hill and Wang, 1977), 142–48.

37. Wolff, *Social Production,* 137, citing Pierre Bourdieu, "Intellectual Field and Creative Project," in *Knowledge and Control: New Directions for the Sociology of Education,* ed. Michael F. D. Young (London: Collier-Macmillan, 1971), 185.

38. An example of a recent psychoanalytic study of the subject is Paul Smith, *Discerning the Subject* (Minneapolis: University of Minnesota Press, 1988).

39. Katie King, "Bibliography and a Feminist Apparatus of Literary Production," *Text* 5 (1991): 91–103; hereafter cited as "Feminist Apparatus."

40. King, "Feminist Apparatus," 94. King refers to Mark Schulman, "Gender and Typographic Culture: Beginning to Unravel the 500-Year Mystery," in *Technology and Women's Voices: Keeping in Touch,* ed. Cheris Kramarae (New York: Routledge, 1988), 98–115.

41. For a discussion of Gabler's synoptic text as "the set of relations between transcribed documents," see Patrick McGee, "The Error of Theory," *Studies in the Novel* 22 (1990): 152.

42. G. Thomas Tanselle, "Textual Criticism and Deconstruction," *Studies in Bibliography* 43 (1990): 1, 2; discussing Harold Bloom, Paul de Man, Jacques Derrida, Geoffrey Hartman, and J. Hillis Miller, *Deconstruction and Criticism* (New York: Seabury, 1979). Tanselle's essay cited hereafter as "Deconstruction."

43. A parallel analysis could be done on Roland Barthes's "From Work to Text," an essay intriguing in this context because it contrasts the two problematic terms. It does so, however, only in relation to opposed attitudes toward the author as a grounding for meaning: "the work is caught up in a process of filiation"; it "refers to the image of an *organism*"; "The author is reputed the father and the owner of his work: literary science therefore teaches *respect* for the manuscript and the author's declared intentions." "The metaphor of the Text," on the other hand, "is that of the *network*"; "it can be read without the guarantee of its father"; "It is not that the Author may not 'come back' in the Text, in his text, but he then does so as a 'guest'." Roland Barthes, "From Work to Text" (1971), in *Image-Music-Text,* ed. and trans. Stephen Heath (New York: Hill and Wang, 1977), 160, 161.

Notes on Contributors

George Bornstein (University of Michigan) is the editor of *W. B. Yeats: The Early Poetry* for the Cornell Yeats; *W. B. Yeats: Letters to the New Island* for the Collected Edition of the Works of W. B. Yeats; and several books of literary criticism, including most recently *Poetic Remaking: The Art of Browning, Yeats, and Pound.*

Ronald Bush (California Institute of Technology) is the author of *The Genesis of Ezra Pound's Cantos* and *T. S. Eliot: A Study in Character and Style.* He is currently at work on an edition of the *Pisan Cantos* manuscripts.

Richard J. Finneran (University of Tennessee) is co-general editor of the fourteen-volume Collected Edition of the Works of W. B. Yeats and is series editor of Poetry for the Cornell Yeats and editor of *Yeats: An Annual of Critical and Textual Studies.* He has recently published editions of Yeats's *Poems* and *Collected Poems.*

Eugene Goodheart (Brandeis University) is the author of several books of literary criticism, including *The Utopian Vision of D. H. Lawrence* and *The Skeptic Disposition in Contemporary Criticism.*

Michael Groden (University of Western Ontario) is the author of *"Ulysses" in Progress* and general editor of *The James Joyce Archive.* He is coeditor of the forthcoming *Johns Hopkins Guide to Literary Theory and Criticism.*

Andrew J. Kappel (Hofstra University) is the editor of a collection of essays on Marianne Moore that appeared as a special issue of *Twentieth Century Literature* and is at work on a book about Moore.

A. Walton Litz (Princeton University) is coeditor of *The Collected Poems of William Carlos Williams, Volume I,* and is the author of numerous books on modern literature, including *Introspective Voyager: The Poetic Development of Wallace Stevens.*

Christopher MacGowan (College of William and Mary) is the author of *William Carlos Williams' Early Poetry* and editor of *The Collected Poems of William Carlos Williams, Volume I* (with A. Walton Litz) and *Volume II.*

Vicki Mahaffey (University of Pennsylvania) is the author of *Reauthorizing Joyce.*

Edward Mendelson (Columbia University) is W. H. Auden's literary executor. He is the editor of the new Princeton *Complete Works of W. H. Auden* and author of *Early Auden,* among other books.

Noel Polk (University of Southern Mississippi) is textual editor of the Faulkner Concordance series and has edited three of Faulkner's novels for Random House and four for the Library of America.

Lawrence S. Rainey (Yale University) is the author of *Ezra Pound and the Monument of Culture.*

Brenda R. Silver (Dartmouth College) is the editor of *Virginia Woolf's Reading Notebooks* and the textual edition of *"Anon" and "The Reader": Virginia Woolf's Last Essays.* She is at work on a book on feminist polemics.